From Sailing Ships to 902 Elm

Compiled, Coordinated, Copied,
Written, Edited
1963-1975
by
Margaret Pollock Campbell
for the joy of
Cora, Mary, Jo Ann and Joe
and in loving memory of
Dad, Mother, Bob, Jean, Stevie and Mike

ISBN: 978-1726275125

TABLE OF CONTENTS

FOREWORD

"Sailing Ships to 902 Elm" was written in 1975 by Margaret Pollock Campbell. This chronological essay weaves the personal stories of her Pollock, Stoakes, and Granger ancestors with the world, national, and state history. There were a few faded mimeographed copies floating around in the family, and it was decided that the unusual family history information and format should be preserved. The result is this project.

Many people have contributed to this project. Unfortunately, some are no longer with us to celebrate the completed project. I thank Mary Ellen Stoakes Sievers for being my partner in crime to start this and Ruth Ann Kuhn Stoakes for helping with proofing and suggestions; this book is finished in memory of them. I also wish to acknowledge the Stoakes cousins Gwyn Jones Augustine, Ruth Stoakes Calderwood, Carol Stoakes Fuller Bruene, Aze Stoakes, and second cousin Jeanne Stoakes Hughes for their contributions. Thanks to my daughter, Sara Stoakes Kvidera, for helping with editing and for designing the cover. Additionally, I would like to thank Don Sievers for helping to finance this publication in Mary's honor.

I hope to continue this history by collecting stories of the Eleazar Stoakes family. If you are a descendent of Eleazar Stoakes and would like your information and family story or stories included in the upcoming update book, please contact me. My information is listed below

Sharon Ingle Stoakes
2970 150th Street
Traer, Iowa   50675

Ph. 319.478.2574
Cell 319.415.3767
Email redhawk8223@yahoo.com

PREFACE

Dear Family,

Have you ever wondered from where our forefathers came? How, when, and where they fit into the American picture? 'Tis said that we can not know where we are going until we know from where we came.

I have been curious, very curious. To satisfy my desire to know, I started delving into family papers, genealogies, old letters, diaries, legal documents, national and local histories, and every place where a scrap of information about our family background could be found. Older relatives gave all of the assistance they could. Many of you added treasured bits.

All of the pieces were put together like a giant jigsaw puzzle. Although incomplete, the results give quite a fascinating picture. Other bits may show up later. If you have information to add, I am sure the rest of us would enjoy hearing about it.

My plan was to locate as many ancestors as possible as they left Europe and sailed to America. Then, I traced the family stories in chronological fashion down through the years correlating them with the story of America and the westward movement climaxing in the marriage of Mother and Dad and their establishing their home at 902 Elm, Rolfe, Iowa.

The early ancestors are numerous, and sometimes difficult to keep in mind in the first part of this chronology. Keep the yellow bookmark at hand for ready reference. Our ancestors' names have been capitalized throughout the pages to give emphasis to them. Other family members have been included only as they help complete or add to the stories of our own ancestors.

May this account satisfy some of your curiosity, and may it some day do the same for your children. Thank you all for your contributions, all of which are appreciated.

Margaret Pollock Campbell

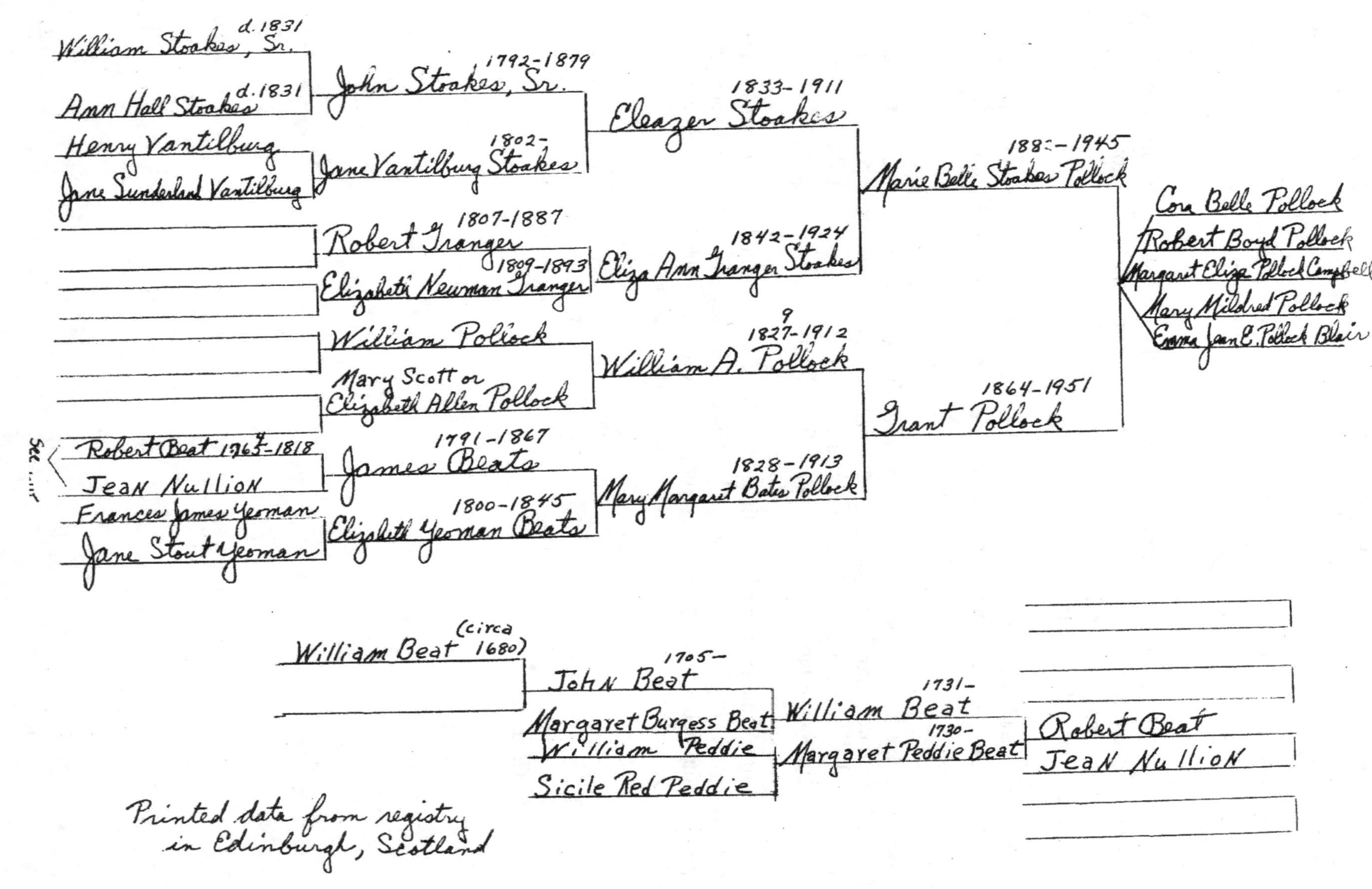

William Stoakes, Sr. d. 1831
Ann Hall Stoakes d. 1831
John Stoakes, Sr. 1792-1879
Henry Vantilburg
Jane Sunderland Vantilburg
Jane Vantilburg Stoakes 1802-
Eleazer Stoakes 1833-1911
Robert Granger 1807-1887
Elizabeth Newman Granger 1809-1893
Eliza Ann Granger Stoakes 1842-1924
Marie Belle Stoakes Pollock 1883-1945
William Pollock
Mary Scott or Elizabeth Allen Pollock
William A. Pollock 1827-1912
Robert Beat 1765-1818
Jean Nullion
James Beats 1791-1867
Frances James Yeoman
Jane Stout Yeoman
Elizabeth Yeoman Beats 1800-1845
Mary Margaret Bates Pollock 1828-1913
Grant Pollock 1864-1951
Cora Belle Pollock
Robert Boyd Pollock
Margaret Eliza Pollock Campbell
Mary Mildred Pollock
Emma Jean E. Pollock Blair
See .....
vi
William Beat (circa 1680)
John Beat 1705-
Margaret Burgess Beat
William Peddie
Sicile Red Peddie
William Beat 1731-
Margaret Peddie Beat 1730-
Robert Beat
Jean Nullion
Printed data from registry in Edinburgh, Scotland

FROM SAILING SHIPS TO 902 ELM

The ancestors of Grant and Belle Pollock came by sailing ships from Holland, Ireland, England and Scotland to the shores of America, and wended westward on foot, on horseback, by covered wagon, raft, canal boat, river steamer, the iron horse and stagecoach. After stopovers in New York State, New Jersey, Pennsylvania, Ohio, Michigan and Illinois, and the elapse of 135 years of American history, the paths converged on Iowa and came together at 902 Elm Street, Rolfe, Iowa.

When HENRY VANTILBURG, the first of our ancestors to come to America, came with his four brothers in 1770 from their native Holland, they settled in New Holland (New York.) Already the Dutch dominated the population there and along the Hudson River.

The five brothers, HENRY, Daniel, John, Peter, and Frank came from Tilburg in south central Netherlands, now a city of 114,312 population. What connection the name Vantilburg has to the city named Tilburg, we do not know.

The brothers arrived in the New World in exciting times. Two million whites lived in the thirteen colonies. "The English settlements were settled up to the mountains," Benjamin Franklin had said a few years earlier. Opportunity on the seacoast seemed monopolized by the rich and influential. New frontiers had begun to form back of the back lines of the old settlements. The seaboard was English, populated, wealthy, safe and cultured. Colleges of Harvard, William and Mary, Yale and Princeton, Dartmouth, Rutgers and Brown had come into being. Twenty-three public libraries had been founded. English actors and musicians were giving concerts in America. American painters were giving exhibitions. Good American newspapers were being published.

New York was a cosmopolitan city when the Vantilburg brothers arrived. Eighteen languages were spoken there. It and Philadelphia and Boston were the principal ports. Montreal was an important fur trading center. Charleston was the big city of the South. Already the North and the South had taken on different characteristics. In the South, there were big country homes with black slaves working the land.

In 1770, the Spanish still had control of Florida and the Gulf Coast. The British had just defeated France in the French and Indian war. In order to keep the territory of Louisiana from England, France had deeded it secretly to Spain. The territory included the area that would become Iowa; also, the new fur trading town of St. Louis built on the confluence of the Mississippi and Missouri rivers to limit the trade in the upper parts of the river to the Spanish and French. In the Far West in the late eighteenth century, the Spanish Jesuits were establishing missions up and down the coast.

One hundred and fifty years or more had passed since the English had founded Jamestown in Virginia, since the Pilgrims had settled in Plymouth, Massachusetts, since the Spanish had founded Santa Fe, New Mexico, and the French had founded and fortified the port of Quebec and started missionaries, fur traders and explorers west and south.

The early New Englanders had tried to transplant the English way of life to this continent, but struggle, hardship, savages and wilderness sometimes dominated, and many arts and crafts and finer things in life had been abandoned. But, through the years, the settlers in general had prospered under colonial government and built up a strong and vigorous civilization. Far back from the sea, the Indians were still a menace when the Vantilburgs arrived, and pirates lurked off the coasts, but violence was incidental.

Now in 1770 the new frontier had begun to form. The old settlers looked down on the men of the New West and called them "Buckskins". Some were Swiss and German, and others were Irish and Scotch. They had no love for England. The older settlers, too, were wanting more rule for themselves and less for England.

The colonists' objection to being taxed without representation was flaring into violent affrays. Three years after the Vantilburgs arrived in America, the colonists dressed as Indians and tossed a shipload of tea into the Harbor in Boston, an act that became known as the Boston Tea Party. The British closed the harbor and forbade town meeting in Massachusetts. The other colonies rose in sympathy. The first Continental Congress was held the next year in Philadelphia.

War seemed likely and colonial volunteers began to drill. Minutemen pledged to meet at a minute's notice. Provisions and munitions were collected.

On the night of April 18, 1775, a thousand British redcoats left Boston for Lexington. Warned by the midnight ride of Paul Revere, the Lexington Militia of sixty men were barring the way to Lexington at dawn. The British swept the band aside and the British marched to Concord and destroyed the colonists' military stores. On the way back to Boston, the British were shot at from every hill and stone wall, shots that were heard around the world and are still reverberating!

Patriots from New England arose and formed more militia groups. But many colonists remained loyal to the king. The second Continental Congress gathered in Independence Hall in Philadelphia in May 1775, adopted its own army and appointed Colonel George Washington as commander-in-chief. The English Parliament closed all American ports and burned a couple of towns. Tom Paine issued "Common Sense." Congress chose a committee to draw up the Declaration of Independence.

England would be a powerful foe, so the colonies solicited and obtained some money and supplies from France before issuing:

> "When in the course of human events, it becomes necessary for one people to dissolve the political bands which have connected them with another... We hold these truths to be self evident, that all men are created equal, that they are endowed by their Creator with certain unalienable rights, among these are life, liberty and the pursuit of happiness."

The powerful British could raise money, train and equip an army, and block American ports. However, the king had trouble getting enough Englishmen to fight, so hired additional fighting

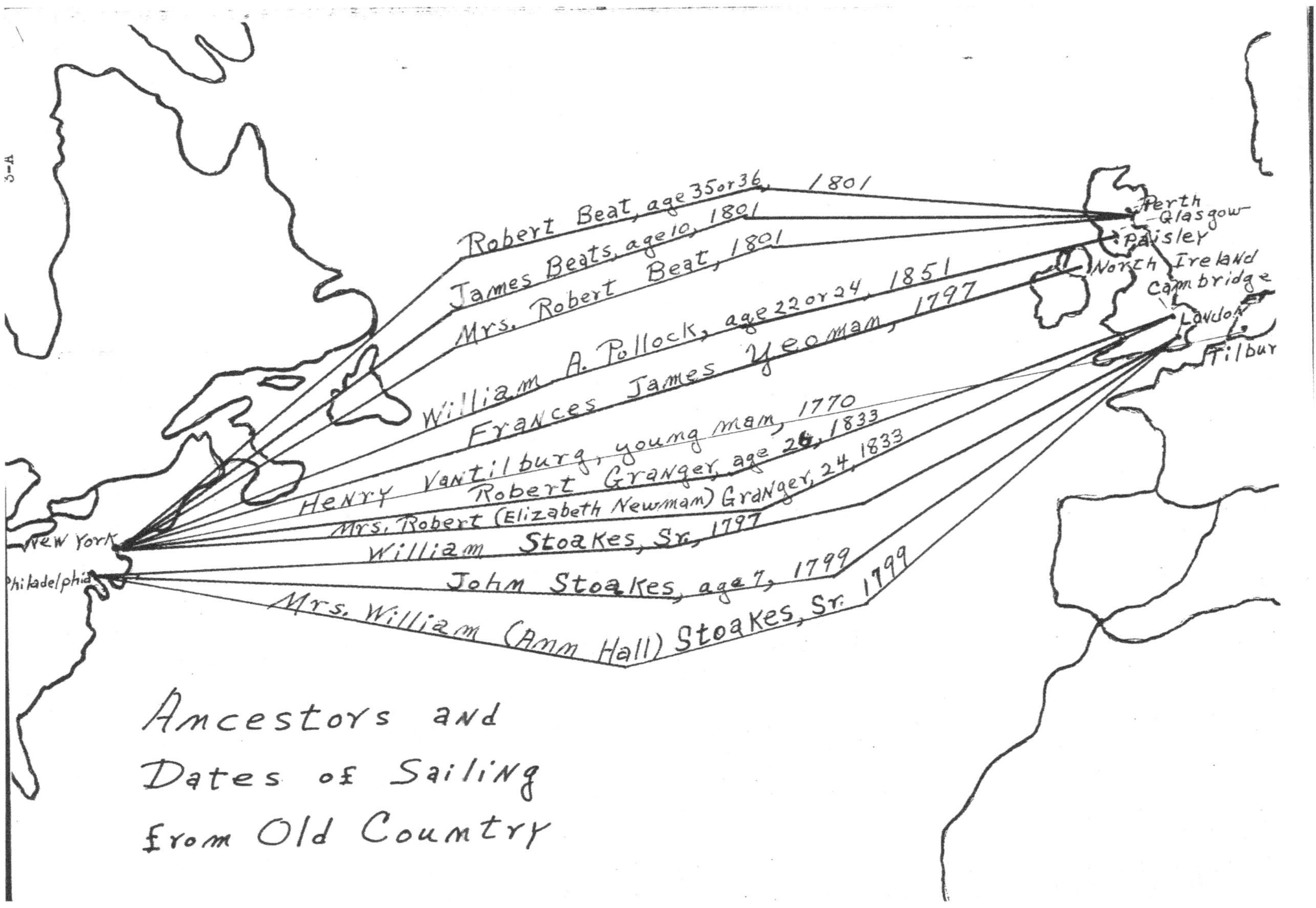

5-A
3
Robert Beat, age 35 or 36, 1801
James Beats, age 10, 1801
Mrs. Robert Beat, 1801
William A. Pollock, age 22 or 24, 1851
Frances James Yeoman, 1797
Henry VanTilburg, young man, 1770
Robert Granger, age 26, 1833
Mrs. Robert (Elizabeth Newman) Granger, 24, 1833
William Stoakes, Sr, 1797
John Stoakes, age 7, 1799
Mrs. William (Ann Hall) Stoakes, Sr. 1799
Perth
Glasgow
Paisley
North Ireland
Cambridge
London
Tilbur
New York
Philadelphia
Ancestors and
Dates of Sailing
from Old Country

men, the Hessians and the Brunswickers, from German princes. These men had no interest in the war and deserted in large numbers when free land was offered to them.

Washington, who with his men were to receive no pay, began to train but they needed supplies and ammunition. Ethan Allen and his Green Mountain Boys of Vermont surprised and captured Fort Ticonderoga from the British in northeast New York without firing a shot, and obtained quantities of ammunition and guns to equip Washington's forces.

Washington early in 1776 with 25,000 men, probably the biggest army he ever commanded, met the British around New York and had to retreat losing thousands of men as prisoners. He had no regular army and men enlisted for terms of three to six months and came and went, some leaving to return home to plant and harvest or to fight Indians to protect families. By the end of 1776 Washington had only 3,000 men. The British in New Jersey, and the Philadelphians expected their city to be occupied any day.

In this black hour, late on Christmas night, Washington crossed the ice filled Delaware River, and after a quick march, fell upon the Hessians at Trenton. Taken by complete surprise, the enemy was driven from town with heavy losses. This victory welded a discouraged nation together and gave it renewed heart.

HENRY VANTILBURG and his brothers John and William who had crossed into New Jersey from New Holland, enlisted in the Revolutionary Army under Washington and were in the battle of Trenton.

HENRY'S wife, while standing in the door of her home near Trenton with a babe in her arms, was shot and killed by a Hessian soldier. Her maiden name was Jane Holman and they had three children, Samuel, William and Polly. Enemy troops at Trenton, mostly Hessian, had committed numerous outrages on the inhabitants and made themselves thoroughly hated. (This information about the Vantilburgs comes from the "Stoakes Family History" by J.S. Hopkins.)

A few days later Washington defeated three British regiments at Princeton and retook New Jersey. He went into winter quarters at Morristown. In 1777 for the third time he had to build a new army from raw recruits. That autumn the British occupied Philadelphia. Washington went into winter quarters at Valley Forge, some 30 miles away. His army was cold and hungry and moneyless. The farmers preferred to sell their produce to the British who had gold to pay for supplies. Our congress had no authority to raise money by taxation, and had issued paper money that had become nearly worthless.

The French and the Spanish, who had been giving secret aid to America, came into the war openly. Holland, an enemy of Britain, also joined the Americans. The British, to keep Americans at home protecting their families, encouraged Indians to attack frontier settlements.

The British were ordered to concentrate its army in New York and abandon Philadelphia if necessary. With abundant supplies, the British marched northward through New Jersey. Washington followed closely, and on July 28, 1778, forced the British to fight at Monmouth. However, part of the American attack was led by Charles Lee, who had conspired to betray the

Americans, and the British escaped to New York safely. Lee was court-martialed. The three Vantilburg brothers, HENRY, John and William, were with Washington in this battle at Monmouth.

After 1778, the fighting was nearly all south of the Potomac River. The British fought on for three more years and surrendered in 1781. Many historians agree that Washington by sheer force of character, courage and indomitable will, held a divided and disorganized country together until victory was achieved.

In 1781, the last of the states ratified the Articles of Confederation, drawn up in 1777, which provided for a weak central government.

Colonists retained their loyalty for their individual colonies and developing a national government was difficult. The event that did most to develop national unity was a step that brought operating money to the national government and enlarged the nation at the same time. It was the establishment of the Northwest territory in 1786.

Seven states that claimed land west of the Appalachians ceded these lands to the nation as a whole. The nation could sell the land and pay the national debt and gain financial support for the national government. The agreement was that when 5,000 free men lived in any part of the new territory, they could take steps to form their own government, new states for the union, not less than three states nor more than five. The territory included what is now Ohio, Indiana, Illinois, Wisconsin, Michigan and part of Minnesota.

Necessity for working together slowly evolved step by step, and in May 1787, 55 distinguished citizens gathered in Philadelphia to draw up a constitution. George Washington presided. He was still holding his disunited countrymen together by their love and respect for him. He was inaugurated president in April 1789 in New York City, the temporary capital. Do you suppose that HENRY VANTILBURG might have ridden a horse the fifty miles from Trenton to New York to see his old commander become president?

When HENRY returned home from the army, he married a second wife whose maiden name was JANE SUNDERLAND. They had ten children, five boys and five girls. In these times very few men or women could support themselves except as part of a family group. In most occupations a man could not get ahead without the combined labor of himself, his wife, and his children. Both men and women married young and remarried promptly if the marriage partner died.

France declared war on England in 1793 and the new American government had difficulty remaining neutral. Many wanted to join France in her fight for liberty. Ninety percent of our imports came from England, and we could not afford to be at war with her. Trouble arose with Spain. Settlers beyond the Appalachians had only one way to send their produce to market which was to float it down the Ohio and Mississippi to New Orleans and transfer it to ocean going vessels. Spanish authorities in New Orleans demanded such a big tax that there was no profit left. Spain was induced to give Americans free use of the Mississippi and free duty land accommodations at New Orleans while awaiting ocean going ships. Now America had full possession of her own lands.

The Spanish, who had built a fort at St. Louis in order to protect the Upper Mississippi and the Missouri rivers for the Spanish and French, and repel the British and the Americans, decided to encourage white settlers to live in key spots along the Mississippi. Spanish protection was offered white settlers who would move into the area and cultivate friendly relations with the Indians. Already the first permanent white settler had located in the area that is now Iowa. He was Julien Dubuque. He had obtained permission from the Indians in 1788, the year before Washington became president, to operate the lead mines at the site of the Iowa town that now bears his name. He had imported laborers from Canada, but the Indian women did most of the hard work. Twice a year, he and his men took their great flatboats filled with lead and fur and floated down the river to St. Louis. They floated down with only the necessity of steering to keep the boats in the channel and then poled back up stream with great labor.

Now Washington had completed his service as president and John Adams was in office.

Two men who have places in our family tree emigrated to America in 1797 namely FRANCES JAMES YEOMAN and WILLIAM STOAKES, SR.

FRANCES JAMES YEOMAN came from North Ireland to take the southeastern section of New York state where the Scotch-Irish and the Irish settled. He located at Delhi, N.Y. His exact home location in North Ireland is not known. North Ireland, predominately Protestant, had two principal industries, boat building and the manufacture of linen. YEOMAN was Reformed Presbyterian, Scotch-Irish Protestant.

His new home was on the western slope of the picturesque Catskill mountains, conspicuous in song and story for loveliness and grandeur. There were majestic peaks and forest glens and lovely valleys. Fountains of pure water gushed from the hill sides. This is Delaware county, New York, fitted by nature especially for agricultural pursuits. The pioneers converted the area to farms and the valleys resounded with the lowing of the kine, the county now being in the front ranks of the dairy industry. New York City is 150 miles away.

The year that YEOMAN arrived, 1797, was the year that six towns were founded in the county. A little later another town was created named Walton for William Walton who in 1770 had obtained a grant of twenty thousand acres from the King of Ireland. The grant extended from the Delaware to the Susquehanna river. The first houses there were built of logs, as were all the houses in the great wilderness.

The first settlers in Delaware county arrived a decade ahead of YEOMAN and one of them described his situation thus:

> "I have built a house and have a good winter's store laid in. I have a very pleasant situation on the side of Pine Hill. The Delaware river runs on the south side of my house. I think I have laid the foundation for all the happiness this world can afford. It is very expensive moving to this new country, and expensive and difficult getting provisions, however, I hope the worst is over. We have four acres of wheat, half an acre of rye and one of timothy sown. I think I could write a long story about the beauty of this place, wild and

romantic. Fish in great abundance, the finest trout ever was. Pigeons in countless numbers. I kept little Joe to drive them off the grain after sewing, but he could scarcely alarm them. Elk and deer are very plenty. I saw fourteen elk in the river a few rods below my house at one time. Wolves are plenty and frequently come up to our house and around our tent at night. We had to sleep with our children between us to prevent their being carried off; but Prince, king of dogs, has killed three of them and the rest have become more shy. Prince went out alone one day on Pine Hill and brought home a beautiful fawn in his mouth that he had killed. The meat was very fine and quite welcome. We have a variety of wild apples and mandrakes very plentiful in the woods, and every kind of wild berry."

When YEOMAN arrived, the grist mills were crude in construction, only one run of stone. Early settlers carried their grist on horseback and often had to go a considerable distance. There were no mail facilities until later, and the grist carrier performed a double duty by carrying the mail, too. After the mills came the construction of tanneries. Brick kilns were established. Before long potash was manufactured. Clothing was made by hand, the wool from the sheep being carded by hand into rolls. Log churches were erected. Bryant wrote of this country:

"The hills, rock-ribbed and ancient as the sun: the vales
stretching in pensive quietness between
The venerable woods; rivers that move
In majesty, and the complaining brooks
That make the meadows green."

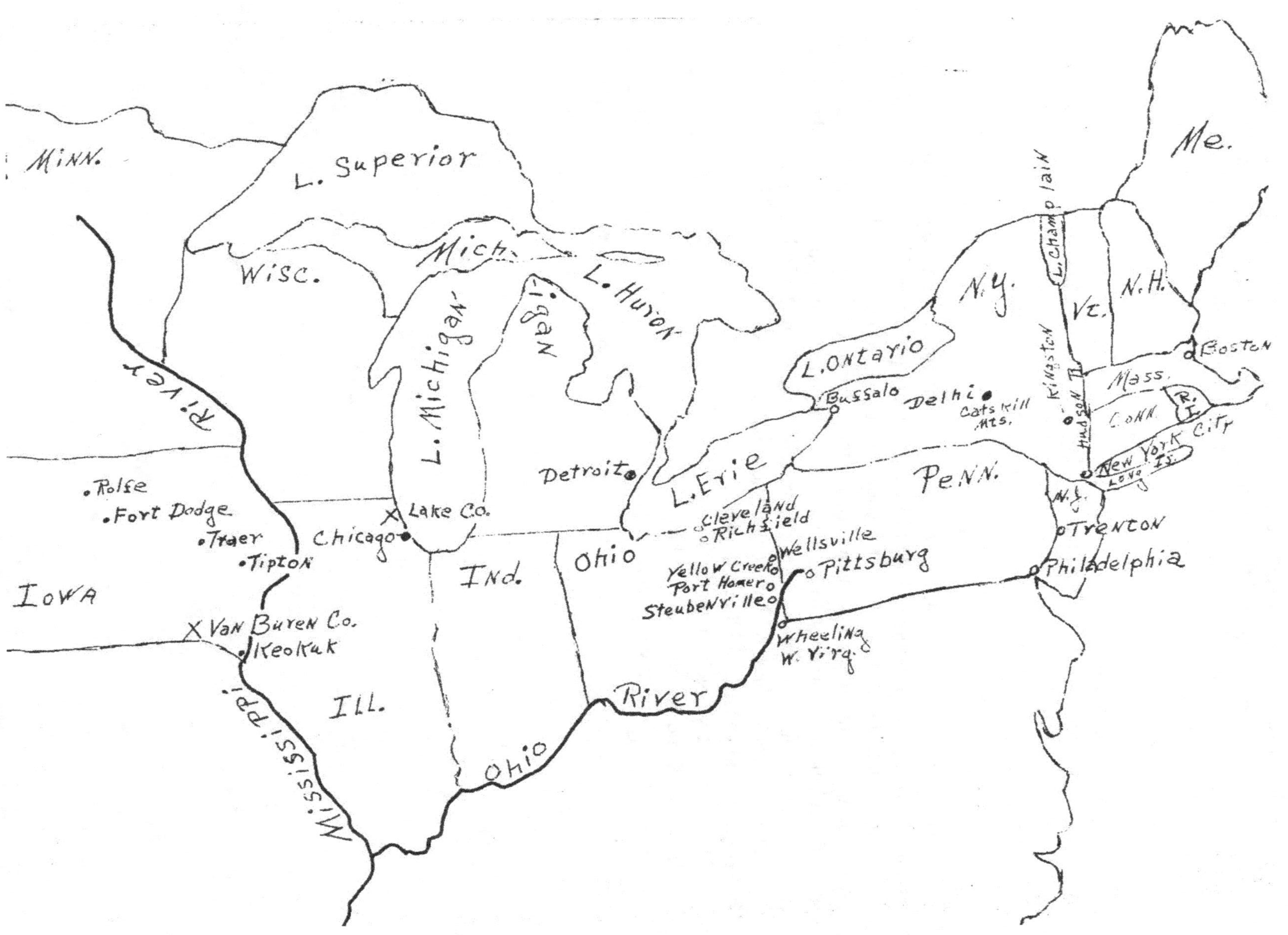

Minn.
L. Superior
Me.
Wisc.
Mich.
L. Huron
L. Michigan
igan
L. Champlain
N.Y.
Vt.
N.H.
L. Ontario
Kingston
Boston
Bussalo
Delhi
Catskill Mts.
Hudson
Mass.
Conn.
R.I.
River
Detroit
L. Erie
Penn.
New York City
Long Is.
Rolfe
Fort Dodge
Lake Co.
Cleveland
Richfield
N.J.
Trenton
Traer
Chicago
Ind.
Ohio
Wellsville
Yellow Creek
Port Homer
Pittsburg
Philadelphia
Tipton
Steubenville
Iowa
X Van Buren Co.
Keokuk
Wheeling
W. Virg.
Mississippi
Ill.
River
Ohio

YEOMAN married JANE STOUT YEOMAN. Nothing is known of her background. They were the parents of ten children. In a listing made of the ten children about 1912 or 1913 by their great grandson, Henry Bates, ELISA was listed first. She was born in 1800, according to her tombstone in Downsville, N.Y. where she is buried as ELISABETH her death having come in 1845. If she were the oldest child, born three years after her father came to America, YEOMAN and JANE may have been married after he arrived in this country. The ten children, in order of their listing: ELISA, David, Jane, Peter, Francis, George, Ellen, Harriet, James and Margaret.

The other ancestor who decided to try his fortune in America the same year that YEOMAN came was WILLIAM STOAKES, SR., a retired merchant from London. Stoakes was a Quaker but there is no reason to believe that he came to America for religious reasons. "The Stoakes Family History" gives this detailed information about him:

Before leaving England, he requested a letter of introduction from his friend, Benjamin West, to West's relatives in Pennsylvania. STOAKES' plan was to come across the Atlantic himself and leave his wife and children behind until he had purchased land and made improvements on it, and then send for the family. West wrote a letter of introduction to his brother, Samuel West, and gave it to STOAKES.

STOAKES crossed the ocean and landed at Philadelphia. He was kindly received by Samuel West. After consideration of STOAKES' object in all of its bearings, they concluded that he had better go West and locate as the Territory of Ohio was then opening to settlers.

Samuel sent a letter of recommendation to his nephew, Isaac Morris, who was a farmer in western Pennsylvania and had resided there ten or twelve years. STOAKES took the letter and wended his way over the mountains on foot to the Morris residence. It being autumn and the roads good, he got along very comfortably on his long walk.

The westward way by now was well traveled for the ever-swelling stream of humanity into the new frontier had started approximately 12 years ahead of STOAKES. A couple of years of prosperity had followed the Revolutionary War and then an economic crash had come, and a great exodus to the new frontier had begun. The government was offering land in the Northwest Territory for one dollar per acre. One section in every township was being reserved for public education and slavery was prohibited.

STOAKES, at the end of his long walk, approximately 250 miles, presented the letter to Morris, who not being able to read, requested that STOAKES read it. On hearing the contents, he gave STOAKES a hearty welcome. Morris was delighted to hear from his uncle.

"The Stoakes Family History" continues the account:

> As the shades of evening were drawing on soon Isaac wished to be excused for
> a little time to attend to some fires in the field below the house before the night
> came. "May I go along?" STOAKES asked. "Oh, no," was the reply, "Thee
> must be weary from thy long journey and perhaps hungry. I will be back soon

and we will have supper." "Nay," said STOAKES, "I am not much tired and would like to go along?" Isaac consented and off they went.

In taking the deadened timber off of the field which he was clearing, Isaac had planned so that each log would burn off the stump, and thus leave the ground entirely free of stumps, hence more attention was necessary than for common log heaps. Soon the men returned to the house and enjoyed the evening with much satisfaction as this little work had rendered them social. Isaac was an early riser and next morning while watching for the first break of day, he observed an unusual light beaming through his chamber window. Rising, he learned the cause. He beheld the fires in his field glowing brilliantly for STOAKES had risen quietly and had the fires in elegant trim. When asked why he had taken so much trouble, he said, "I expect to settle in the woods and I want to learn all I can." The two men formed a friendship that lasted through the years.

Isaac proposed that he put his own farm work into shape and go to Ohio with STOAKES where they could probably make the most judicious selection of land. A land office had been opened recently in the small village of Steubenville. They crossed the Ohio river near that place and STOAKES selected and purchased a tract of land about eleven miles north of Steubenville in Knox township, a little south of Knoxville, in what is now Jefferson county.

Here STOAKES built a log cabin and cleared a small piece of land, which was the beginning of a large farm. STOAKES was a man of splendid physique and well fitted to endure the hardships of pioneer life. The country was heavily timbered and wild game was plentiful, which contributed largely to the bill of fare of the early settlers.

Even panthers were encountered occasionally. STOAKES had the unpleasant experience of being followed by one when returning from getting his laundry from a neighbor's home, several miles distance from his own cabin. At one time, the panther became very bold and threatening and approached quite near. Not being armed, STOAKES resorted to strategy by taking a white shirt from his bundle and taking a sleeve in each hand, threw it above his head, at he same time giving a loud yell. The panther sprang up the hillside and kept a safe distance afterward. However, it followed him home and prowled about his cabin the entire night, but had disappeared when daylight came.

STOAKES made improvements on his cabin and land, and in about two years sent for his family which consisted of his wife, ANN HALL STOAKES, and two sons William, aged nine, and JOHN, aged seven, also a daughter, age unknown. Her name was Sarah.

They crossed the ocean in a sailing vessel and landed in Philadelphia, Pennsylvania, having been three months on the ocean.

The hardships they may have suffered on that trip can only be imagined. Such a trip should have taken from six to eight weeks. Storms sometimes drove ships from their courses making voyages last three months. There were no regular lines of ships nor regulated dates of sailing. The traveler after bargaining with the sea captain for passage, had to wait until the ship was ready to sail and the winds favorable. Meanwhile, he was using up his store of food and supplies he had brought for the journey. Ships were small and completely lacking in comfort. Contagious diseases frequently broke out.

"The Stoakes History" says that ANN HALL STOAKES and her children remained three months in Philadelphia before the husband and father came. They had almost despaired of his coming. He finally arrived having walked the entire distance of about three hundred miles from his claim. He wore a broad brim hat and was clad in frontier garb, quite a morphosis from the fashionably garbed London merchant. So great was the change that his wife and children scarcely knew him at first sight.

STOAKES at once went to work to improvise some conveyance to get his family to their future home in the wilds of Ohio. He purchased an outfit composed of a horse and a side saddle, on which MRS. STOAKES rode, the boys riding alternately behind her. The little daughter had died during their stay in Philadelphia. The father led the horse. In this way, they traveled across the state to Pittsburgh at the head of the Ohio river. They sojourned a few days with Isaac Morris.

At Pittsburgh, STOAKES constructed a raft which his family floated down the Ohio river about eighty miles to a point eleven miles from their cabin, and thus they reached their home.

"The Ohio fever" had swept the nation. The chief entry to the West was over the mountains and down the Ohio river. After crossing the mountains on foot, horseback or in Conestoga wagons, thousands upon thousands floated and poled their way down the Ohio. Sometimes rafts were large enough to carry wagons, livestock, ploughs, and household equipment as well as people. Sometimes several rafts were lashed together.

The settlers of the Steubenville locality at this time, as far as can be learned, were not troubled with Indians, either hostile or peaceable.

By perseverance and industry, the STOAKESES cleared a farm, planted an orchard, and elevated themselves from their first rustic log cabin to a comfortable hewed house situated on the public road running from Steubenville to New Lisbon. Their home was frequently the recipient of many of the first settlers of Columbiana County, nearby, in passing to and from the land office in Steubenville. In those days public houses were few and far between, hence the name of WILLIAM STOAKES became known to many travelers. The Morris and the STOAKES families continued their friendship. STOAKES' oldest son, William, visited Morris and attended school one term. "The Morris Family History" tells of WILLIAM STOAKES, SR. going with Morris' son-in-law to purchase land and of advancing the money to pay for it when other buyers were crowding to buy the same land.

The orchard the STOAKESES planted must have grown well, for the Morris history tell of STOAKES having a large crop of fruit, and of his sending invitations to three families of new settlers to come and get all they wanted. They accepted and took home three wagon loads of peaches.

With almost solid backing of the South and the West and the support of many poor farmers and mechanics in the North, the Republican party swept into power and Thomas Jefferson was elected president in 1800. He was the first president to be inaugurated into the new capital of Washington, hardly more than a village of shabby houses. He paid respect to the poorest citizen as well as to the highest officer. The Federalists had lost control after 12 years. They had put the constitution into operation, created a judicial system, firmly established the national government, and had helped build up commerce and industry. Now Jefferson was in office, a president who had great sympathy for the common man.

Shortly after the turn of the century, HENRY VANTILBURG, whose first wife had been killed by the Hessian soldier, and who had remarried and lived on in New Jersey, now rode into eastern Ohio looking for land. He bought land in Jefferson county near Port Homer, a government fort.

Under the new Land Law of 1800, a settler could buy a small tract of land paying down fifty cents an acre, and the balance of a dollar and a half an acre being spread over four years. HENRY and his brothers had lost their property in New Jersey by the failure of the government to redeem currency issued during the Revolutionary War. The paper money issued by the Continental Congress had declined to zero and the phrase "Not worth a Continental" was coined.

In the fall of 1801, HENRY brought his family from New Jersey. He was so late that he could not get his cabin completed before winter. The family was obliged to spend the winter in the fort, where the youngest daughter, JANE, was born early in the spring of 1802. She was welcomed by five brothers and four sisters namely Daniel, Henry, Peter, John, Frank, Elizabeth, Kathern, Nancy, Keziah, besides two half-brothers and a half-sister, children of the mother killed by the Hessian.

HENRY had limited means to start a new home on the frontier, but he and his family were industrious and frugal and soon acquired a competence. In the Ohio country in those days, neighbors joined together to build rough houses. Large families meant additional workers. Food came from the farm. Clothing was homemade.

The VANTILBURGS arrived at Port Homer only a couple of years after MRS. STOAKES and two boys had come to Steubenville. The two farms were only a few miles apart.

Turnpikes, 3,000 miles of them were being built in New York state by private companies. The companies built the roads and bridges and collected tolls from the users. The state government gave the companies the land. The population was not great enough yet in Ohio to interest private companies in building roads and bridges there. President Jefferson tried unsuccessfully to get congress to aid in these improvements as a means of helping sell public lands in the West.

The year before JANE VANTILBURG was born in the Ohio fort, another man and wife emigrated to America. ROBERT BEAT and his wife Isabel Rodger Beat came from Moneidie, Scotland. They brought with them, his children: Ann, age 12 and JAMES, age 10, and ROBERT and Isabel's son Robert, age 5. All the children had been born in Collertown (or Cottertown) Scotland. They arrived in America in 1801.

Ann and JAMES were the children of ROBERT BEAT and JEAN NULLION BEAT. JAMES was born April 17, 1791. (A friend of Mary Pollock's from St. Abbs, Scotland went to Edinburgh and traced family genealogy in the official registry there as a courtesy to Mary. This was done in 1969. Her research took the Beat family back to around 1680 in Scotland).

ROBERT BEAT was born May 27, 1764 in Letham and had three sisters, Jean, Margaret and Anna, and a brother John. They were the children of WILLIAM BEAT, born in Letham Sept. 26, 1731, and MARGARET PEDDIE BEAT, born in Letham Sept. 13, 1730. She was the daughter of WILLIAM PEDDIE and SICILLE RED PEDDIE. WILLIAM was the son of JOHN BEAT, born at Gollybanks Dec. 30, 1705, and MARGARET BURGESS BEAT. Besides WILLIAM, they had seven other children: Margaret, Patrick, John, Gilbert, Robert, Charles and David, all born at Letham. JOHN BEAT's father was WILLIAM BEAT, probably born around 1680.

ROBERT BEAT brought with him to America two little letters of introduction which said:

Moneidie, 16 April 1801
This is to certify that the bearer Robert Beat and his wife and family resided in this parish from their infancy and behaved themselves civilly and inoffensively and that nothing has been known or delated in this kirk session to obstruct their admission   into any Christian society where Providence may order their lot. This certificate was given by the High session of Moneidie at their meeting this day and is attested   by

George Frazer, Moderator   Alex Robertson, Session Clerk
Donald Drumond, Elder   Charles Beat, Elder
     (Charles Beat, Elder, may have been ROBERT'S uncle)

Perth, 17 April 1801
We the undersigned hereby acknowledge that the bearer Robert Beat has acted honestly in whatever transactions he has had with us, and previous to his leaving this place has fully paid or otherwise settled such accounts as were betwixt him and us and to the best of our knowledge and belief there is not any claim against his person or property.
     (This was signed by twelve merchants and dealers.)

The original copies of the above two letters are now the treasured property of Charles and Vida M. Bates of Walton, N.Y., great great grandchildren of ROBERT BEAT. We are deeply indebted to Charles and Vida for furnishing information on both the Yeomans and Beats coming to America and their early years in this country.)

ROBERT BEAT first settled on Long Island. He sold that farm and went up to Scotch Mountain near Delhi in beautiful Delaware county, New York, on the western slopes of the Catskills near where YEOMAN had settled a few years earlier.

Perth, from where the BEATS came, is in the Lowlands of Scotland between the Firth of Clyde and the Firth of Forth. It resembles fertile England and contains a dense population and large industries.

ROBERT BEAT from Scotland spelled his name "BEAT." His son JAMES added an "s." JAMES' sons Robert and Gurdon spelled it "Beates." Some other descendants changed it to "Bates".

While the BEATS were settling down in New York state, the endless stream of settlers continued pushing on westward. A few thousand had even crossed the Mississippi River into what was then Spanish territory. They believed Spain was weak and could not long oppose the expansion of the United States. When the news came in 1801 that Napoleon had forced Spain to give the great land called Louisiana back to the French, the West was aflame with excitement. The mighty Napoleon was dangerous. He could block the territory west of the Mississippi. He could close the New Orleans port through which three-eighths of the U.S. produce went to market. From flatboat to flatboat and all through the Ohio valley this news spread. It undoubtedly brought consternation to the STOAKES and VANTILBURG homes as it did to all the new homes of the West. Their whole economy was based on exporting down the river. There was no way to take produce in quantity over the land to the East. The State of Ohio alone by now was raising crops valued at $700,000 for export.

President Jefferson acted quickly. He sent men to see Napoleon who was about to renew fighting in Europe. He was willing to turn over uncertain liabilities in the New World for cash in the Old. He offered to sell Louisiana to Jefferson for $15,000,000 and Jefferson readily accepted. The transaction was completed in 1803. The Western settlers could breath easy again. Their economy was safe.

The purchase had doubled the size of America! The next year, the president sent Lewis and Clark west to explore and report on the new land. They wintered in St. Louis in 1804 before starting up the Missouri River for the far west. As they moved along the western boundary of what is now Iowa, they shot deer, bear, turkey, grouse, beaver, catfish, geese and buffalo. They encountered and talked to Indians.

Soon after Lewis and Clark started up the Missouri, Zebulon M. Pike was sent up the Mississippi to explore the upper part of that river. On his trip along the eastern boundary of Iowa-to-be, he visited the Sauk and Fox Indians and found Julien Dubuque a cagey and uninformative host at the Mines of Spain.

The area that is to become Iowa had become, by the Louisiana Purchase, part of the youthful American Republic. This had ended 130 years under French and Spanish rule.

By the fall of 1808 a fort and stockade, first called Bellevue and later Fort Madison, manned by 60 or 80 blue coated soldiers, had been built on the Mississippi above the turbulent Des Moines River rapids. The Americans had given the Sauk and Fox Indians a $300 in trade goods for the land.

Now France and England were locked in a deadly war. Neither would recognize the right of America, as a neutral, to trade with the enemy. American exports were our life blood. Both sides kept capturing our ships, especially those filled with foodstuffs. Between 1803 and 1812, the British captured 917 and the French 558. American lawmakers decided to stop all trade with foreign ports, but this ruined the ship owners, put sailors, merchants, bookkeepers and longshoremen out of work, tumbled farm prices and hard times hit. Then America offered that if either would stop interfering with our commerce, we'd trade with her alone. France agreed. Britain said we were no longer neutral and blockaded our coast.

On the wilderness side of America, 48 million acres of Indian hunting grounds had been taken by treaty by the Americans. Two great Indian leaders, Shawnees, arose: Tecumseh and his brother The Prophet. They determined to save their race. Then William Henry Harrison, governor of Indiana, got some Indians to cede him Tecumseh's hunting ground. The famous battle of Tippecanoe in east central Indiana ensued, Nov. 7, 1811 and Harrison defeated Tecumseh. The Americans suffered heavy losses and blamed the British in Canada for giving guns and ammunition to the Indians.

Urged on by the fiery young frontiersmen with unlimited faith in their country, and lead by the youthful Henry Clay, congress declared war on England. Clay wanted to take Canada to make up for losses to American shipping, and declared that Indian attacks would continue until Canada was ours.

Canada, with one-sixteenth our population, did not wish to be a part of United States, and fought hard aided by several thousand regular British soldiers, to defeat three American expeditions sent in 1812 to capture strategic points on the Great Lakes. An American column of 2,000 men had to surrender Detroit and the other two expeditions failed.

Most of British men living in the old fur trading town of Prairie du Chien, just across the Mississippi from the northeast corner of Iowa-to-be, had left their village to help the British and Canadians at Green Bay and Mackinac on Lake Michigan. The Americans in St. Louis chose this time to strike Prairie du Chien. Two hundred men in five barges went up the Mississippi and took Prairie du Chien without firing a shot. They erected a stockade and named it Fort Shelby.

When the men who'd gone to Mackinac learned this, they headed for Prairie du Chien, accompanied by Canadians in British uniforms and their Indian friends. A total of 120 white men in barges and 500 Indians in canoes attack Fort Shelby. The Americans held successfully for awhile but finally agreed to surrender if the British would protect the Americans from the Indians. This was agreed upon and the Americans went back to St. Louis.

A few months later the Americans at St. Louis dispatched Zachary Taylor and 334 officers and men in fortified boats to chastise the Indians. Word of this reached Prairie du Chien and soldiers were sent to reinforce the 1000 to 1500 Indians who were going to attack the Americans as they came upstream. In the engagement, at the present site of Davenport, Taylor soon decided that his forces were inadequate to cope with the enemy, and he dropped back to St. Louis.

Encouraged with success, some dissident Sauk and Fox known as "the British Band" and led by Black Hawk who had been fighting with the British in Canada, increased their harassment of Fort Madison on the Mississippi just above the Des Moines River. One day the Indians opened fire on the soldiers who were chopping wood near the fort. The Indian siege kept the soldiers from coming outside the fort for their wood. Then the Indians started shooting flaming arrows into the fort. This resulted in the soldiers, themselves, setting fire to the fort in September 1813 and slipping away in the night by boats for St. Louis.

Back in Indiana and Ohio, William Henry Harrison took charge of a large, new force of soldiers. In the fall of 1813 he recaptured Detroit aided by Commander Oliver Perry's clearing Lake Erie on the north border of Ohio of British warships.

The Stoakes brothers, William Jr. and JOHN fought with Harrison at Detroit. They had grown to manhood in Ohio assisting in clearing and improving the large tract of land taken by their father at the turn of the century near Steubenville. The brothers had had limited opportunity outside of the home in the line of education, as educational facilities were limited. They had received considerable education at home, though, for their parents were both well educated. JOHN took great interest in public affairs, was a strong Whig, and a great admirer of Henry Clay, The Stoakes History says.

A descendant of Isaac Morris wrote:

> "In 1812, during the panic among the Columbiana county settlers because of the false rumors that the Indians were on the warpath, the father of Morris Miller and his family and many others fled from their homes. Two of the families decided to go to WILLIAM STOAKES. They rested awhile at the salt works on Yellow Creek and at midnight started on their journey again reaching the home of their friend, STOAKES, about daylight, where they were kindly received and their necessities relieved."

The account continues:

> "That day was to be remembered with them as well as ourselves. Their elder son William, Jr. was a captain of a military company and that day they were to rendezvous at their father's house and commence their march for the frontier, their provisions and baggage wagon having been prepared the day before. The company assembled at the appointed time, and their captain took them through a short drill and then addressed them in a brief but very appropriate speech standing on his father's doorstep. A little later Henry Boyles and his rifle company arrived and all marched off toward Steubenville. Recruiting was in progress everywhere at that time."

The younger son JOHN went into the service as a private a month after his brother left. In order to comfort the brothers' parents, Isaac Morris sent an eleven year old son, Mordecai, to live with the STOAKESES and do chores during the winter.

William Jr. and JOHN served under General Harrison on the northwestern frontier until the close of the war. They were in the Battle of the Thames in which the enemy, under the British General Proctor and the great Indian Chief Tecumseh, were defeated. Tecumseh was killed. William Stoakes Jr. was promoted to a major and at one time was a member of a company organized by General Harrison to capture and burn several British ships which were ice bound not for from Detroit, but a high wind came up the night before the attack was to be made, and broke up the ice and the ships escaped. The Americans charged that the British had promised the Indians that if they would fight bravely and help defeat the Americans, the American prisoners would be turned over to the Indians to be dealt with as they saw fit. These Indians entertained a bitter hatred for General Harrison who had defeated them only a few years earlier at Tippecanoe.

The British and the Americans fought a big sea battle on Lake Chaplain in northeastern New York state and the British were trounced. But on our eastern coast, the British drove our navy off of the sea and controlled our coastline landing raiding parties at will. In August 1814, the British marched on Washington, our government fled, and the British burned our capitol and executive mansion. Britain was preparing to attack New Orleans. We wanted peace. After 22 years of war, and having recently defeated Napoleon, the British wanted peace, too. A peace treaty was signed in Europe by the two nations on Christmas Eve 1814, but news of it did not reach America until 49 days later. Meanwhile, the greatest battle of the war was fought at New Orleans with a great victory for America and it made Andrew Jackson a hero.

The war left bitterness on both sides. We had fought England twice in our short history, and decades had to pass before friendship returned. England did develop more respect for us as a nation. We turned our face from Europe to westward expansion. During this war, Francis Scott Key wrote "The Star-Spangled Banner" and our feeling of being a nation became more fixed.

> "At the close of the war the militia had been discharged without any provision for transportation home and the Stoakes brothers with many others were obliged to walk through the almost roadless wilderness to their homes several hundred miles distant, the best walkers getting there first," according to Stoakes history.

The Indians were assembled at Prairie du Chien and told that the United States and Great Britain were now at peace. The chiefs accepted the news stoically and smoked the peace pipe, but some of the Indians in the Upper Mississippi Valley received the news with despair. They felt as though they had been deserted for the influence of the British trader over the Indians was still strong. The British evacuated Prairie du Chien and the U.S. took over control, established fur trading, factories, Indian agencies and military posts. The government decided to establish forts at Chicago (Fort Dearborn), Green Bay (Fort Howard), Prairie du Chien (Fort Crawford), near the Falls of Saint Anthony (Fort Snelling), at Rock Island (Fort Armstrong), and opposite the mouth of the Des Moines River (Fort Edward).

Three years later, in the spring of 1818, fur traders brought their season's catch to the trading post at Prairie du Chien. Boats from St. Louis began to arrive at the post with provisions, whisky and supplies of all kinds, a welcome sight to the garrison and the traders. Many boats loaded with furs left for Mackinac and St. Louis. In June a fleet of Winnebago Indians arrived and erected their teepees on the island opposite the fort. The braves, naked except for a breechclout and painted all colors, danced through the streets of the village. On the nation's birthday, the troops fired a cannon at daybreak, and later marched out of the fort and fired a salute by platoons. The Indians, reportedly, were greatly impressed.

Back in the East, the states were trying to figure a way to bring produce from the rapidly growing new West to the East coast. Smoothing a road between the western settlers and the eastern seaboard had been advocated as early as George Washington's administration. Now the talk was to build canals. Pennsylvania and Maryland wanted a canal that would connect the Great Lakes to the Susquehanna River and thus to Chesapeake Bay. The BEAT and YEOMAN households probably took great interest in this idea for the headwaters of the Susquehanna were in their own county.

New Yorkers as a whole, though, advocated a canal east and west across their state from Lake Erie to the Hudson River. Of this idea, Jefferson wrote, "Talk of making a canal 350 miles through the wilderness is short of madness." But New York was afraid the Susquehanna and the Mississippi Rivers would capture the bulk of the western trade, so under the leadership of the governor, DeWitt Clinton, started digging the Erie-to-the-Hudson canal July 4, 1817. It quickly was scoffingly labeled "Clinton's Ditch".

The next year ROBERT BEAT, the Scotchman from Perth, died. He had come to America when he was 36 years old and died at the age of 53. His daughter Ann (or Anna) had married James Stoddard and her father is buried in the Stoddard family lot at Delhi, New York and his stone is marked 1765-1818. (The official registry in Edinburgh lists his birth as 1764). The burial place of his wife is unknown. Robert Jr. died when a young man. He was returning from New York City and landing at Kingston on the Hudson. He dropped from the plank he was walking into the water and never rose to the surface again. His body was found and buried at Kingston. He had two sons: August became a businessman in New York and Brooklyn, and Andrew went to sea and was never heard of again. ROBERT SR. was survived by his son JAMES who is part of our family tree.

Out in Ohio, in the Steubenville and Port Homer neighborhood, this was the wedding year, 1818, for JANE VANTILBURG, who had been born in the fort, and JOHN STOAKES, who had recently fought in the War of 1812. She was 17 and he was 26. Both of the Stoakes brothers had been attracted to the HENRY VANTILBURG home, a short distance from their own, by the two youngest daughters in the family. William Stoakes Jr. had married Keziah Vantilburg after the war. They made their home with his parents and reared a family of nine children. JOHN and JANE, after their marriage, located on the north part of the Stoakes farm near Yellow Creek, where they lived nearly thirty years and reared a family of ten children. We have no idea what kind of a house they had on Yellow Creek in the first years of their marriage.

The government was wondering just what it had out beyond the Mississippi and was beginning to send military expeditions on foot to explore. The first of these to explore Iowa-to-be was headed by Stephen W. Kearny in 1820. Kearny and his men went up the Missouri River to the present site of Council Bluffs and then struck out toward the northeast. They shot deer and buffalo and prairie chickens, visited Indian villages, saw miles and miles of waving grass, were soaked by sudden rains, crossed marshes and treeless areas, swamps and timber land. Their route took them to the present site of Emmetsburg and to the Falls of St. Anthony.

The VANTILBURGS and the STOAKESES were seeing their dream unfold and become reality. Statehood came to their Ohio in 1821. The future looked good to the two young couples: William Jr. and Keziah, and JOHN and JANE.

The Scotch born JAMES BEATS (he now added an "s" to Beat) had grown up on his father ROBERT'S farm on Scotch Mountain near Delhi, and in 1822 married ELISA (ELISABETH) YEOMAN, the daughter of FRANCIS JAMES YEOMAN of North Ireland. Apparently she, too, had grown up on a farm for her younger sister Ellen married a Presbyterian minister, Aaron A. Shaver, minister for many years at Shaverton, and they reportedly lived on the YEOMAN home farm.

When JAMES and ELISA were married, he bought a farm in Bovina township in Delaware county. There they lived for nine years and their first children were born there.

Looking Westward

Out West on the Mississippi, the first steamboat chugged its way up to Fort Snelling (Minneapolis). It was a 20 day trip from St. Louis. Only the Indians, a few miners, fur traders, missionaries and soldiers probably saw the boat chugging upstream. The crew stopped many times to cut timber for the boilers. Passengers were: an Indian agent, an Italian traveler, a Sauk chief, a missionary, a Kentucky family of settlers.

Fifty miles north of the young BEATS, the Erie Canal was completed. The builders had wisely constructed "the long level" first, and completed that easier part swiftly thus adding impetus to the more difficult portion of the project. Underwater cement was discovered and was a boon to construction. This canal (four feet deep, 28 feet across the bottom, 40 feet across the top with 81 locks) had crossed 350 miles of wilderness, rocky barrens and miasmic swamps by 1825. Jefferson had called the idea "short of madness", and skeptics had labeled it "Clinton's Ditch", but its success was immediate and it was soon referred to as "The Grand Canal". Forty thousand persons passed her locks the first year... a guide book of that year said 500 persons a day were going West through the canal.

Western produce poured East through the canal. Along with the grain and pig boats, and passenger packets, there were occasional library boats, theatre and waxwork boats to entertain and educate the people of the canal towns. The boats were propelled by animals hitched to the boats and driven along the towpaths along side of the canals. The drivers, known as "hoggies", sang rousing songs, told tales, joked and fought. A new type of folklore sprang up along the canal. America prospered and living standards rose.

In a giant effort by the United States government to get the Indians of the Upper Mississippi Valley to bury the tomahawk and agree to confine their excursions in search of game within specific boundaries, the Indians were called together in "The Great Council of 1825" at Prairie du Chien. The government especially desired to put an end to the bloody clashes between the

Sioux and the confederated Sauk and Fox, and the equally sanguinary Sioux-Chippewa feud to the north. This was one of the most imposing councils ever held with the red men. Chiefs, principal men, warriors and their families arrived from all directions. From the region of Fort Snelling came 400 Sioux and Chippewa. From distant Sault Ste. Marie, 150 Chippewa. Hundreds of Winnebago from Wisconsin. Many, many Sauk and Fox. A total of 2,000 Indians.

Up from St. Louis came a government keelboat loaded with provisions and presents for the Indians- rations valued at $6,750. The tobacco, salt, sugar, gun powder, lead and liquor for presents were valued at $2,000. Pay of the interpreters, help, transportation and other expenses brought the total cost to $10,400.

This was in impressive historic sight: The Indians arriving from Fort Snelling area stopped above Prairie du Chien and prepared for an impressive arrival. They arranged their canoes in columns and swept down the river with flags flying, drums beating and guns firing. They stopped at the levee in an imposing array. Soon the buffalo skin tepees dotted the prairie for miles above and below the village. The tall and warlike Chippewas and Winnebagoes from Lake Superior and the St. Croix Valley jostled the Menominee, Potawatomi and the Ottawa Indians from Lake Michigan and Green Bay. Sioux Indians carried war clubs and lances decorated with every imaginable device of paint. The Sauk and the Fox and the Ioway were the last to arrive. In their finery and singing songs, they swept up the river and back again. As the prairie was already filled with teepees of the early arrivals, these Indians camped on an island.

The council began and the Indians were told that the Great White Father in Washington did not ask any of their lands, but wanted them to stop their bloody fighting and live in peace as brothers of one great family, and to establish boundaries for their hunting grounds. The Indians agreed to this idea. The chiefs argued for days over the boundaries, but at last agreements were made and signed, and the wampum belt was passed, the calumet was smoked as a solemn pledge that the war tomahawk was buried "never to be raised again as long as the trees grow, or the waters of the river continue to run." Then tribe by tribe the Indians departed.

Eight years had passed since JOHN and JANE STOAKES married and established their home on Yellow Creek in eastern Ohio, on the north part of his father's farm. Four children had come to bless their home. Now the Stoakes built a fine brick mansion (the ruins of which were still standing in 1915). And William Jr. and Keziah had just completed a brick home, too, about a half mile south of Knoxville, on the Steubenville and New Lisbon road. Not long after JOHN completed his brick house, he built a mill on Town Fork, a branch of Yellow Creek, where he ground grist for the settlers for many miles around.

Textile factories had recently come to New England. Spinning, carding, weaving by power were being done in this country now, as well as in England. The production of raw cotton to finished cloth was being completed under one roof.

The first public transportation in any large city in America had just been introduced to New York City in the form of horse-drawn bus lines. Before that, everyone walked to work except the rich who had private carriages.

On the farm in Bovina township, Delaware county, New York state, JAMES and ELISA BEATS welcomed a new daughter, MARY MARGARET, into their growing family in 1828. Often peeping into her cradle was a brother Robert, 5, and a sister Sarah, 2.

When MARY MARGARET was three, her parents sold the Bovina township farm and purchased a 500 acre farm near Downsville, N.Y., still in Delaware county. That year a fourth child was welcomed into the family and named James after his father JAMES.

The senior JAMES BEATS' parents had brought two little letters of introduction and endorsement from Scotland when they came to America. Now JAMES and his wife took a little letter from their Bovina church, signed by the acting minister, to Downsville with them. This letter, written in ink in fine penmanship on a piece of paper now yellowed with age, is the property of Charles and Vida Bates. They also have the two little letters brought from Scotland.

The Bovina letter says as near as can be deciphered 130 years after it was written: "This is to certify that Elisabeth Beats was in full communion with the Ansoite preabler or cave Church of Bovina when she was married to Mr. Beets and nothing to hinder her to be taken into any Christian Church as far as known to me at the time of her marriage. Bovinea 11 of July, 1831. Walter Doig E. Der."

Out in Ohio, sadness came to the STOAKES households. That staunch English couple, WILLIAM STOAKES SR. and ANN HALL STOAKES, both died. They had brought their little family from London more than three decades earlier and had carved out a home in the Ohio wilderness. Now both of their sons lived in fine brick homes and had growing families. ANN died March 7, 1831, and WILLIAM SR. Nov. 18, 1831, after 42 years of marriage.

The Sauk and Fox Indians, under the leadership of Keokuk, had sold their lands east of the Mississippi in Illinois by treaty to the whites. The Indians, however, were not required to vacate their property until the government sold it to private buyers. Soon, though, the white settlers began to flood the land. George Davenport, later the founder of Davenport, bought the great Sauk village of Saukenuk on the Rock River, a short way upstream from the Mississippi. Keokuk, understanding the treaty and resigned to the inevitable, took his loyal band of Indians across the Mississippi into Iowa, which was reserved at that time for Indians. But Black Hawk, a Sauk warrior, did not want to leave his home village of Saukenuk and crossed into Iowa reluctantly. There Black Hawk longed for his old home, and thinking his old friends the British and other friendly Indian tribes, would help him. He recruited other disgruntled Indians and made plans to return to Saukenuk. Keokuk, who commanded the loyalty of most Sauk, warned Black Hawk not to go. Black Hawk went and the Black Hawk War ensued bringing death to his 400 followers and capture and humiliation to himself.

Peace was made in September 1832 at a great council held at the present site of Davenport. The Indians were forced to give up six million acres of land in Iowa. The government agreed to pay $640,000. This was the Black Hawk Purchase.

When the Indians vacated this land in eastern Iowa, future white farmers were already lined up with their covered wagons to claim new farms. The settlers moved in rapidly. Prior to this practically the only white people who lived in Iowa were the 400 who lived in the mining village of Dubuque.

As Iowa was opening to these very first white settlers, a new son was born to JOHN and JANE STOAKES back in Ohio in their new brick home and they called him ELEAZER. He arrived on March 4, 1833 and was welcomed by three sisters and three brothers, the oldest 14 years old. They were: Martha Jane, Nancy Ann, William M., Henry C., John R. and Elizabeth. A few fields away lived ELEAZER'S uncle and aunt, William Jr. and Keziah and their bevy of children. The old folks had come from England, WILLIAM SR. and ANN HALL STOAKES and both had died two years earlier. ELEAZER'S maternal grandparents, the VANTILBURGS, may still have been living nearby.

Eleven days after ELEAZER'S birth, a couple destined to play a major part in his future life, sailed from England for America. MR. and MRS. ROBERT GRANGER sailed May 27, 1833 from St. Catherine's Dock, London, on the American Packet Ship Sampson. It was ROBERT'S twenty-sixth birthday. She was 24.

Information compiled at a family reunion by their grandchildren years later says:

> "The spring following their marriage ROBERT GRANGER'S health was very poor and they decided an ocean voyage might be of benefit to him, so planned to come to the new country, America, and make a home for themselves here... After a voyage of 56 days on the ocean, they landed in New York July 22, 1833, approximately a year after their marriage. ROBERT GRANGER, born May 27, 1807, and MISS ELISABETH NEWMAN, born Feb. 22, 1809, were married in their native town of Cambridgeshire, England, July 29, 1832.
>
> ELIZABETH'S folks did not want her to come then with ROBERT," the family information says, "for she had a tiny baby girl, Harriet by name, to care for, and they thought it was too big an undertaking for her at that time, but she would not stay so came when he did. They said that as soon as they were on the water ROBERT began to feel better and was in good health when they arrived, but ELIZABETH did not fare so well. It worked just the reverse for her, she was not so well on the ocean, in fact sick most of the time.
>
> From New York, they journeyed by tow-boat up the Hudson River to Albany, thence on the Erie Canal to the city of Buffalo situated on the shores of Lake Erie. From Buffalo they took passage for Cleveland, Ohio on the steamer Uncle Sam, the first steam boat that plied between Buffalo and Cleveland," the Granger Family Story says.

The canal was a busy picturesque place with the boats carrying farm products, hides, wool, wheat, other grains and such things as potash, pearlash, staves, shingles and salt, and sometimes a great deal of meat and way-freight between all the places along the route. These boats were much slower than the passenger and packet boats which had relays of horses at stations and went quite fast. They had good cabins for passengers, too, and cooks and stewards served fine meals.

The tow-path drivers, many of them orphan boys, urged on the mules or horses in loud picturesque phrases. As on the sea, chanties sprang up or were adapted from older chanties from the old country and there was much singing as folk moved westward. The sound of the friendly boatman's horn rolled over meadows and farmyards.

After the canal and the steamboat ride on Lake Erie, the GRANGERS disembarked at Cleveland, a boom town which was to grow from 1076 to 6081 population in that decade. Cleveland was a boat building town and this was a time when many, many steamboats were being constructed. The Ohio Canal had been newly completed connecting Lake Erie across the state to Ohio River thus opening up water transportation on down to the Mississippi and thus to the Gulf.

ROBERT and ELIZABETH and little Harriet went inland, south from Cleveland about 20 miles, half way between that city and the present site of Akron. They settled in Summit county on the banks of a little creek called Furnace Run. This creek still goes by that name.

ROBERT had learned the trade of carpenter and wagon maker in his native land and engaged in that and mechanical work for many years in the new country. Wagon making was an important occupation when thousands of persons were moving westward, many of them on wheels.

This was the Jacksonian Era. Andrew Jackson, hero of New Orleans in the War of 1812 and popularly known as Old Hickory, was president. The new western states had made their influence felt. The Westerner's voice and opinions were worth as much as those of the aristocratic merchant and planter of the East. Real democracy was blooming. Social rank had greatly diminished. Vigor, self-reliance and industry, not birth, privilege or wealth, were the marks of distinction. The test of a man was what he could do: manage a wild horse, drive an axe deep, repel and Indian attack. Head and hand were engaged in invention and industry. The McCormick reaper had just been patented. A steam locomotive on a new 13 mile track of the Baltimore and Ohio railroad gave promise of the future. There was talk about the settlement of Oregon, but some Congressman scoffed at this idea explaining that it would take a whole year for a man to journey beyond the Rockies and back to Washington, our capital.

A military expedition was sent to explore the central, and as yet unsettled portion, of that land what would become Iowa. Three companies of dragoons, mounted infantrymen, went up the Des Moines River to the present site of Des Moines, then swung northeast across Iowa into Minnesota and up to Lake Pepin, turned west and circled back south. They returned by the way of the present Kossuth county and went down the Des Moines River valley. They stopped one night where the north branch of Lizard Creek flows into the Des Moines River. This is the first record of white men in what is now Webster County, and which a little more than two decades later would be the home of the POLLOCKS. Kearny and Albert Lea commanded the dragoons and Lea made many notes. He found the soil rich and fruitful and the climate pleasant- mostly prairie but with timber usually available in the neighborhood. He encouraged families to come and settle on this rich land. His use of the name Iowa District encourage others to call this new area- Iowa. This was 1835.

While the dragoons were exploring Iowa, the last of JAMES and ELISA BEATS' family of six children was born on the 500 acre farm near Downsville, New York. She was named Harriet N.

Her big sister MARY MARGARET was then seven. Robert was 12, Sarah 9, James 4 and Gurdon E. 3. Both JAMES and ELISA apparently held members of their own families in great affection for they passed on to their children names from previous generations namely Robert, James, Margaret and Harriet. They were names destined to go on down through subsequent generations, too.

The six Beats children grew up on this farm near Downsville, in a house later described by two of Robert's grandchildren who knew it in their own youth. "It was a frame house with a fireplace at each end," Emma Foster says. She lived on this same farm as a little girl. Charles L. Bates, who himself lived in the old house until he was six years old, (and who lives at Walton, New York with his sister Vida as this is being written) recalls, "As I remember it, while we lived there, it was a long house with a stone chimney at each end- the fireplaces were no longer in use- a big heater stove at the west end and a cookstove at the east end- several rooms in between. I remember the east door where I was playing one day when a black sheep butted a chair after me into the room. The chair had been placed across the door to keep him out. I think the back side of the house slanted down to one story. There was an orchard around the house and a big watering trough in the backyard fed from a large spring on the hill nearby."

This must have been a big roomy house in which MARY MARGARET and her brothers and sisters grew up. The nearby hillsides were covered with maples and hemlocks. The stand of hemlock trees from Pennsylvania to Maine is said to be the largest stand of hemlock in the world.

There is a hill called "Money Point" on the north side of the farm. Charles L. Bates, spoken of above, wrote, "At the time of the Revolution there was a Tory settlement at the south end of the farm whose captain, a Reuben Peters, was said to have buried his loot- a kettle of coins- on the hill called Money Point. My brother and I searched for it when we were too young to know any better but in vain!" We might wonder if MARY MARGARET and her brothers and sisters might have done some digging in their childhood, too.

This was maple sugar country! Can you visualize the young BEATS children probably helping with the buckets, the tapping and the gathering? MARY MARGARET must have passed on her enthusiastic liking for maple sugar to her own children for some of them years later were especially fond of it. Charles L. Bates' sister, Vida Bates, a school teacher, wrote in 1928 recalling the old-fashioned way of the seasonal task of sugar making. Excerpts from her account follow:

> "...of wooden spiles (made by hand), wooden troughs, of wooden buckets set on the ground at the foot of trees, gathered by hand with sap yoke or by means of horse-drawn sled with barrels, boiling in enormous kettles over an outdoor arch..."

> Tapping is lots of fun. The sleigh is loaded with buckets and covers and spouts and carefully packed tapping bits. Besides the boring of the holes and driving of spouts, there is the hanging of buckets and fitting of covers, the latter being

often the boy's job. It means traveling miles in rubber boots but it does give the finest introduction to Spring.

While the sap is running, one has time to set up the big evaporator and storage tank, connecting them with some sort of pipe and regulator. The regulator is to determine the flow of the sap from tank to boiling pan. In our neighborhood there are some evaporators with corrugated bottoms to expose a greater surface to the fire, but many of us still use flat-bottomed evaporators. Both admit cold sap at one end and yellow syrup to be drawn off at the other.

The fuel used here is wood. The more provident have a supply already piled conveniently near the arch, perhaps under cover at one end of the sap house. The boiling place varies from the arch of stones out in the open where the storms and flying leaves enrich the color of the syrup to the iron furnace set up inside a well-built sap house with ventilators in the roof to be opened and closed according to the direction of the wind.

The gathering tank is a closed receptacle that can be drawn by the farmer's team... As soon as the right combination of wind and sun has brought a flow of sap, one may see on the hillsides the teams toiling up and down in the sunshine. We watch to see whose smokestack sends up the first signal column of the real opening of the sap session. This is really the beginning. One may tap trees at one's convenience, but the sap may not flow for days afterward. Trees on a sunny slope or in a wet place are affected sooner than those on a drier or colder exposure.

      Probably everybody has heard these couplets:
            Wind in the north, Sap pours forth.
            Wind in the south, Sap has a drouth.
            Wind in the east, Sap flows least.
            Wind in the west, Sap flows best.

We can hardly wait for the first sap to be gathered and boiled in the big evaporator, and brought to the house for the finishing process. How good the hot syrup tastes even when it burns the tongue! Then comes... testing... weighing... longer cooking for sugar... stirring... caking... a delightful business. The first run is often made into little cakes of sugar which sell at top-notch prices. By far the larger proportion is sold as syrup in 50 gallon drums.

After a few weeks the weather gets so warm that the tree buds open and sap sours as fast as it drips from the spouts. This means the end of sugar making and the time to wash all equipment. The next sunny day when the wind is not too strong you may see a stack of sap buckets draining on porch floors and on boards laid out in dooryards. Before dark, everything is put away to await another season."

Out West, Texans declared their independence from Mexico, 1836, the year of the Alamo and the subsequent routing of the Mexican army by General Sam Houston and his Texas volunteers. Fifty thousand Americans had gone into Texas to settle by that time.

A Whig man, William Henry Harrison, hero of Tippecanoe, a former territorial governor and member of congress, was elected president in 1840. A feature of every Whig parade was a log cabin with the latch string out, a coonskin cap nailed to the door, and shouts of "Tippecanoe and Tyler, too." Henry Clay had helped secure the nomination for Harrison. Thus, there undoubtedly was happiness in both the STOAKES and the BEATS households. Harrison was the STOAKES brothers old War of 1812 commander; and MARY MARGARET'S oldest brother Robert Beats was such an admirer of Henry Clay that Robert subsequently named one of his sons "Henry" after Clay. This Henry was the father of Charles and Vida Bates. President Harrison died a few weeks after the inauguration. Tyler so wrecked the Whig program that Clay and all the rest of the cabinet resigned.

Two weeks before Christmas in 1842, ELIZA ANN was born to MR. AND MRS. ROBERT GRANGER, approximately a decade after they came from England and moved westward on the Erie Canal. The baby's next older sister Elizabeth J. was two years old. The two sisters were to live close together and be closely associated all of their lives.

The GRANGERS lived a total of 13 years in Ohio. While there, they were called upon to mourn the death of Harriet, the child they had brought from England, another little girl named Mary and a son named George. They are all buried at Richfield, Ohio.

ROBERT GRANGER apparently wasn't satisfied with his material prosperity and he was depressed over the deaths of his children. Among old letters saved in a little trunk by his daughter ELIZA is a faded epistle written to ROBERT in 1844 by a sister back in England in which she expresses her sorrow in the death of his children, sympathizes with his material problems, and tells news from home. The letter says in part:

Aldreth April 16, 1844

My Dear Brother Sister

It was with great pleasure we received your letter... we console you in your great affliction and loss of your dear children... to lose mine dear girl was one of my greatest trials in life... my dear Brother you have great cause to rejoice and be thankful that God in mercy and pity to you spare your dear Companion and snatch her from the yearning grave. Save you from being a lonely Widower in afar distant country away from most of your friends, me think you would have been a very unhappy man left with your dear children almost destitute and desolate... you my dear Brother I hope will love and cherish Your Wife and Family... I am aware afflictions are expensive a great pull backs, but we can make but little as respect this worldly good unless we be diligent in business, fervent in spirit, serving the Lord. It grieves us all to hear you are so destitute, that you have nothing now but what you work for and your health so precarious... hope you will soon be enable to write the blessing of God as smiling upon you that you are in more comfortable circumstance, for it must be a great trial for your Wife who left her Native land so much against her own will. It is a sad thing to leave all your friends for a better living than be disappointed, as your mind so strongly lead you to America we hope you would have had a better home than hear. Times so very moderate here... corn yield so little per acre and price low... the fields have been inclosed you must think there is a great alteration in appearance... Sister Waters is very poor... obliged to keep her bed, but is now mending and able to get in to the garden... Brother Wm. as taken Aunt Camps farm last Lady day at Willburton... my Betsy went to live with him till Vichuslmas... Sister Harriet as got 5 little girls... Ann and Eliza have sweethearts but not marry at present.

We have a new Chapel... Mr. Howlett as been in Chapel... he will tell you about it... Mr. Howlett was so kind as to say he would take a parcel for me. I have sent you some of my dear Maryann things... they are but little worth... I hope they mother make them for the Children as I expect you will receive them free of expense. Sister Sarah as sent you a sovereign in a slip of paper put in the letter. She wishes no one to know of it... when you receive it write a letter and direct it to me... acknowledge the sovereign... my dear Brother as we don't expect to meet in this world or have any other intercourse then by letter let us have one soon. Your loving sister till death,   E. Effindell

ELIZA ANN GRANGER was two years old when this letter was written. She probably was named for some dear ones back in England referred to in this letter "Ann and Eliza have sweethearts but not marry at present." (This is of particular interest to me, this story's compiler because from my grandmother ELIZA ANN GRANGER STOAKES I received part of my own name, Margaret Eliza.)

The Oregon country, what is now the whole northwest corner of the United States and extending into Canada, was opening up to settlers. By 1843, about 1,000 settlers lived there. A couple of years later, Americans were branching off of the Oregon Trail and going to California. California had about 2,000 white inhabitants under Spanish rule in the early part of that decade. Texas was annexed by the United States and became a state in 1845. The cry "fifty-four forty or fight" was echoing through the country as we disputed with Great Britain over our northwest boundary line. Mexico was unhappy with us over our demands in the south and southwest and was threatening war, so we grew less demanding on Great Britain and settled the Oregon boundary at forty-nine degrees.

On the big farm near Downsville, N.Y. great sadness came to the BEATS home. Elisa (Elisabeth) YEOMAN BEATS died in 1845, age 45. She left her partially grown family and her husband JAMES who was 54. MARY MARGARET was 17. Robert was 22 and Sarah J. 19. The younger ones were James 14, Gurdon 13 and Harriet 10.

Sarah J. and MARY MARGARET may have become the homemakers then for their father and older brother and the younger children in the family, but we have nothing that tells us this. Sarah J., years later, taught school, we do know. What MARY MARGARET'S training or schooling was, we do not know. (Her daughter-in-law, Anna Pollock, the only one of that generation left when this is written, believes that MARY MARGARET was trained as a tailoress and practiced that craft.) One other thing we know: JAMES BEATS remarried. How soon, we do not know.

The last of the Sauk and Fox lands in Iowa-to-be, the whole central and southern part including as far northwest as most of Webster county, had been purchased by the United States government. The Indians had been given three years to get off of the land. The Indians stayed as long as they could. Now in 1845, they packed their teepees and belongings, downcast and in stolid silence, they left for the Kansas reservation to the southwest. The Sauk and Fox had sold their hunting grounds in central Iowa for $1,058,566.34. There was little homesteading in Iowa. This land and most of the rest of the state was offered to settlers at the going price of $1.25 an acre. This acquisition was known as The New Black Hawk Purchase. No settlers were permitted until October 10, 1845.

At midnight October 10, 1845, guns were discharged by the dragoon soldiers and amid shouts and wild uproar, settlers rushed across the line which had barred them. They carried hatchets and axes and by the light of torches, they laid out their claims with utmost speed. In days that followed, woodland and prairies were alive with human beings. There were tents, covered wagons, tethered horses and oxen, and children everywhere!

The next spring, war broke out with Mexico. United States earlier had offered Mexico $25,000,000 for California and $5,000,000 for New Mexico. Abolition had been a burning issue for years. Now the abolitionists, bitterly opposing the war on moral and political grounds, charged the administration with wickedly precipitating the war only to get "bigger pens to cram with slaves."

Iowa became a state in 1846. The Stone Capitol building in Iowa City which had housed the Territorial government since 1842, although the building was not complete, now became the State Capitol. There was immediate demand for legislation to establish roads, ferries and bridges. The old roads had frequently been old buffalo trails and Indian paths skirting the tops of hills and ridges where it was dry. Of course, by now the Dillon road was a well traveled road. A furrough had been ploughed from Dubuque through Iowa City to the Missouri Border in 1839. Trees were cut. Soon the furrow had been paralleled by the beaten paths of wagon wheels. Steamboats were coming up the Iowa river to Iowa City. The territorial governor had built a two story brick home in Iowa City and named it Plum Grove. The house still stands, with plum trees in the yard, and is maintained as a historical site.

When Iowa became a state it had 44 counties in what is now mostly its eastern and southern parts. Some of the state land already acquired had not yet been organized into counties. That year more land was added. In June the Potawatomi sold the Western Slope, all of the Missouri slope east of the Missouri river and the Little Sioux river. The government paid $700,000 for it. In October, the Winnebago sold their land in north central and northwestern Iowa for $190,000.

The Mormons made a trail from east to west across Iowa in 1846. A whole religious community was moving from Illinois, where they were not wanted, to found a home in Utah. By July, 15,000 had moved across Iowa in 3,000 wagons. Each wagon had five persons, horses and oxen, sheep, cow, flour, sugar, rifle, ammunition, tent, seeds, cooking equipment and farm tools. The Mormons gathered in Council Bluffs on the Missouri River, built cabins and stayed the winter, planted gardens in the spring for those Mormons who would come later, and then moved on westward. The exodus took two years.

Settlers were pouring into Iowa. It began statehood with a population of 102,000.

The first white settler came that same year, 1846, to what became Webster county and built himself a cabin on the Des Moines and Boone rivers. He was Henry Lott. He came from eastern Iowa where he had a flourishing trade with the Sauk and Fox Indians. In his new location he started trading with the Sioux Indians but his relations with them deteriorated. Some historians say that he stole the Indians' ponies and sold fire-water to the red men. He was warned by the Indian leaders to leave but he did not go. His wife and son were murdered by the Indians who crept up on his cabin one winter day when he was gone.

After 13 years in Ohio, the ROBERT GRANGER family decided to move on westward. They left Summit Township in August 1846 and moved overland by team and wagon to Cook county, Illinois. The wagon probably was of GRANGER'S own making, he being a carpenter and wagon maker. Three little girls went with them: Elizabeth J. 5, ELIZA ANN 4, and Mary H. 1 ½. The family stopped a few weeks near Chicago, at that time a town of 25,000. Word-of-mouth tales passed on down to later generations were about mud holes, and of lanterns and lamps – "quite grand affairs." Back east, a new mode of transportation, the railroads, were connecting principal cities and proving their superiority over the canals.

The GRANGERS tarried only a few weeks near Chicago and later that fall, still 1846, they moved to Fremont township in Lake county, Illinois... just north of Chicago along Lake Michigan. "At that time, Lake was a very new county, for GRANDPA told us of attending the first election in Fremont township, Lake county," the Granger family story says. It continues, "They bought and improved a forty acre farm there, remaining seven and a half years."

"While in Illinois," the story says, "they added two more children to their family, a girl they called Alice R., born June 24, 1847, and a son George E. born April 2, 1850." Apparently the parents were fond of the names Mary and George because after losing an older daughter Mary, they named a younger daughter Mary H. before leaving Ohio, and now named the youngest son George E. An older son George died in Ohio.

The State University of Iowa was founded in 1847 at Iowa City. The year earlier the Congregationalists had started their fund for what subsequently was to become Grinnell college. The Methodists, who blessed Iowa with the earliest and most persistent circuit riders, had founded their college in Mount Pleasant in 1842.

Steamboating was in its full glory. In one summer more than 600 steamboats from the Upper Mississippi docked in St. Louis. Some of them were ornate floating palaces. Others were working freighters carrying iron ore, furs and crops grown by the settlers. Immigrants were crowding the boats with farm implements, animals and tools for their first farms. Steamboats were not only plying the water of the Great Lakes, the Ohio and Mississippi rivers, but were puffing their way up many of the lesser streams of the nation.

February of 1848, the Mexican War had come to a close. Mexico acknowledged our title to Texas, New Mexico and Upper California and in return we paid Mexico $15,000,000. The Rio

Grande was agreed upon as our southern boundary although the United States had fought all of the way to Mexico City and raised the Stars and Stripes over the "Palace of Montezuma." Thus, the United States completed 100 years of expansion. Slavery was a hot issue in the election. General Taylor, hero of the of the Mexican was and affectionately called "Old Rough and Ready," was elected president. He was a sugar planter and the owner of 300 slaves.

ELEAZER STOAKES was 15 years old when his parents, JOHN and JANE STOAKES, left their Yellow Creek farm and grist mill business to move up the Ohio river 3 or 4 miles to Wellsburg. The oldest daughters, Nancy Ann Rider and Martha Jane Hopkins were married and living in Wellsville. The oldest son William M., also married, stayed on the farm to continue the farming operation. When JOHN and JANE moved to town, he went into the wholesale grocery business with his second son Henry C., 22, and with the son-in-law, J.P. Hopkins. The third son John R. was already employed in Wellsville in the new business of railroading, a work he'd follow all of his life. Elizabeth, 18, ELEAZER, 15, and the younger children Sarah E., California and George W. were still living with their parents.

Gold was discovered in the Sacramento Valley in 1849. Merchants, farmers, physicians, artisans, shopkeepers, servants abandoned their businesses and jobs to go West and stake out claims. Some men made nine months trips around Cape Horn, others crossed the pestilence-laden Isthmus of Panama and fought for passage in crowded ships plying up the coast of California. Others went overland braving starvation, the fever of alkali wastes and dangers of Indians. Hordes of people crossed Iowa on their way to easy wealth. In the single year of 1849, California increased its population from 6,000 to 85,000. The new residents began right away to organize for statehood and within a few months had attained that status.

Death twice this year brought sorrow to the STOAKES family. JANE'S sister, Keziah Vantilburg Stoakes, died. They had been the youngest in a large family and had married brothers and reared their large families only a few fields apart. Death also came to J.P. Hopkins leaving the Stoakes daughter Martha Jane, 28, a widow with one son. And the STOAKESES waved good-bye to their oldest daughter Nancy Ann Rider, her husband and three little ones, as they headed for a home in Wisconsin. From there they moved on in the gold craze to California and lived out their lives in Sacramento rearing eight children.

To open a new region in Iowa for settlement, the government in 1850 ordered a military fort established on the Des Moines river near the fork of Lizard Creek. This was done by early fall and called Fort Clark. The following spring of 1851 the first flurry of settlement began and the fort was renamed Fort Dodge. The merchants in Dubuque, with an eye for more business, petitioned the government for a road to the new fort, but nothing was done about that during the two-year life of the fort. The fort was a tranquil one. When the soldiers came, the Indians departed for regions north and west of Fort Dodge, and when the Indians did return, always in small groups, they were on peaceful missions. Guns of the soldiers were idle except in pursuit of game.

That year of 1851 was a happy, adventurous year for the STOAKESES of Wellsville. Three of the young people were married. The rest answered the call of the westward movement. The widow, Martha Jane, 30, the mother of the little boy, married L.S. Cope, a widower with a young daughter. Elizabeth Stoakes, 21, was wed in her parents' home to a merchant, Hugh Gaston, from nearby Knoxville. John R. Stoakes, 24, employed by the railroad, took a bride.

JOHN and JANE, now 59 and 50, themselves answered the call of the West and said goodbye to their newly married children in Wellsville and to JOHN'S widowed brother and life long companion, William Jr. William's children were all grown and most of them married except one 16 year old daughter.

JOHN and JANE leaving for the young state of Iowa were accompanied by their unmarried children and their oldest son William and his wife Caroline and their two little children. Did JOHN and JANE personally feel an urge for the West or did they foresee the best future for their young people there? Besides ELEAZER 18, the unmarried children were Henry C., a bachelor of 26 years, Sarah E., 13, California (fondly called Callie) 10, and George W. 8. A daughter Katherine had died ten years earlier at the age of five.

These were the first of our ancestors to come to Iowa – to Van Buren county in the southeast part of the state, where the Des Moines river empties into the Mississippi. How they came we do not know. Probably they came overland by wagon with farm equipment. They could have. JOHN and his two sturdy sons, Henry and ELEAZER, could have been the drivers. Maybe, like Elizabeth and John Gaston, who followed later, they came by water. The Gastons, young and unencumbered with possessions, took passage on board a steamer, went down the Ohio river to St. Louis, then up the Mississippi to Keokuk, and thence to Van Buren county.

When JOHN and JANE arrived, steamboats were servicing the bustling Van Buren county towns of Keosauqua, Bentonsport and Bonaparte, towns founded on the north bank of the Des Moines river more than a decade earlier. Farmers from 100 to 200 miles away were bringing their wheat and corn to the five story grist mill at Bonaparte. This town boasted a huge brick woolen mill for the carding of wool. Bentonsport was building a two story brick general store. The Mason House there had served the public for a number of years as had the black walnut post office next door, seventh post office in Iowa. The two story brick, oak and walnut courthouse at Keosauqua had been in use (and still is) since its completion in 1843. The STOAKESES also found on their arrival a goodly number of modified Georgian style brick, and "steamboat Gothic" homes –

some with walnut circular stairways. (Now in the nineteen sixties, these beautiful old buildings are being restored as the "Williamsburg of Iowa".)

The STOAKESES arrived the year the last of the Indian territory in Iowa was purchased. The Sioux sold the remaining territory in northern Iowa for a little more than $340,000. Iowa had been purchased in a series of parcels for roughly three and a half million dollars. Now all of Iowa was open to settlement.

The United States had grown from a seaboard people of 3,929,000 when the first census was taken in 1790 to a continental people of 23,192,000 as the second half of the nineteenth century began. More than 10,000,000 people now lived in the great central basin of the Mississippi, and only 120,000 in California and Oregon. The population increase was due in great part to the reproduction of native stock. Early marriages and large families were the rule, especially on the frontier, where homesteads were easy to get and sons and daughters grew up to a life of wholesome toil crowned by the clearing of their own farms farther west. Also a great influx of immigrants had come to our shores from Europe as the first half of the century was drawing to a close. This was partially due to the demand for laborers in the United States and partially due to various forms of distress in Europe. Utter ruin of the potato crop had brought famine to Ireland, and revolution had thrown central Europe into political turmoil.

As the first of our ancestors were arriving in Iowa, the last of our ancestors to leave the old country was setting sail for America. A young man who had learned stone cutting in his native Scotland, WILLIAM A. POLLOCK, came to America in the early fifties, probably in 1851, when he was in his early or mid twenties. His brother Thomas came with him and two other young men. Thomas' descendants say that William's and Thomas' brother David came with them. One of the four was believed to have been a cousin – maybe two of them were.

Thomas' descendants also tell that the Scottish young men had a rough crossing and they thought they'd never get to America. The trip took nearly six weeks and their food supply was reduced to just beans. They were delighted to land and get something else to eat.

As the story comes down to us, by word of mouth, the boys accidently became separated in New York City and after due time, struck out on their separate ways. The California gold rush attracted Thomas. He later came back to Seaforth, Ontario, Canada, married and became the father of a large family. WILLIAM went across Pennsylvania to Pittsburgh. He is believed to have cut stone there a couple of years or more. He may have worked there with some relative with whom he had cut stone in Scotland.

Many boys in Scotland did learn stone cutting because of the Balmoral granite there. America came to know quite a few of these skilled young men. Anna Pollock, daughter-in-law of WILLIAM, says that she always understood that WILLIAM first learned to be a weaver and later became a stone cutter. We believe he was born in the Paisley area which is a few miles west of Glasgow. Paisley was noted for its weaving, especially for its scarves.

Authoritative sources vary on dates and information on the Pollock brothers' birth. The death record in the Webster county clerk's office lists WILLIAM'S birth date as July 3, 1827 in

Scotland, son of WILLIAM POLLOCK, and gave his mother's name as ELIZABETH ALLEN. The informant for this information was listed as WILLIAM'S daughter, Jennie Pollock. Date of death was June 14, 1912. His tombstone in Oakland Cemetery at Fort Dodge carries these same dates.

Thomas' tombstone in Oakland Cemetery says he was born June 16, 1829 and died Aug. 12, 1918. His obituary in the Adrian, Mo. Paper of Aug. 12, 1918 carries these same dates and mentions that he was born in Bellshill, Scotland and among his survivors is a sister in Derby, England.

A younger brother Robert, who came to America years later, is also buried in Oakland Cemetery. His tombstone says Nov. 11, 1844 – Jan. 3, 1915.

Mary Pollock's friend from St. Abbs, Scotland, who traced the Beat family records in the official registry in Edinburgh, Scotland, also traced the Pollock records there. Officially recorded in Edinburgh is this information:

21st Feb. 1823 – David, lawful eldest son of WILLIAM POLLOCK, labourer in Bellshill, and his spouse, MARY SCOTT, was born 21st Feb. and baptized at a Diet of Visitation at Bellshill by the Rev. M. Gardiner 27th of the month, 1823.

24th Nov. 1824 – Janet, lawful daughter of WILLIAM POLLOCK, feuar and labourer at Bellshill and of his spouse, MARY SCOTT, was born 24th Nov. and baptized 12th Dec. 1824.

6th April 1827 – Thomas, lawful son of WILLIAM POLLOCK, thatcher, at Loanthank, and MARY SCOTT, his wife, was born 6th April and baptized at Bothwell church 22ndnd April 1827 by Dr. Matthew Gardiner.

15th July, 1829 – WILLIAM, lawful son of WILLIAM POLLOCK and MARY SCOTT, was born 15th July and baptized by Dr. Gardiner at Orbiston 9th Aug. 1829.

Sept 17, 1841 – Elizabeth Leckie Pollock, lawful daughter of WILLIAM POLLOCK and Elizabeth Robertson. Baptised 3rd Oct.

16 Dec. 1844 – Alexander Rennison Pollock, lawful son of WILLIAM POLLOCK and Elizabeth Robertson. Baptised 5, Jan. 1845.

The above are all registered for the County of Lanark and the parish of Bothwell. Mary's Scottish friend explains: "The word 'feu' (pronounced few) is a Scottish legal term which exists to the present day. It means ground rent, (usually for land on which a house is built), payable by the house owner to the land-owner.

"I hazard a guess," she writes, "That it comes from the French word for fire; probably any building which had a fireplace would at one time be classed as a dwelling house.

"In those days 'labourer' usually meant 'farm worker', but the fact that WILLIAM POLLOCK is referred to as a thatcher and a feuar probably means that he was not attached to any specific farm (because he would be given a house by the farmer for the duration of this employment with him and would therefore pay no feu). He probably owned his own house and gave his services to several farmers and possibly house-owners as well."

The information from Scotland presents both mysteries and illuminations. There is an apparent carelessness in the handling of dates, but why are the years of Thomas' and of WILLIAM'S birth dates reversed from Scotland to America? Which <u>was</u> the older? And Robert Pollock and Alexander Rennison Pollock were born at approximately the same time. Are they the same person? The older children are all listed as the sons of MARY SCOTT POLLOCK. WILLIAM POLLOCK'S death certificate in Fort Dodge, Iowa lists his mother's maiden name as Elizabeth Allen. Could that have been the name of WILLIAM'S first wife?

When the older Pollock brothers left home to come to America, a young brother followed them down the lane crying and begging BILL to take him along. WILLIAM always remembered that with a pang of homesickness. The account of this incident was passed down from WILLIAM to his son GRANT and thus to his children.

Glasgow was a big seaport with ships taking off for all parts of the world. Surely those ships would beckon young adventurous men! But America was beckoning not just as an adventure but as a future. Just across the North Channel from Glasgow, a potato famine in Ireland (1845-49) was one of the great tragedies of history. Historians say that 1,500,000 Irishmen perished – most of them starved to death. They wandered the roads and died in ditches. Beggars could get nothing when all were beggers. Whole villages became rotten cemeteries. A visiting Frenchman found in Ireland, "the extreme of human misery, worse than the Negro in his chains." The Irish blamed the English and to this day hate the English. A system evolved through the centuries of conquest, rebellion and confiscation in which the land was owned by absentee and irresponsible landlords, and Irishmen had been driven into smaller and smaller patches of land until whole families were trying to exist on an acre of even a half acre of land. The cheap and easy 'tater' was their crop. When it failed, starvation came. A million Irishmen managed to escape to the U.S, Canada, England and Australia. The English government did advance a large quantity of sterling for the purpose of feeding the starving Irish but historians say the administration of it was bungled. America with its boundless acres of cheap land in the West must surely have looked like great opportunity to young men from all over the British Isles.

Sixty years after the Pollock brothers came to America, at least Thomas was still receiving letters addressed to "My Dear Brother" from two sisters back in the British Isles. Some of these letters are preserved by Thomas' descendants. One sister was Elesabath (also called Lissie and Lizzie and recorded in the Edinburgh registry as Elizabeth Leckie Pollock.) She often signed her letters "E.A." WILLIAM POLLOCK'S daughter-in-law, Anna Pollock, says that WILLIAM named his own youngest daughter "Exie" after someone dear back in Scotland. The name may well have come from "Leckie."

Most of the preserved letters came from Lizzie or "E.A." and were written on small sheets of fine quality stationary printed with her address "Glenrosa, Grafton Road, Derby," and on others

"Glenrosa, Littleover Hill, Derby." In one letter she writes that her husband is "7 years older than me but he has a young spirit." In a 1918 letter her husband "had entered his 85th year." The registry gives Elizabeth's birth date as Sept. 17, 1841. The other sister who writes is Jeannie or "Sister J.P." as she sometimes signs her letters. In 1913 letter she writes "70 3 I be the 12 of Aughe." This would make her born in 1840. The sisters would have been 10 and 11 years old when their brothers went to America. Mary Pollock's friend did not find a "Jeannie" listed in the Edinburgh registry.

In letters written from Glenrosa in July 1913 and received in the same envelope by Thomas, "Your loving sister E. Boyd" writes "I have Jeannie with me since May. She feels very much the better for the change and we have had some nice talks on olde times." And "Sister J.P." writes "I come up to Derby for a change and i can say i feel much better for it and Sister Lizzie and her daughter had been so kind to me I never for get." She also writes, "a for Brother David cannt hear anything abath him. Ask garing Wife and Guy. She does not hear anything abath him He used to came to see them but has not been for years to see them."

Lizzie was the wife of George Boyd. (This is where WILLIAM POLLOCK'S grandson Robert Boyd Pollock, son of GRANT POLLOCK, received his middle name.) Lizzie and George Boyd had four children: Lizzie, Tom, Bob and Lily. The daughter Lizzie had four sons in World War I and a younger boy in school. Lizzie and George's sons, Tom and Bob were both married. Their mother wrote, "Bob is still in Birmingham and doing well...not called up yet....is very busy getting out plans for a large town house for Builders Cargo Shapeyards. Tom is kept very busy...cant get men in his work...In Terland (?) they are belding shapes as fast as they can...Tom has more to do than he is able. He has lost the most of his men but nothing matters but to get this war settled. The mother writes that Lily is still home "doing her best for us. I don't know what we'd do without her."

Sister Lizzie's husband George Boyd is aged and in poor health. She reports on farm crops, speaks of the garden, dreads the war raids, is concerned about the welfare of her grandsons in the war. She speaks of the sea shore:

> "We are at the Sea Side for six weeks so ought to feel the better for that... Tom
> and his wife want me to go with them to the Sea for two weeks... you see we
> all used to go but Father is not able to go now so the Holidays are not so
> enjoyable as they were when we all could go together."

After Lizzie's and Jeannie's brother, Robert Pollock, died in Fort Dodge, Iowa in 1915, his widow Jean went back to Paisley, Scotland. She wrote from 4 St. James St., Paisley, Care Mrs. Hart, to a niece "Annie bell" and said "well I got hear last friday night. I stay in Liver Pool for a few days... had a good passage... but it is a long way to go all by your selfe... I find great changes... I had a letter from Lizzie from Dearby." And she signed her letter "your auntie Jane Pollock." She found her friend in Paisley "well" but added "everyone don't know me to be the same." She took sick shortly after arriving there and died soon afterward.

Lizzie wrote from Derby in April 1917 to her Brother Thomas and said about Jean:

"We were looking forward to Having her in the summer – I wanted to have a long chat about you all – It seems She just came Home to die. It is very sad." In 1918, this time signing herself "E.A.", Lizzie again wrote to Thomas, "How are all WILLIAM'S family getting on? I suppose they are all scattered now. You see I have never seen any of them – nor yours. I should like to have seen them but they are all so far away..."

In 1970, Mary Pollock (granddaughter of WILLIAM and daughter of GRANT) went to the British Isles. She decided to go to Derby. She did not find "Littleover Hill" but found "Littleover." After inquiries and persistence she found not "Grafton Road" but "Crafton Street" printed on an old stone wall. Down the street a short distance above the arched doorway of a two story brick house were the stone letters "G ENROSA." Only the letter "L" had fallen away. A white panel door with stain glass made a welcoming entranceway. Flowers bloomed by the front steps. There were bay windows on the front and big chimney pots on the roof. The woman of the house invited Mary into the garden back of the house, an attractive shrubbery surrounded area and colorful with roses and other blooms, neat and well tended as a little park. Mary was invited inside and shown the four rooms downstairs and the six bedrooms upstairs, together with the downstairs and upstairs hallways and lovely stairs. (Anna Pollock says that his aunt at Glenrosa never liked the upheaval of spring house cleaning so, to avoid it, always had one room cleaned thoroughly each month of the year. This worked neatly because there were 12 rooms in the house.) Mary was invited to take all of the pictures she liked and she came home with many pictures of the sturdy, well built old home and garden. The present owners had purchased the house 12 years earlier and knew nothing of former owners.

"The name Pollock was of Saxon origin and was given to a large feudal barony in Renfrewshire, Scotland," Cora Belle Pollock has learned from the Media Research Bureau of Washington, D.C. "The family of Pollock is believed to have descended from Fulbert the Saxon of the Barony of Pollock in the eleventh century." Later King David I of Scotland gave the lands of Paisley, Pollock and Cathcart to the man from whom the Scottish royal family of Steward descended. The county of Renfrew (a county was formerly called a shire) is immediately south and west of Glasgow and includes the towns of Renfrew and Paisley.

The year 1854 could well be called "Moving Year" for our ancestors: for WILLIAM A. POLLOCK, for the GRANGERS and for the STOAKESES.

That was the year the first railroad reached the mighty Mississippi river! The Chicago-Rock Island track was completed Feb. 22, 1854 linking the East coast with the Mississippi at Rock Island. Six first-class passenger cars handsomely decorated with wreaths and garlands came out from Chicago to Rock Island on Washington's birthday to celebrate the link-up. Three hundred passengers gazed out of the car windows upon the Great Father of Waters. A great booming of cannon heralded the first train's arrival. A huge temporary building had been erected in which to entertain the guests. The iron horse moved with lightning speed. Now the people of Rock Island could go the entire distance to New York in 42 hours! The United States boasted more than 14,000 miles of iron rails.

Ferry boats were still the connection between the east side and the west side of the Mississippi. The ferries were doing a huge business in the fifties. The Iowa population tripled in that decade from 195,000 in 1850 to 674,000 in 1860. The reports of cheap land, lush crops, friendly Indians, available water and timber brought the settlers. They waited in line on the east side of the river for the ferry so they might cross over and strike out across the prairie in search of a farm. Many came with as much equipment as possible. To start a farm one needed a breaking plough, a heavy wagon, a grain cradle, an ox team and a grind stone. Grain was scattered by hand. Corn could be grown by cutting a gash in the sod with an axe and dropping in a few kernels of corn.

A network of stagecoach routes over the dirt roads now linked the principal towns of eastern Iowa and extended across the southern part of the state to Council Bluffs on the Missouri river. Great rivalry for passengers and to carry mail existed between the stagecoach lines. The brightly painted oval shaped Concord coach mounted on leather braces and pulled by four horses was a favorite. Every ten or fifteen miles, a fresh team was waiting and could be harnessed onto the coach in a couple of minutes so as not to detain the stage. The driver, a colorful character and expert handler of horses, had to content with mud roads and blizzards but took great pride in keeping his stage as nearly on schedule as possible.

After being a stone cutter in Pittsburgh a few years, WILLIAM POLLOCK moved westward. His mode of transportation is unknown. He could have boarded the steam cars in the East and followed the gleaming rails westward as many a young man was doing and been carried away to the irresistible western lands. He could have taken a steamboat that plyed across Lake Erie and thus to Michigan. The country was awakening to a new age. The old order was passing: the men in the three cornered cocked hats and the big buckle shoes had grown old and were becoming few in number.

A grandson, Raymond Pollock, has the impression that WILLIAM POLLOCK lived awhile in Michigan. At his death, WILLIAM owned two lots in Crawford county, Michigan. Subsequently, he went to Tipton, Iowa, Anna Pollock says. She says that he was married and lost his first wife and baby in childbirth and that they are buried at Tipton. Among old family papers is a tax receipt from the Treasurer of Cedar county, Iowa and marked Tipton, made out to WILLIAM POLLOCK, Nov. 27, 1856 for taxes on 120 acres of land. County tax was .72, state .60, school .48, and roads .24 totaling $2.04. The property is described as E1/2 SE1/4 and SW1/4 SE1/4 section 1, town. 81, range 4, acres 120. His coming on to Fort Dodge was thought to be in 1856. Anna Pollock suggests that he may have continued to own this Tipton land after coming to Fort Dodge.

(One day, years later WILLIAM'S son GRANT and his daughter Margaret – compiler of this account – stopped and walked around on the old family farm northwest of Fort Dodge near Clare. A small triangle of land in the corner of a field was fenced off – a little grassy spot with trees nearby. GRANT said that some unknown woman and her new born child, enroute West in a covered wagon caravan, died and were buried there and the caravan moved on. GRANT said that his father WILLIAM always kept that unmarked grave enclosed with a fence in respect to the pioneer mother and child, and also as a gesture of memory to his first wife and infant child.)

No doubt while living in Tipton, WILLIAM visited the state capital, Iowa City, only a few miles away. Being a stone cutter, he probably took interest in the fine capitol building, in use then for a dozen years but still unfinished. WILLIAM may have gone out north to the Clinton street quarry from where the first stone of the capitol was taken, and on to the quarry ten miles up the Iowa river from where stone was obtained to complete the building. The stone from the latter quarry was carried down the river in flat boats. During the time that POLLOCK lived in Tipton, there was talk of moving the state capital to the center of the state, to Des Moines.

About the time POLLOCK came to Tipton, the ROBERT GRANGER family left Lake county, Ill. where they had lived for seven years and they came on west to Tama county, Iowa. During their stay in Lake county, Chicago to the south of them had become a boom city. The railroads had arrived and connected it to the East. The population had grown from 25,000 and was pressing 100,000. Property values had increased 500 percent.

The Granger Family Story says, "Having decided to emigrate farther west, they started in May 1854, coming by covered wagon pulled by two yoke of oxen.

"On this trip they were accompanied by other families traveling westward. One family's name was van Vliete, while another one was Whitney, and the others, none of us can remember our parent ever saying what the names were.

"Grandpa (ROBERT GRANGER) also brought along twelve head of cattle. The Granger daughters took turns walking and driving those cattle. Their father (here referred to as 'Grandpa' for the account is written years later by granddaughters) had to drive the two yoke of oxen and the mother had all of the culinary work to do and looking after the younger children so they thought it best she rest whenever she could.

The account continues, "The Mr. Whitney who came with the group had a team of horses to pull his wagon and his wife could drive them, and that way he was able to help the Granger girls with the cattle, but when he did, one of the girls rode with his wife and held the baby."

The oldest one of the girls was Elizabeth. She was 13, ELIZA ANN was 11 1/2, Mary H. 9, Alice R. 7 and the youngest child was George who was 4.

"In coming from their old home in Illinois to where they settled in Tama county took three weeks of travel. They used to tell how they would begin about four o'clock to look for a camping place for the night, for they had to stop where they could get water. They never traveled more than 18 miles a day – sometimes less.

"The first Saturday on the road grandpa made better preparation than usual for one night's camping and some of the party wanted to know why, and he said that he was going to rest on the Sabbath day, for he and his family and his stock would all be better for the rest, and would stand the long trip better.

"Some of the other families, which we do not know the names of, said they wanted to hurry, so they went on never carrying for the Sabbath. When grandpa's crowd was ferried across the river at Cedar Rapids, they asked the ferryman if he had taken anyone across the river lately. He said, 'Yes, about an hour ago,' and went on the described the outfit, and it was people that had started with the crowd grandpas were with, but could not stop to rest on the Sabbath. And in all that time of traveling, which was nearly three weeks, one hour was all they had gained by traveling on the Sabbath. Grandpa's children always thought grandpa had done right by resting on the Sabbath, so followed that idea in their own lives and taught it to their children."

One of the Granger granddaughters, Ermina Kober, added this to the Granger Family Story, "The Grangers were the only ones in the caravan with cows but there was plenty of milk for all.

"The Grangers had a five gallon jug in one corner of their wagon which they kept filled with milk which soured. All of the caravan used it to make hot breads for the families. The Grangers had an iron Dutch oven with an iron cover in which they baked their biscuits. Live coals from the campfire were spread on the ground, the Dutch oven placed on these and covered with more live coals. In about twenty minutes, the biscuits were nicely baked. Sometimes when the soured milk was poured from the milk jug, small chunks of butter had formed."

Another traveler from the East heading toward Tama county with his wagon this same spring wrote, "There is nothing but one unbounded expanse of rolling prairie, the richest country I ever beheld. The soil is 2 and 3 feet deep, as black and mellow as any country in the world... Been looking all day for timber, found none. Why could not Providence set down some timber in this vast prairie – seems to me the distribution of the timber in this world is not as it should be to serve the needs of pioneer settlers."

The Granger Story continues its account, "As the Grangers were traveling along on the prairie one day they saw a nice place where they thought they would like to stop for awhile. It was in Tama county, Iowa on the banks of a stream called Wolf Creek. It was June 3, 1854, at 2 p.m. when they stopped at this place."

The camping spot was on the south side of the creek between the present site of the T.F. Clarks State Park and the present town of Traer. In that area the stately elm trees, the hickory, ash, linden and iron wood are native. There are walnut trees. Wood ivy and grass are lush green. The cool shade must have been inviting and no doubt Iowa's many birds were singing that June day.

The prairie would have been in bloom with wild roses, with indigo spider wort, white anemone and other early summer beauties.

"At one of our family reunions lately, "The Granger Story written in 1940 continues, "Different ones were reminiscing of what they could remember: grandparents and parents telling of early days. BELLE STOAKES POLLOCK (daughter of ELIZA ANN GRANGER STOAKES) says she can remember her mother telling about the day they stopped at the creek. When the yokes were pulled off of the oxen and thrown on the ground, snakes from the thick tall grass crawled up on the yokes to sun themselves."

"The Grangers lived on the creek for a while, then grandpa entered 120 acres of land of his own, it being the W1/2 of the SE1/2 and also the SE1/4 of the NW1/4 of section 36, Buckingham township, and ten acres of timber land on the creek not far from where they had camped."

Ermina adds, "The nearest post office was Iowa City and when anyone went down for supplies, that person brought all the mail and left it at different homes until a post office was established."

ROBERT GRANGER lived until he was nearly 80 years old. His obituary says, "Settling along the creek bottom he had the ague nearly all of the time until he moved this house back on more rolling ground." The Granger Story says, "He built a log cabin that fall and moved into it before cold weather. The log cabin stood near the south end of the W1/2 of the SE1/4 of section 36, and later the frame house was built near the same location. They lived in the log cabin a few years and then grandpa built the frame house which was their home until 1875 when they moved into Traer." They later moved back to the farm.

While GRANGER was building his cabin, an advance group of the Stoakes family arrived in North Tama to look for possible land. The first of the Stoakes contingent in Iowa had been living in Van Buren county for three years when they were joined by the two married daughters left behind in Wellsville, Ohio: Martha Jane and Elizabeth and their husbands, L.S. Cope and Hugh Gaston. Each daughter had one child at that time. After a stop in Van Buren county, Cope and Gaston, joined by their brothers-in-law, William M. and Henry C. Stoakes, went up to Tama county to investigate land. They found what they wanted in Perry township.

Henry took the southeast quarter of section two and the south half of the northeast quarter of the same section; Gaston took the southwest quarter of section two and bought land in section 3. Cope chose the northwest quarter of section one. William went farther south and selected the southeast quarter of section 21. William built a cabin on this land that year before returning to his family in Van Buren county. Gaston's land already had a large hewed log cabin on it and he brought his wife Elizabeth and their little daughter to the new home yet that year. Henry was a bachelor when he entered his land. William selected the SE1/4 of section 21.

The first of February, 1855, two prairie schooners started a week's journey from Van Buren county to Wolf Creek settlement in Tama county. In one wagon was Cope, his wife Martha Jane and her son, 13 years old. In the other was William and Caroline and their four children. They arrived at the Hugh Gaston cabin and all were able to get lodging there.

The old folks, JOHN and JANE, arrived four months later in June with the unmarried members of their family: Henry, ELEAZER, Sarah E., Callie and George.

Henry, 30 years old, who had already entered the land in section two, was joined there by his father JOHN, age 62, who also took land in that section 2 range 14. ELEAZER, 22, entered 80 acres of government land in this same section and continued to make his home with his parents.

Now Father JOHN, his two unmarried sons and his two sons-in-law had land together in a cluster, adjacent northeast of what later became the town of Traer. The other son, William, and his family lived a mile or two south of Traer-to-be. They had staked their fortunes together in the New West, would build their homes and rear their families in Tama county.

(The ROBERT GRANGER farm was in the section just to the north of the cluster of Stoakes farms, closer to Buckingham.)

Martha Jane Cope's son by her first marriage, John S. Hopkins, the boy of 13 wrote of the arrival of these prairie schooners and explained farther, "The Wolf Creek settlement this spring of 1855 consisted of about twenty log cabins, most of them built near the timber as a protection from the blizzards which swept from the north. Prairie land was mostly broken by oxen in the late fifties. The oxen could live and work on the prairie grass while horse teams, not plentiful, required grain in order to work.

Very little grain had been raised yet, especially corn which required several years cultivation of the soil for good results. Those able to raise crops had a good home market at good prices. The new settlers usually brought enough money with them to pay for their own land and buy supplies to live on until they had raised a crop."

Buckingham was a couple or three miles north of the Granger and Stoakes farms. It had come into being in 1853. The year before that, the first white settlers had come to live in the Valley of the Wolf in North Tama. A few settlers had come into the southern part of the county a little earlier. Herds of buffalo had lived in Wolf Valley. One herd had consisted of 300 head.

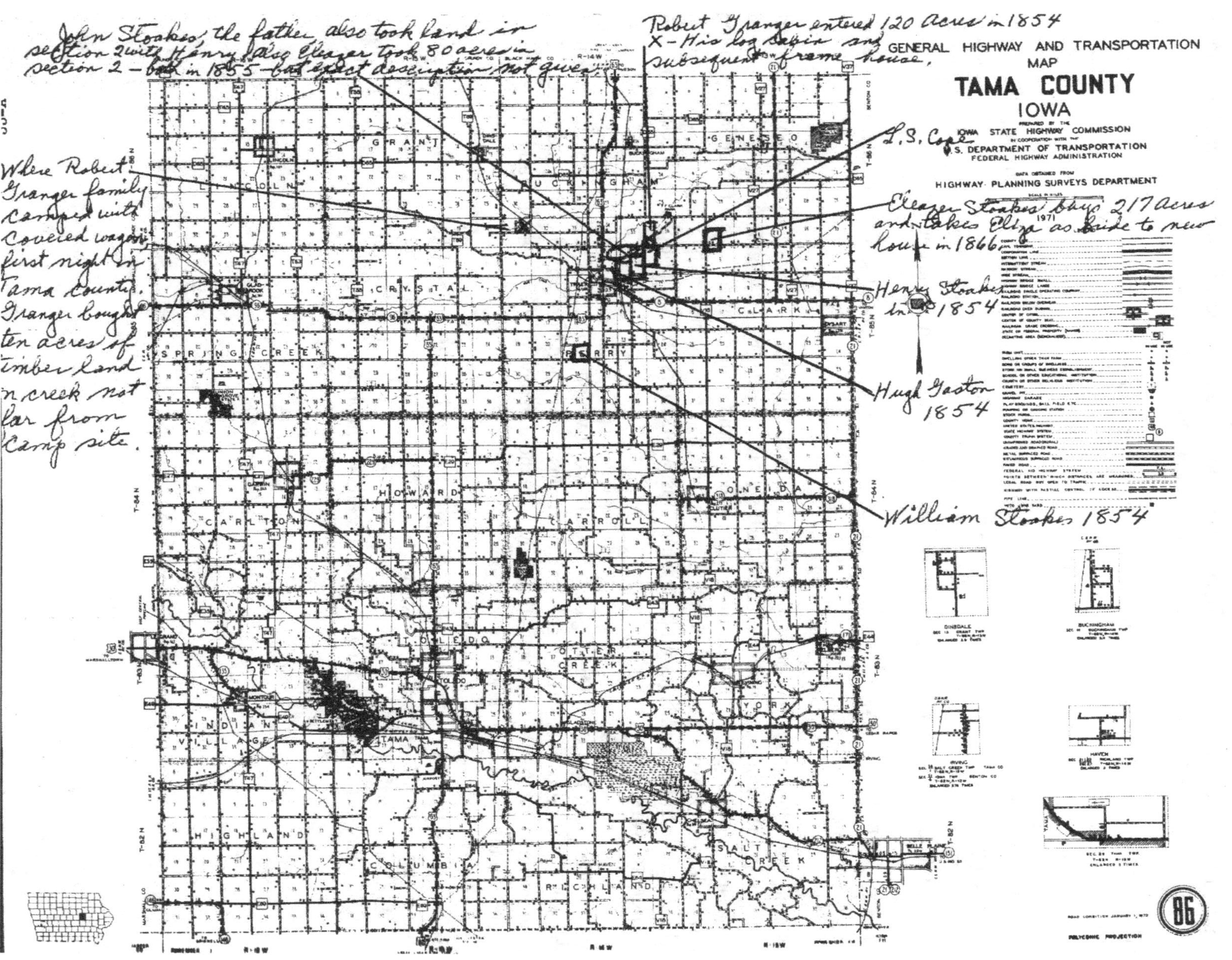

John Stoakes, the father, also took land in section 2 with Henry. Also Eleazer took 80 acres in section 2 — both in 1855 — but exact description not given.
Robert Granger entered 120 Acres in 1854
X — His log cabin and subsequent frame house.
Where Robert Granger family camped with covered wagon, first night in Tama county. Granger bought ten acres of timber land on creek not far from Camp site.
GENERAL HIGHWAY AND TRANSPORTATION
MAP
TAMA COUNTY
IOWA
PREPARED BY THE
IOWA STATE HIGHWAY COMMISSION
IN COOPERATION WITH THE
U.S. DEPARTMENT OF TRANSPORTATION
FEDERAL HIGHWAY ADMINISTRATION
DATA OBTAINED FROM
HIGHWAY PLANNING SURVEYS DEPARTMENT
L. S. Cope
Eleazer Stoakes buys 217 Acres and takes Eliza as bride to new house in 1866
Henry Stoakes in 1854
Hugh Gaston 1854
William Stoakes 1854
POLYCONIC PROJECTION
86

A Methodist circuit rider from Vinton already had held services in the settlement before the Grangers and the Stoakeses arrived. The town already had celebrated one Fourth of July: the huge sum of those days of $9.75 had been collected from 20 men in 1853 and a lumber wagon went to Cedar Rapids for lemons, sugar, flour, flags and other necessities. The Grangers had arrived in time for the second Fourth of July celebration which was held near Tama City with 500 present, a table of 200 feet spread for all and a novel feature was ice water. A grist mill was being built in Buckingham in 1854. Prior to that the settlers had to go to Cedar Rapids for flour and cornmeal.

Buckingham was to grow to a fine town of 300 before the coming of the railroad would cause the town's near demise. Buckingham had a kiln for making pottery to be sold to the surrounding towns, a general store, boot and shoe business, drug store, harness shop, saloon, shingle cutter, cooper shop (L.S. Cope was the cooper), and on a nearby farm a blacksmith shop. Buckingham was on the north side of Wolf Creek. On the south side another little town, West Union, soon cropped up and the rivalry of the two towns was described as "the bane of the countryside." West Union was to have a store, post office and a boot and shoe business, but it never was to prosper like Buckingham did.

The Granger and Stoakes children were not long without educational facilities. A school was built in Buckingham in 1856. A Fourth of July dance was held there before the builder turned over the keys.

The school house was used for church and Sabbath school purposes, too. Years later at the death of ROBERT GRANGER, the editor of the Traer Star Clipper would recall, "We remember way back in the old school house in Buckingham of Father GRANGER giving us and a row of other boys seated on the rear bench, valuable lessons from the Great Book." The Toledo Chronicle at that time wrote, "Mr. GRANGER was always an earnest Christian wherever found. We well remember whole family used to go to church and Sabbath school with an ox team and wagon." Grangers were Methodists at first, but when a Congregational church was organized, they transferred to that church.

The Stoakeses were Congregationalists. Once when money was being raised at church, and when time after time someone by the name of Stoakes had made a contribution, the visiting minister suddenly and fervently exclaimed, "God bless the Stoakeses." Years later when the new church was being built and half of the sixteen families of Stoakeses had subscribed, a visiting churchman inquired, "How many Stoakes are there anyway?" To which the reply came, "There are enough to build a church if necessary, and they are that kind, too." The newspaper which reported this, continued, "The Stoakes families have all been successful – at least we never heard of an unsuccessful Stoakes – and a majority have remained in North Tama and in the Congregational church." Another story of the Stoakeses found its way into print regarding a new minister, "I remember his anxiety over his first sermon; his attempt to familiarize himself with the names of his parishioners and his look of relief when he saw a whole page of Stoakeses in the church manual. 'If I can't remember who they are,' he added, 'I'll just call them Stoakes. I can't miss it many times.'"

The government had taken over the lands of the Sauk and Fox Indians in the southern part of Tama county years ago and the Indians had been banished to Kansas. Now in 1856 they came back to their old hunting grounds. They had longed for their old home and now they had requested, and by a special act of the General Assembly, been given the right to buy land in the same manner as white men did. The Indians acquired 80 acres at Tama in the south part of the county and set up eight wickiups. The number of acres and the Indian population would increase. This is not a reservation. The village is known as "Mesquakie."

In the history of North Tama, one old settler recalls, "I've never forgotten the Indians who left their Tama home each summer to hunt and fish in North Tama, and how Buckingham business men would put a penny in a slit in a stick forty feet away. Every penny the Indians hit with their bows and arrows, they could have. They missed very few."

Roughly forty miles southeast of Buckingham and forty miles west of Tipton, a religious body from Germany had just purchased 26,000 acres and was founding a cluster of communities to be know as "The Community of True Inspiration." Down through the years they would come to be known as the Amana Colonies. These people had come to America to avoid persecution in Europe and had settled first in New York state. Theirs was a communal enterprise.

The middle fifties were great times in Iowa. In one day, 700 immigrant wagons crossed the Mississippi at Burlington and the same influx was being felt at Muscatine, Rock Island and Dubuque.

The second contingent of Mormons crossed Iowa in 1856. The first had been in wagons. These were on foot. Mormon missionaries had gone back to England and Europe, and these were the converts enroute to join the other Mormons in Salt Lake City. The converts came by boat and then by railroad train to the end of the railroad lines, which at that time was Iowa City. A railroad bridge recently had been completed over the big Mississippi river at Davenport, so now trains came a ways into Iowa. In Iowa City, the Mormons, without money, tarried and built handcarts and gathered supplies for the long, long pull to Utah. Thirteen hundred of these people on foot pulling all of their worldly possessions in sturdy two-wheeled carts crossed Iowa in five groups from Iowa City, to Homestead, Marengo, Newton, Des Moines, Adel and Council Bluffs and thus on westward.

This same year, 1856, WILLIAM POLLOCK is believed to have gone from Tipton to the booming two-year-old town of Fort Dodge. The year earlier, a U.S. land office had been opened there, a newspaper had been established, logs had been hauled from the woods and cut into boards at a mill for the first frame building, a bank. School had been taught for a couple of years in a log cabin. The old fort established in 1850 had gone out of existence. The town boasted a postmaster, a physician, an attorney, a land broker, a boarding house that could accommodate 100 guests, and a small log cabin store. A brick schoolhouse was being built.

A supply train, one man with a team and wagon, was running between Muscatine and Fort Dodge competing with the weekly stage in carrying passengers and supplies. He often exchanged the groceries he hauled to Fort Dodge for furs, deer skins and other such commodities that could stand transportation back to the Muscatine market. Frequently on his return trip to the Mississippi river, he'd have the receiver of the Fort Dodge land office and his guard and boxes of gold coin.

Squatters had moved into Webster county the winter of 1855-56. It was a cold winter with deep snow.

The county seat fight took place the year Pollock arrived. Webster county had been created three years earlier combining Yell and Riseley counties, and still included the present county of Hamilton. The county seat had been established at Homer in the southern part of the county.

John F. Duncombe, a newly arrived political figure in Fort Dodge, and Walter Wilson, who owned a saw mill at New Castle (now Webster City), had put their heads together and decided that the county should be divided and that Fort Dodge should be one county seat and New Castle another. New Castle was nothing but a saw mill, and Fort Dodge was a very small settlement compared with the thriving town of Homer, population 600.

Duncombe and Wilson arranged an election before Homer became aroused as to what was happening. It was a bitter election fight. Election day came. The pioneers thronged to the polling places. The votes of the children nine and ten years old were stuffed into the ballot boxes by both factions, the leaders of both the Homerite and the New Castle-Fort Dodge factions voted as many as a dozen times, according to old stories. Travelers passing through the towns were compelled to vote for the party fortunate enough to collar them. Homer with a greater voting strength than the combined Fort Dodge-New Castle forces was strangely defeated.

After the ballots were counted at Homer and Homer had lost, Judge John D. Maxwell of that little county seat was infuriated. He and other Homer residents encountered Duncombe and Wilson in front of the Snell Merchandise Store in Homer. Then the fireworks began. Wilson pointed out to the irate Maxwell that the election had decided the question fairly, that it represented the wishes of the people, that the good of the whole community had been at stake. At this Maxwell exploded. There were plenty of things on his mind and he didn't mince words. He had a certain vigorous impression of Duncombe and Wilson. Duncombe and Wilson were the essence of such things as horse thieves, murderers, cut-throats and white livered Democrats. To this, the latter replied in their own original ways and tempers rose higher and higher. A Homer man suggested that they fight it out and Duncombe accepted. The match was held in the Homer public square. The whole town turned out to watch – it was one of the great events of the year. Duncombe won. Shortly after the match, the county records were moved to Fort Dodge in a prairie schooner. Accounts of the event say that Maxwell spit on the fire, called his dog and moved up to Hamilton county where he became the first county judge.

The election was contested but the legislative assembly sustained the majority. With the county seat gone, Homer went into decline and nearly disappeared from the map.

POLLOCK located land that he wanted nine miles northwest of Fort Dodge. This was deep black rich soil on the north fork of Lizard Creek. There was plenty of timber. The area was marked with swamps like much of Iowa was in those days. Vegetation was lush. This was

Jackson township and school was taught for the first time in the township the year before POLLOCK arrived.

Being a stone cutter, before locating land he probably had ascertained that there was an abundance of limestone and sandstone of fine quality in the county which would work up into excellent building material. There was plenty of gypsum, too, available for the construction of foundations, cellars, well walls and even houses. Its cheapness would lend its use to a variety of purposes.

When WILLIAM POLLOCK bought his first land or how soon he built a cabin we do not know. To break five acres of ground was generally recognized as ownership and would hold a claim for six months. To build a cabin eight logs high with a roof was sufficient to hold a claim for another six months. Most claims could be bought for $1.25 an acre. Some land was government bounty land – had been assigned years before to some officer or soldier for engaging in the military service of the United States. If it was not settled by the owner, the land would be assigned by the owner, through the government, to the man who had located upon it....for a price, of course.

A document in family hands today, and signed by Abraham Lincoln, president, shows that WILLIAM POLLOCK acquired 160 acres of this bounty land in 1861. The document reads:

THE UNITED STATES OF AMERICA, TO ALL TO WHOM THESE PRESENTS SHALL COME, GREETING: Whereas, In pursuance of the Act of Congress, approved Mar. 3, 1855, entitles "An Act in addition to certain Acts granting Bounty Land to certain Officers and Soldiers who have been engaged in the Military Service of the United States," there has been deposited in the GENERAL LAND OFFICE, Warrant No. 43395 for 160 acres, in favor of John M. Sharp Private Captain Barkers Company North Carolina Militia Mar. 1812 with evidence that the same has been duly located upon the South East quarter of Section Thirty six in Township Ninety north of Range Thirty West in the District of Lands subject to sale at Fort Dodge Iowa containing One hundred and sixty acres according to the Official Plat of the Survey of the said Land returned to the GENERAL LAND OFFICE by the SURVEYOR GENERAL the said Warrant having been assigned by the said John M. Sharp to William Pollock in whose favor said tract has been located.

Now Know Ye, That there is therefore granted by the UNITED STATES unto the said William Pollock as assignee as afore said to his heirs the tract of Land above described: To have and to hold the same tract of land, with the appurtenances thereof, unto said William Pollock as assignee as afore said and to his heirs and assigns forever.

In Testimony Thereof, I, Abraham Lincoln PRESIDENT UNITED STATES OF AMERICA, have caused these letters to be made Patent, and the SEAL OF THE GENERAL LAND OFFICE to be here unto affixed.

Given under my hand, at the City of Washington, the Eighth day of November in the Year of Our Lord one thousand eight hundred and sixty one and of the Independence of the United States the Eighty Sixth

BY THE PRESIDENT Abraham Lincoln
By WV Stoddard, Sec'y.
Recorded, Vol. 350 Page 35   Martin Buell, Acting,
                                  Recorder of the General
                                  Land Office

When a man located his land, settled upon it, he filed a claim with the U.S. land office. Farmers organized into claim associations and were strong enough so that settlers cooperated at the first land sales to protect their farms. The newly created land offices gave squatters the right to preempt their farms. When a neighborhood would be for sale, settlers would ride their horses to the office, have cash in hand and through a spokesman would buy their farms for the usual price. No other bidder would dare to bid. After farmers already on the farms had bought their land, the newly surveyed lands would be offered for sale to the new arrivals. Webster county had such a claim association called "The Mutual Protection Claim Association."

The above land transfer signed by Abraham Lincoln was in 1861, and POLLOCK came to the Fort Dodge area in 1856. He had not been in this area many months when a frightening alarm spread over the settlement. Three men had gone to see their claims in the vicinity of Spirit Lake and had hastily arrived back in Fort Dodge on March 21, 1857 to report that the Indians had massacred the Spirit Lake settlers. The next day a public meeting was held in the brick schoolhouse at Fort Dodge and the following day two companies were organized to go to the relief of the settlers.

The first school was being taught in the new brick schoolhouse that winter. Fort Dodge was growing fast and by 1857 had a population of 800, two hotels, five dry goods stores, three grocery and provision stores, one drug store, one printing office and newspaper, two brick churches, lawyers, physicians, two saw mills and a grist mill.

When the news of the massacre 100 miles to the northwest reached Fort Dodge, school was dismissed, and the schoolhouse became a shelter for the settlers north and west of Fort Dodge, all of whom fled into town with their wives and little ones for protection from the Indians.

WILLIAM POLLOCK'S son later told of their father's going with the Fort Dodge men to the relief of the Spirit Lake settlers, but said his group only went part way, probably until advance men came back saying the settlers were all dead and the Indians gone. Then his group turned back to Fort Dodge. However, the William Pollock who went on the expedition is listed in historical records as William P. Pollock. Our ancestor is WILLIAM A. POLLOCK. This may be an error in recording. There is no reason to believe that WILLIAM A. did not go on the expedition.

John F. Duncombe, who headed one of the three relief companies (two companies came from Fort Dodge and one from Webster City) later described the extreme trials and hardships of that trip in a speech, from which the following information has been taken:

The companies were furnished with teams and wagons, provisions, clothing and blankets and such arms and ammunition as were available consisting of nearly every kind of gun, from double-barreled shotguns to the finest rifles.

After the first day of fighting snow drifts, the men had advanced only seven miles. They rolled themselves in blankets, covered their heads and lay down in the snow near timber on Badger creek to sleep.

The next day the men shoveled snow, tramped it down for their teams and when no other method was possible, fastened a long rope to the wagon and every man grabbed a hold to pull the wagon through a drift. Often the horses and oxen were hauled through the drifts in the same fashion. That night after traveling ten miles, some of the men found shelter in cabins and sheds at Dakotah City, but others slept on the snow again.

A scout was sent ahead the next day across the trackless prairie to select the best route and signal back how best to avoid the huge snow drifts. The crust of the snow would sometimes permit a light man to walk five or six rods, but a heavier man would break through and go in to his hips, and then have to extricate himself from the hard crust to make another plunge. They camped that night at McKnights Point on the Des Moines river, a few miles west of Ottosen. Each day was a repetition of the preceding one until the relief party reached the Irish Colony, a few miles northwest of the present town of Emmetsburg.

Beyond the Irish Colony, signs of Indians were found: a few cattle shot, moccasin tracks. Every little grove was searched. Moving objects in the distance thought to be Indians were sighted. A detail was sent ahead to investigate. A nearer view revealed an ox team and sled. White people! This party mistakened the approaching Fort Dodge reliefers as Indians and had put themselves in an attitude of defense. The joy of these 17 or 18 people at finding the reliefers were friends was great indeed. The party was escaping an Indian attack at Springfield, Minn. (now Jackson) where one person had been killed and several wounded.

After giving the refugees food, the supply for the Fort Dodge men was almost exhausted and they went on half rations. However, raw meat supplemented the short meals. Some was beaver meat. Each man had a stick or ramrod to hold his own meat over the night fires until cooked for his own supper.

The last few days of the march, constant expectation of meeting Indians put everyone on guard. Watchers were posted at night. This shortened sleeping hours. Constant shoveling of snow, dragging teams and wagons through drifts, traveling with sore, wet and swollen feet made advancing most difficult. Some men became snow blind. After leaving Mud Lake, scouts were dispatched ahead to search all timber for Indians. No Indians were found. The party reached the Granger cabin (no relatives of ours), where several white men had been massacred, beyond Estherville and met a soldier there from Fort Ridgely, Minn. He said that from Springfield, the Indians had fled to the northwest and probably were 100 miles away by then.

The officers of the Fort Dodge expedition held council and concluded that they could not overtake the Indians. The sun had come out, the snow was melting and the streams were rising.

The officers called for volunteers to bury the dead around the Iowa Lakes. Chief Inkpaduta and his Sioux Indians, starting at the Rowland cabin on the south shore of West Okoboji Lake on March 8, had murdered 32 men, women and children and had kidnapped four young women.

Leaving a 20 man burial detachment behind, the rest of the Fort Dodge command started the return march toward home. The fast melting snow had raised the streams and in places they were almost impassable. After a hard, toilsome march, the Irish Colony was reached.

But the burial detachment, after completing its job and heading for the Irish Colony, became bewildered on the prairie and disagreed as to the proper course to take. Some remained all night on the prairie with their clothing frozen and feet wet without food or shelter. In the morning, those who had taken off their wet boots could not get them on again. The group separated into squads each taking the route thought best. During the day, most of them reached the Irish Colony but some were so crazed, they did not recognize companions. Two of the men were frozen to death on the prairie, and although a great search was made for them, their bones were not found until years later together with one of the men's rifle.

At the Irish Colony, the command was so short of food, they tried to buy a steer, but the people there refused to sell without receiving cash, so the command took the animal by force.

The Fort Dodge men moved down the Des Moines river keeping to the hills to avoid the water. Two hours before dark, they arrived at the flooded Cylinder creek. It covered the flat land for half a mile in width. Two officers rigged up a wagon box for a boat and calked it with a bed quilt, took two other men and started across, hoping in this manner to move the command across the flooded stream. The wind came up, the men baled constantly and barely reached the opposite bank when the boat swamped and sank. Night was coming on fast. All of the blankets had been left behind on the other side of the creek. The two officers and the two men, with wet feet, frozen boots and clothing, knew their chances for the night were slim unless they could get to a cabin three miles distance. This they did.

The night brought a snow storm, sub zero weather and fifty mile an hour gale. The men of the expedition, stopped by the flood, piled up together as close as they could lie, covered themselves with blankets and canvass from the wagons. Scarcely a person moved from Saturday night until Monday morning by which time ice had frozen so solid that loaded wagons and horses, as well as men, could cross over the creek.

Meanwhile, the two officers at the cabin twice fought their way through the blizzard back to the creek. All they could see across the stream was a snow covered hump where the men lay covered with blankets and canvass. The officers did not know if the men were frozen to death or alive.

When the ice had frozen solid enough and the men and wagons crossed the stream, the group was short on food, so the men broke into squads and headed for Fort Dodge picking up what food they could enroute. All of the men, except the two who froze to death on the prairie, reached home by April 11. Fear of the Indians hung over Fort Dodge for some time, but new settlers continued to arrive.

A newly married couple from New York state, Jared and Sarah J. (Bates) Fuller arrived in Fort Dodge this summer of 1857. Sarah was the daughter of our ancestors, JAMES and ELIZABETH (YEOMAN) BEATS. Jared had been born in Colchester, N.Y., not far from Sarah's home at Downsville. His ancestors had come to America on the Mayflower. Jared's parents did not want him to marry. He married Sarah and his parents would not let Sarah into the house, not because they disliked Sarah, but because they did not want Jared to marry, Anna Pollock says. The young couple came West and built a cabin three or four miles west of Fort Dodge on the south side of what is now highway five.

The Biographical Record and Portrait Album of Webster and Hamilton Counties, Iowa, published 1888, says "Jared Fuller came West in 1857 and through the influence of his brother-in-law, G.E. Bates, to Webster County. Mr. Bates afterward went to Junction City, Kansas and during the Civil War served in a Kansas regiment. After the war he devoted himself to politics and became quite prominent, serving several times in the Kansas legislature. He died Jan. 6, 1888."

MARY MARGARET BATES (who became our grandmother) came West later this year to join her sister Sarah and the brother Gurdon Beates (sometimes recorded as G.E. and sometimes G.W. Bates.) Only two years separated the sisters in age, Sarah being the older. Their mother had died twelve years earlier. Their father had remarried.

MARY MARGARET left behind in the East, her father, two brothers, her youngest sister and at least four nieces and nephews.

The oldest brother, Robert, father of the children, had bought the home farm from his father nine years earlier and carried on farming and lumbering. Robert had added 200 acres to the original 500 acres and had a sawmill and rafted his own lumber to Philadelphia. He had a dairy herd of 40 cows. On this farm was a bluestone quarry which furnished the stone for the county courthouse and other buildings. Robert was an elder, a trustee and a Sunday school superintendent in the Presbyterian church at Downsville for 25 years. He became a state representative to the assembly at Albany.

James Yeoman Bates, the brother two years MARY MARGARET'S junior, had his heart set on becoming a minister. As a young man, he made speeches to the family and to the horses practicing for his calling. He studied at some school and realized his ambition, and became a Methodist minister in Sing Sing Parish at the then fabulous salary of $3,000.

The next youngest brother was Gurdon Beates (he used that spelling), who like Robert once was Sunday school superintendent at Downsville.

Harriet N., the baby of the family, was 22 years old when MARY MARGARET came West. Harriet married Simon Bolivar Horton and may well have been married by this time. More about these brothers and sister as the years pass.

MARY MARGARET probably came West by train as far as she could come, likely Iowa City, and then she would have had to take the stage coach the rest of the way. Can you imagine her excitement to see her sister as the stage rumbled across the rough trails of the prairie, fording the creeks and circling or crossing the sloughs? If there wasn't dust, there was mud. There were rest stops for a short time, a pause for a meal or for a night's sleep. With a rush of wheels, creaking leather, and a blare from the driver's horn, the stage approached each stop.

She may not have gotten off at Fort Dodge, but likely continued with the stage as it left Hay Market Square, rumbled down Market street hill, forded the Des Moines river, and climbed the western bank to the prairie again for Powers Crossing on the south fork of the Lizard creek. This two story brick inn and farm house would have been almost new having been built in 1856. The passengers entered a walnut paneled room. A big dining room and a kitchen accommodated the travelers. The inn had eight bedrooms and a ballroom. (This handsome inn is still standing in 1962.) This probably was not far from Jared Fuller's cabin. Sioux City was 125 rough uncomfortable miles beyond.

MARY MARGARET may have been with Sarah when the first of Sarah's family of sons was born.

This was the year the capital of Iowa was moved from Iowa City to Des Moines. The first settlers to select claims in the northern part of Pocahontas county (the county eventually to be our family home) chose them on the future site of Old Rolfe in May 1857 in what is now Des Moines township. Of the three men who selected these claims, two had spotted the location a few months earlier when going to Spirit Lake with the relief corps from Fort Dodge. Land had been settled in the southern part of the county two years earlier... just a couple of years after the last Indian battle had been fought in that county. Eighteen war-like Sioux Warriors hunting on the Little Sioux River near the present town of Sioux Rapids had learned that the peaceful Winnebagoes were camped on Pilot creek near where it flows into the Des Moines river. The Sioux decided to take the Winnebagoes by surprise and get some fresh scalps. The Winnebagoes were camped to feast and prepare furs for market at the trading post in Fort Dodge. In the hand to hand fight, ten Winnebagoes were killed. How many Sioux were killed is not known because a Sioux would rather die than leave any of his dead behind on a field of battle.

Some of the trails in northwest Iowa were getting quite passable in 1857. One settler bragged that it took him only 12 days to move his wagon from Dubuque to Estherville.

The Spirit Lake massacre was in March. Late in the fall, ROBERT and ELIZABETH GRANGER on their farm in Tama county received a letter, now yellow with age, from Charles Porter Senior back in Richfield, Ohio. He wrote, "Did you ever hear or know about a murder done on big creek by the Indians. The paper stated that 7 families were murdered and one family by name of Granger and not hearing from you so long, we supposed it must be you." (There was a Granger murdered in the Spirit Lake massacre, spoken of earlier in this book, but was no relative of ours.)

Porter was wedded to ELIZABETH GRANGER'S sister. They were Newman girls from Cambridgeshire England. The Porters had followed the GRANGERS to America and both families had lived for a period of years at Richfield, Ohio. The GRANGERS had left Ohio 12 years ago and Mrs. Porter had said to ELIZABETH, "I followed you to America but I won't follow you to the West." When the GRANGERS left Ohio, they had three daughters 5, 4 and a year and a half. The Porters at that time had daughters 12, 6 and an infant, and sons 10, 8, 4 and 2. Later they had one more daughter.

Porter must not have been too convinced that ROBERT GRANGER was murdered by the Indians, though, for in the same letter he ardently inquires about the West, "I whant you wright and let us know how you are giting along and how you are situated and how much land you have and how the country is elevated wither it is leavel or gullee and how much timber according to prary land and how much land is worth per acre is there any congress land to be sold near you how are you situated for school and meeting and gristmill and how fare from a store or market and what kind of timber you have and what kind of animals and let us know wither you hav heard from England or not. Let us know how fare you are from railroad it is not unlikely that some of us shall come out and see you what sort of climate you have thare and whether you like the country or not."

The same letter continues, "We have got as far as talking about going to England, but not fully desieded yet.......This is a few lines from MOTHER, "My Dear Children i send these few lines hoping to find you all well my thoughts are allways thinking about you i hope you will pray for you pore MOTHER as lost her all my pore boy as been very bad if i lose him what shall i due i hope we shall meet in heaven at last no more this time i still remain your affectionate MOTHER NEWMAN.'"

And the Porter letter goes on, "Concerning pore FATHER affares MOTHER takes one third four will take two-thirds but things are not settled at present i expect we shall hear more about it in the next letter." ELIZABETH GRANGER in Tama county, as well as her sister back in Ohio, must have cherished every bit of news they received from their MOTHER and the rest of the family back in England.

This summer following the massacre, WILLIAM POLLOCK, the man from Scotland, undoubtedly was breaking his land and maybe building a cabin northwest of Fort Dodge. As he went back and forth to town, he could have gone past the cabin home of Jared and Sarah Fuller, and there made the acquaintance of her sister, MARY MARGARET BATES, newly arrived from New York state.

Sometime late that year or early in 1858, WILLIAM and MARY MARGARET, the girl of ScotchIrish descent, were married. She was a third generation American. The Rev. L.C. Coffin, a prominent and colorful minister of early Fort Dodge, pronounced them man and wife. Where the ceremony took place we do not know. She was 29. He was 30.

The POLLOCKS would know Rev. Coffin for a period of years. He had railroad interests and invented the automatic coupling device to link cars together, thus eliminating a dangerous task, Anna Pollock says. She tells that Coffin built a seventeen room house northwest of Fort Dodge. One side was a chapel, the other side was family living quarters, and the upstairs was used at different times for different purposes. At one time he kept ex-convicts there, instructed them and had them farm his land. At another time, he used the house as a home for wayward girls. WILLLIAM POLLOCK and Jared Fuller built a big red round barn on that place which was still there in the nineteen sixties.

The newlyweds' cabin home nine miles northwest of Fort Dodge was prairie country, different than MARY MARGARET had known in the foothills of the Catskills. The cabin was in a pretty wooded area – plenty of wood for building, for fuel and for fence posts. Lizard creek meandered through the trees and a tributary flowed past the cabin home. The streams ran clear as gold in those days. After a heavy rain, the sloughs and bogs on the prairie held the surplus water for several days but by the time it had filtered through the ground, the water entered the streams as clear as could be. The sloughs in Webster county were often no less than small lakes. When they had outlets in a river or creek, they were full of fish. In the winter, they made ice skating ponds; and in the fall and spring, fine places to hunt geese and duck and other waterfowl.

Plenty of high ground was available for cultivating. The farmers mowed the choicest wild grass early in the season for hay. The prairie rule was that any likely looking hay looking hay was yours if you mowed a swath around it. Prairie grass often was six feet tall.

Prairie fires were something to fear. When the grass dried in the late summer or early fall, settlers mowed wide swaths around their buildings to break any blaze that might develop.

Supplies of salt and sugar and whatever else couldn't be grown or obtained from the land, the woods or the streams came from Fort Dodge, the trading center. Usually trips to town were made about every two weeks. Winter trips to market were shorter than summer ones. With ponds frozen, a beeline could be made to town, but in the summer a wide circle was made around every slough and bog. Travel was difficult. Horses or oxen drew the lumber wagons and occupants sat on hard board seats. When the deep snow and intense cold came, people did not leave their houses for weeks at a time.

When spring came, bears came out of hibernation, poked around the streams looking for food. Bass and other fish could be had for the catching. Otters played on the river banks. They made slides on the banks, then slid down these ending in a splash, a sport they never seemed to tire of. Otter pelts brought seven dollars and a beaver hide five. Muskrats brought 25 cents. Plenty of prairie chickens were available for the hunting.

A few maples in the woods could be tapped for the sugar but most settlers raised cane and made sorghum. Sometimes settlers who had no coffee made a substitute of rye grain that tasted something like postum.

Dairy cows were permitted to graze across unfenced prairies. A few pigs and a span or two of oxen and maybe a team of horses usually made up the rest of a farmer's animals. These meant milk, butter, cheese and meat for the family. Warm steaming johnny cake, oatmeal mush, sorghum, dried fruits, nuts from the woods, fish from the streams were all a part of the pioneer menu.

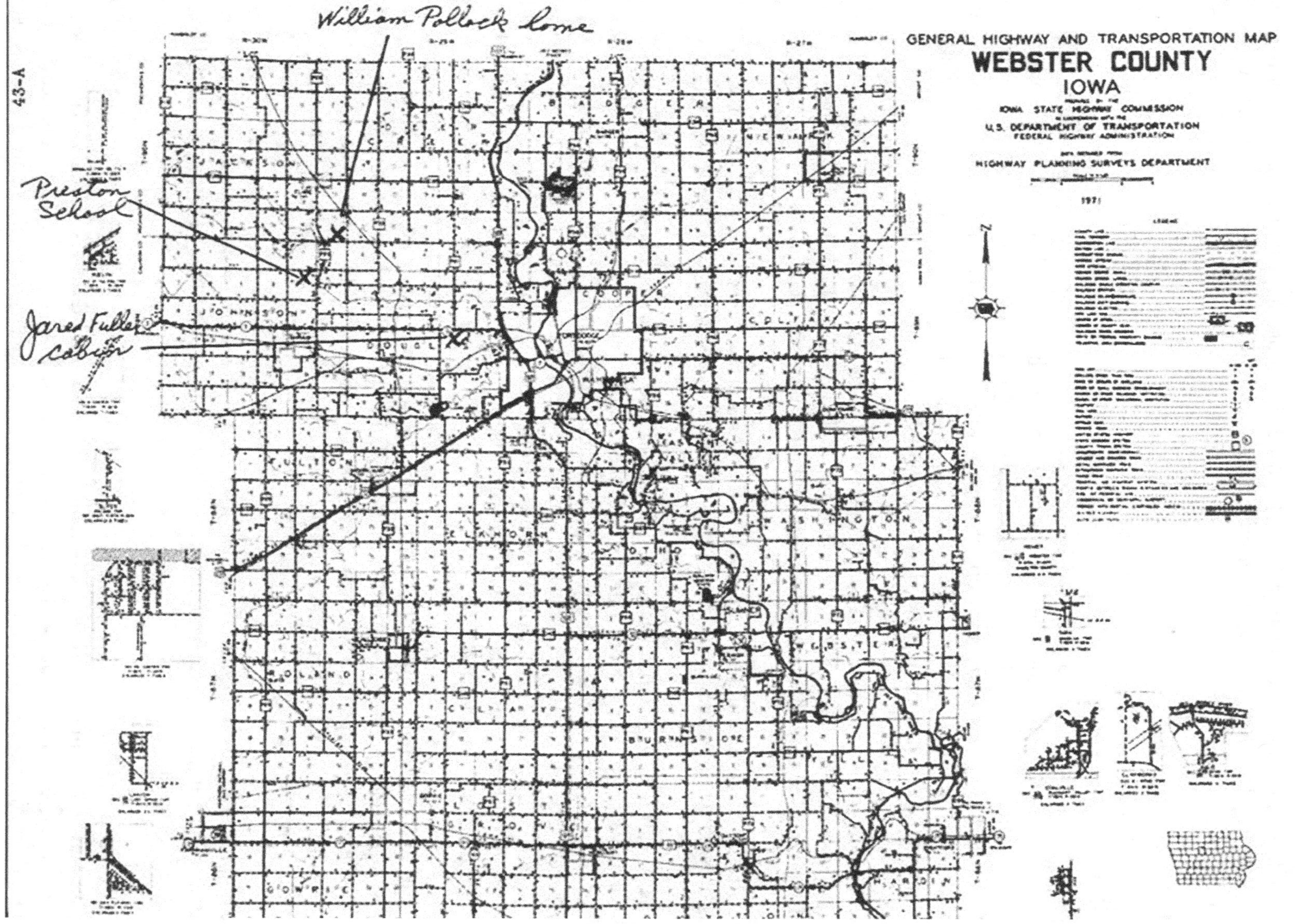

William Pollock home
Preston School
Jared Fuller cabin
GENERAL HIGHWAY AND TRANSPORTATION MAP
WEBSTER COUNTY
IOWA
IOWA STATE HIGHWAY COMMISSION
U.S. DEPARTMENT OF TRANSPORTATION
FEDERAL HIGHWAY ADMINISTRATION
HIGHWAY PLANNING SURVEYS DEPARTMENT
1971
43-A

The young people enjoyed themselves at dances called cotillions. Music was often just a single violin. Dresses were made of homespun and reached the floor. Calico cost 45 cents a yard. Husking bees, sleighing and skating parties, hunting and fishing trips were part of the pioneer fun.

The POLLOCKS were a newly married couple when the Fort Dodge countryside was aroused by a murder and the subsequent trial. Two families had settled along opposite banks of the Des Moines river north of Ft. Dodge. Both claimed the same tract of timberland. Timber for building, fuel and posts was of primary importance to the early settlers. A teen age boy of one family shot a twenty-year-old son of the other family when he and his brother were caught cutting wood in the tract. The boy who did the shooting disappeared but a brother was held by officials and charged with "second degree murder, an aider, abetter and accessory." The trial was sensational, the first murder trial in the county. The most distinguished lawyers in northwest Iowa participated in the case. Settlers from all parts of the county crowded the courtroom. The trial had scarcely begun when it came to an abrupt close. The father of the boy on trial had put up a thousand dollar bail. They forfeited that bail and the father and son slipped out of the country and were never seen again. One of their attorneys wrote in a memoir, "The worst of it all, the fine fat cow that was promised us by way of compensation, they drove away with them."

On the national scene, Abraham Lincoln, a Springfield, Ill. attorney, was gaining more and more prominence as an opponent of the extension of slavery. Stephen A. Douglas of that state was maintaining that the people of each territory should decide whether it should be a free state or a slave one.

ROBERT GRANGER in Tama county again receives a letter from his brother-in-law, Charles Porter in Ohio, dated Nov. 28th, 1858: "i whant to know what you delay in writing for i whant to no if you got that letter i sent to you respecting you natherlization i got captain Weld and Hall to draw up a paper that would qualify you for ofice. they done it and was glad you made application for same when i see any of your old friends they enquire about you and glad to hear you are well there is a company in richfield as got a steem grist mill and saw mill on that brook opsite old Sol Oviatt cidar mill... we had been expecting a letter from England a good wile but have got none... we have no letter from England this 14 months... i must wright soon to no what the matter is they do not wright... I shall wright to you as soon as I get a letter from England without fail... it makes it bad for you if you can not sell what you raise... we have a good market in Cleveland for all we can raise down to mushrooms..."

One of the cousins, who had been attending Richfield Academy in Ohio, encloses a little letter with her father's saying in part, "It has been so long since we separated, they need not think it strange if we have almost forgot each other... Mother says she has not given up going to England yet. We have had no letter and that is the reason why it is not decided... We send our love to AUNT BETSY and UNCLE ROBERT and cousins all..."

Up in Fort Dodge the next January, in 1859, the POLLOCKS' first child was born and he was named William after his father and subsequently called Will. He was the third William Pollock for his paternal grandfather living back in Scotland carried that name, too. Will was welcomed into this world not only by his parents but by his Aunt Sara, Uncle Jared and two little boy cousins whose cabin home was five miles away. The population of Webster county that year was 2,597.

Pocahontas county, to the northwest of Webster, was organized and the first election held in March. The county seat was located in the little settlement on the Des Moines river later known as Old Rolfe. It was first called Highland City, later Milton, and part of the time Parvin. (Pocahontas county and new Rolfe years later would become our family home.)

In Tama county, the GRANGERS were still receiving letters from the cousins back in Ohio. This little epistle written in May, 1859 and addressed to "Dear Cousin ELIZA," says in part:

Eliza Ann Granger
copied from a tin type

"When I left home I started for the South East part of Richfield, a place I never saw before we arrived a little before dark. I commenced my school the next day (as I am teaching now) and as all was strange you need not wonder that I got a little homesick during the week. The first day wore away rather slowly, but since then it has become more pleasant and I like it first rate. It seemed odd to be called maam, but I am getting used to it now. I have 16 scholars. It is a small but pretty school house, situated I was going to say, the other side of nowhere. The furniture composes a stove and two chairs. I have a steady boarding place nearly a mile from the school. I expect to teach three months...Mother talks about you often and would like to see you all. They have not heard from England when I came away...Last winter there was quite a revival of God's work on Hinkley Ridge where we attend meeting... the young folks have prayer meetings once a week in private homes, have meetings twice every Sunday at church, together with a large Sabbath school and Bible class. The Methodists have preaching half of the time and the Baptists the other half and people unite together in worship. UNCLE ROBERT and AUNT BETSY you write, please do, tell Elizabeth and Mary and all the rest to do the same. Now ELIZA you write as soon as possible... be free to speak on all subjects you see fit..."

But the young Elizabeth Granger, known as Lizzie, had other things on her mind. In GRANGERS' house there was excitement and plans being made. The oldest of the four daughters was being married. Elizabeth, 18, became the bride of George Kober who was German born and had come to Tama county five years earlier in 1855. He "worked out" at first and would subsequently acquire land and build a fine house for a growing family just a couple of miles northwest of the GRANGER home.

One hundred steamboats were now plying the waters on the eastern border of Iowa. That spring the businessmen of Fort Dodge had organized a stock company and raised money to acquire a steamboat to navigate the Des Moines river. A captain and others were sent to Pittsburgh to superintend the building of the boat, a small stern wheeler of fifty ton capacity, with adjustable smoke stack and pilot house to enable it to get under the bridge at Des Moines. It was launched and sent by way of the Ohio and Mississippi rivers to Keokuk, then up the Des Moines river to Fort Dodge. The boat was named "The Charles Rogers."

The maiden voyage from Keokuk to Fort Dodge was described thus in an old letter: "In May, 1859, our firm chartered the steamboat Charles Rodgers, a small craft of about 50 tons, we agreeing to load her to full capacity, destination Fort Dodge on the Des Moines river, rate of freight through 50 cents per hundred pounds. We loaded the boat with sugar, coffee, molasses, tobacco, salt, flour etc. and I went on board as super cargo. We left the landing at Keokuk Wednesday, May 18, 1859, at six o'clock in the evening and entered the mouth of the Des Moines river before dark. The boat had no cabin only the pilot house on the hurricane deck. We ate and slept on the lower deck, just back of the engine and boiler. The boat was laid up at the bank whenever night overtook us, only running in daylight, warping through the locks at Bonaparte and Bentonsport. One of the pilots was a violinist and at several places where we tied up to stay for the night, with the assistance of the neighborhood belles and beaux we had old fashioned dances. Our cargo being billed through for Fort Dodge we made no stops for way business and arrived at Des Moines Friday evening where we remained all night. Saturday morning we left Des Moines. Our boat being of light draft and the river a good stage of water we passed over the dam at Des Moines and arrived that evening at Boonesboro landing, several miles from the town of that name. Here we remained for the night and some parties coming over from the town, we had a dance in the building on the shore. Between that point and Fort Dodge we ran out of fuel and had to land several times, all hands going into the woods to gather dead timber to keep our fires going. The shrill whistle every now and then brought people to the river bank for miles back to see the boat. That evening we made a landing at a farm owned by a man name L. Mericle, a short distance below Fort Dodge. The farmer being very anxious for supplies I made my first sale of groceries to him. The next morning, Monday, about noon, we steamed up to the landing at Fort Dodge.

Excitement was great in town. The first steamboat had arrived. One historian wrote, "as the captain came steaming up the river, he blew the whistle so long and loud that the citizens imagined a Mississippi river fleet had arrived, and before he could land at the levee and make fast the bow line, the banks of the stream were lined with men, women and children anxious to get a sight of the newcomer."

The Charles Rodgers made a half a dozen trips up and down the Des Moines river, Fort Dodge to Des Moines to Keokuk and back, while the water was high. Emigrants, groceries and provisions were delivered to Fort Dodge, and the boat was loaded down with potatoes and grain for the down stream trip. Excursion parties went at half rate. Then the water began to lower and the only steamboat ever to ply the Des Moines river as far upstream as Fort Dodge was taken down stream to the White river and sold.

Webster county was making plans for its second annual agricultural fair. The Fort Dodge Sentinel, May 6, 1859, a paper for the family fireside, carried an advertisement in which L.H. Coffin, president, listed the animals and articles to be exhibited in September and the premiums offered. Exhibits were to include: Blood, draught and matched horses, horses of all work, jacks and mules, cattle, work oxen, sheep, hogs and poultry. Farming tools made in the county: breaking plough, stirring plough, one horse plough, shovel plough, cultivator, wagon for all purposes, harrow, field roller, horse rake, fanning mill, hay rigging, cheese press, specimen of horse shoeing. Implement of manufacture: double harness, single harness, saddle and bridle, corn brooms, gents' boots, ladies' summer walking shoes. Mechanical made in the county: sofa, lounge, table, parlor chair, split bottom chair, coopers' ware, tin ware, specimen of upholstery. Best vegetables, grain and field crops. Best sack of flour made in the county, best butter, cheese, honey, sugar made from cane, syrup, loaf of bread, biscuit, soft soap, hard soap, best specimen of coal. Domestic manufacture: woolen cloth, satinet, woolen blanket, flannel, linen, hearth rug, rag carpet, woolen knit stockings. Needlework and wax flowers, ornamental work, ottoman cover, crochet collar, silk patchwork quilt, silk bonnet, straw bonnet. Best lady equestrian, ladies' driving match double or single carriage.

The same newspaper published train schedules from Iowa City to Chicago and from there to Detroit, Cincinnati and New York. Stage and hacks were advertising their services, and the American Hotel at Cedar Falls and the Dubuque Key House were desirous of giving service to travelers. Fort Dodge concerns were looking for business: "Hark ye, Hungry Mortals, Fort Dodge Bakery, Fresh bread, pies, crackers etc."; "Whoa: Hold your horses! Saddler and harness shop, carriages and buggy trimmings"; "Cooking, heating and parlor stoves." One advertisement read: "Wait for the wagon, wait for the wagon, wait for the wagon and we'll all take a ride... Wait for Mrs. C.H. Crosby who will arrive in Fort Dodge about the first of May, direct from New York with a full stock of the latest millinery goods- when she will be prepared to furnish the ladies of Fort Dodge and vicinity with all the articles of her line of business." The paper said that the work on the courthouse was going ahead and the cornerstone would be laid the next Saturday by the judge. The public was invited. WILLIAM POLLOCK cut some of the stone and worked on this building.

With white man's civilization moving fast into the area, there were still some Indians around. They were not entirely trusted, especially by the farm folk who lived separated from the populated centers. The Indians called at the pioneer homes and begged for food. One day WILLIAM POLLOCK saw Indians coming and told his wife MARY MARGARET to get into bed and cover up. He knew the Indians were terribly afraid of smallpox. When the Indians came to the door, he informed them his wife was terribly sick with smallpox. She let out a few loud groans and the Indians fled quickly. This is an incident told by the POLLOCK daughter-in-law, Anna Pollock, a hundred years after the incident happened.

Down in Tama county as the year was drawing to a close, horse thievery roused the countryside. Horses were absolutely necessary for the growing and marketing of crops and for transportation. The loss of a horse was drastic. Several horses had disappeared in the county. Then Lemual Small, east of Des Moines, lost three valuable colts and suspected the notorious Bunker brothers who lived with their mother, three other brothers and four sisters near Eldora. Small and Constable Seaman went to the Bunker home in search of the brothers, whom they finally found at Independence. Small and Seaman with the Bunkers in tow started back for Des Moines and stopped to spend the night at West Union, the tiny town near the Stoakes farms. The Bunkers being in town caused great excitement. A crowd gathered next morning. One brother made a break for freedom on his horse. He was overtaken near the Stephen Klingaman mill. Klingaman was a respected, prosperous leader of the community. The Des Moines men with both prisoners again in tow stopped at the Klingaman house to ask directions to the Ridge road. They wanted Klingaman to go a ways and show them the way but he reportedly declined but after being urged, went along. They started off through a grove. Then apparently to scare the Bunker brothers, who were considered desperate characters, into revealing anything they might know about the Tama county horses that had disappeared, a noose was put around the neck of the older brother Will. Charlie Bunker was tied to a tree for safe keeping. A sapling was bent down and one end of the noose rope was fastened to it. Another rope held the sapling down. Will reportedly was strung up several times but denied any knowledge of the North Tama thefts. Charlie, tied to the tree, suddenly broke loose. Two men went in pursuit. The third tied the sapling rope to a tree to hold the sapling down and joined the chase. Struggling to free himself, Will loosened the rope and the sapling flew up carrying him with it and he was hanged. The trio caught and brought Charlie back and there learned what had happened. Apparently under the theory that "Dead men tell no tales," Charlie was hung, too. Two days later a boy hunting pheasants discovered the bodies. News of the hanging quickly spread. There was great excitement. The coroner charged the trio with murder, but all left the country and were never tried. Klingaman left his family financially and spiritually ruined. There were mixed feelings about the trio, bu horse thieves were thoroughly hated. Great sympathy was felt for the Klingaman family. Years later when Small returned to Iowa to face the law, 2,000 tax payers and all the officers of Tama county signed a petition and the case was dismissed in 1879.

JOHN STOAKES on his farm between West Union and Buckingham received word that his brother William Stoakes, Jr., had died at his home near Knoxville, Ohio. The two had come as boys with their mother from England to join their father in the Ohio wilderness, had fought in the War of 1812 together, married sisters, reared large families close together on the same big farm, built brick houses. There William had lived out his life while JOHN came west to Iowa with his young folk to seek and obtain new land. Time was marching on.

The rift between the North and South was growing wider. James Buchanan was president. ELEAZER STOAKES when he was old enough, cast his first vote for John Charles Freemont, the rugged explorer of the Rockies and Southwest and the controversial Mexican War officer, but Buchanan had won. Now Abraham Lincoln was running on a Republican anti-slavery ticket against Stephen A. Douglas, Democrat. ELEAZER voted for Lincoln.

WILLIAM POLLOCK received his American citizenship in district court at Webster county September 26, 1860 by swearing his support to Iowa and the United States, and renouncing his allegiance "to every foreign king, prince and potentate, state and sovereignty... particularly the Queen of the Kingdom of Great Britain of whom he was late a subject."

A little more than a year later, he received the official document signed by President Lincoln giving POLLOCK title to 160 acres of land in Webster county, as told about earlier in this book.

(These two documents together with POLLOCK'S subsequent Civil War discharge paper are treasured by his granddaughter, Helen Horton Cole.)

The year after POLLOCK became a citizen, his first daughter was born. She was named Jennie Elizabeth. Now the POLLOCKS had a son and a daughter. Sarah and Jared had three sons, a new son Edward having been born in 1860.

Years of the War

In November 1861, ELEAZER STOAKES, 28, enlisted in the Union Army of the War of the Rebellion. He followed into service a number of his North Tama county friends who had enlisted in October. Included among them was B.F. Thomas who was later to become ELEAZER'S brother-in-law. He would marry Sarah Stoakes, a sister five years younger than ELEAZER. Thomas kept a diary which he had published for family consumption. In its printed pages, we go with Thomas, STOAKES, and their friends to war. The following is in part a summation, and in parts direct quotations from that diary called "SOLDIER LIFE, a Narrative of the Civil War by B.F. Thomas."

The boys who went in October joined their company in Toledo; were feted there by the ladies of the Baptist church at a bountiful dinner; went in lumber wagons to Marengo where they took the cars to Davenport. At Camp McClellan every man who could saw or drive a nail built barracks. Thomas says that some of the men were rough and profane and two refused to take the oath of allegiance and were drummed out of camp. The soldiers ate from roughly thrown together tables, and were marched to the river to wash.

One night about 11 o'clock, the men were awakened with the announcement, "The captain has come." He had gone back to Tama county to enlist more men. The soldiers climbed out of their bunks to meet the new men. Thomas wrote, "The captain called me to the door and there I met ELEAZER STOAKES. This was truly a wonderful surprise to me. I had no thought of his coming. We had much to talk about and very little sleep that night."

The soldiers were "examined by four surgeons. They stood two on each side of the parade and we marched singly between them, holding our hands over our heads and moving our fingers. This is all the physical examination we ever had."

The Tama men were sworn in for three years or the duration of the war. They were issued coats, hats, pants, shirts, drawers, socks and shoes and then swapped to get the right sizes.

On November 11, Thomas and STOAKES were with eleven men taken by the captain to Davenport to round up men who'd run the guard to spend the night in a carousal. The captain and men went to one place with a large room, a small counter in the corner and some bottles on the shelves along the wall. A woman presided at the counter. A number of girls finely attired were playing cards and chatting with the soldiers and citizens. The captain demanded to see passes and they all showed them. The captain and men went to other places. At one house as they entered, the soldiers ran upstairs. STOAKES and Thomas followed them to upstairs bedrooms. Thomas caught his man and STOAKES lost his momentarily but thrust his gun under the bed and the man called out that he'd surrender. They were taken, with others, back to the guard house.

The Tama men became part of Company G. of the 14th Regiment of the Iowa Volunteers. On November 26, they marched to Davenport to take a boat to St. Louis but the boat filled up and there was no room for Company G and it had to return to camp. Two days later they again marched to Davenport and took the passenger cars south, crossing the mighty Mississippi on a bridge, and glided over the prairies of Illinois in the darkness. The next night they were in Springfield and then continued by the cars to Alton and went aboard a steamboat for St. Louis. They spread their blankets on the deck of "The Meteor" and slept. At sunrise they passed the muddy mouth of the Missouri river and thence into St. Louis arriving November 30. They marched through the streets, saw their first street cars, were cheered lustily, and arrived at Benton Barracks. The barracks consisted of about eighty acres back of the fairgrounds where there were gardens, a large amphitheater, a fine race track, many flower beds, shrubbery, vases and statuary.

49-A
I
Toledo
Traer
Marengo
Clinton
Davenport
(Camp McClellan)
Sublette
Springfield
Missouri R.
Alton
Ohio R.
St. Louis
(Benton Barracks)
Golconda
Smithland
Cairo
Paducah
Cumberland R.
Fort Henry
Nashville
Fort Donnelson
Columbia
Pittsburg Landing
Pulaski
Chattanooga
Shiloh
Tennessee R.
Memphis
Corinth
Huntsville
Atlanta
Jonesboro
Cahaba
Birmingham
Macon
(Camp Oglethorpe)
Mississippi R.
Canton
Jackson
Montgomery
Alabama R.
Mobile
Eleazer Stoakes'
War Record
Battles Fought
War Prisoner

Dec. 1, The men had their first grand review and inspection, unslung their knapsacks, laid them open for officers to inspect. Guns had not been drawn yet.

Dec. 4, The lieutenant took the company out about six miles into the country. "Found plenty of persimmons- excellent eating. Talked to a number of citizens. Everyone claimed he was 'Union' but his neighbors were 'Secesh'."

Many of the company men were sick and the well ones pitched tents to live in and gave the barracks over to the sick.

Dec. 13, The company took a seven mile trip into the country. Plenty of persimmons. Measles and mumps in camp. Vaccinations for smallpox.

Dec. 25, "'Merry Christmas'- Boys seemed like a merry family of children instead of sturdy soldiers. Received a letter from Miss Stoakes with her miniature enclosed. I was glad to see even a resemblance of her fair face.

Dec. 28, "Our guns came. Proved very poor and were condemned.

Dec. 31, "Guns issued and tested. Out of 35 guns in the squad, 15 burst and one had the tube blown out.

Jan. 7, "ELEAZER STOAKES sick but not very bad.

Jan. 15, "Again given guns, same old Belgian muskets. Wooden guns would be almost as good as these.

Jan. 29, "Tried guns again. Some would not explode the caps.

Feb. 4, "Drew guns. Much better guns and boys well pleased. These were rifled and fired the famous minie ball.

Feb. 5, "Embarked on the steamer 'Empress.' It was heavily laden. There was floating ice in the water. Where the rebs might be dangerous, all steam was shut off, the lights extinguished, and the boat floated noiselessly down stream. Up the Ohio river to Cairo. A turtle back gunboat that had helped capture Fort Henry the day before was anchored next to our boat."

Feb. 8, "We went up the Ohio to the mouth of the Tennessee river and up to Fort Henry where we landed and saw the effects of battle. Our tents pitched and our goods unloaded, we learned there was a much more formidable fort on the Cumberland river 12 miles from here which we were expected to attack and take."

Feb. 10, The men went foraging and found an unguarded beef and butchered it. They found a woman in a log cabin with six children. She was cooking unsalted hominy and shared it with the men. They left her some beef.

Feb. 12, The men's tents, overcoats and knapsacks were placed aboard a boat for Fort Donelson. "We'd heard plenty of this fort's great strength but our boys were eager to press forward. The soil here was brick red and there were pitch pine and yellow gum trees. We built a fire and ate hardtack and sow belly. The boys rolled in their blankets and nestled in the leaves- less than a mile away was a hostile army encampment with guarded walls awaiting an attack from us.

Feb. 13, "This day was equal to a June day in Iowa. The birds sang, squirrels chirped, and the first beams of sun touched the leafless branches of the noble beach trees and turned them into gold. The sunrise gun was fired from the rebel fort and seemed only a few rods away."

The men formed battle lines and moved forward to the brow of the hill when "a single shot from the fort buzzed through the trees and cut the air above our heads. We advanced down the timbered hill, reached the rebels' mass of fallen timber with the tops toward us, impossible to penetrate. We received the heaviest fire I was ever subjected to. We returned the fire as best we could but the rebels were behind breastwork. We fell into the protection of the trees and continued firing whenever enemy heads appeared over the breastwork. A rebel battery to the right opened fire on us and would have had us at its mercy except Birge's sharp shooters, men with homemade squirrel rifles, come up and silenced the battery. They fought Indian style and wore squirrel tails in their hats.

"At four o'clock, the soldiers withdrew to rest and eat. Rain turned to snow and the men couldn't light fires to cook. They laid down in their blankets and by morning every man or group of men was a mound of snow, an army invisible under four inches of snow.

"Union gunboats approached and imbedded shells in the walls of the fort, but the rebels shot through the Union boats and they had to retire or be sunk.

"General Grant proposed to encircle the fort and told the 14th to hold its position in the enemy's front and not to let him escape though our lines.

Feb. 15, "A battle began early on our extreme right. The rebel cavalry escaped but the rebel infantry was held in the fort. Heavy losses on both sides.

"After this, General Smith, a very old man who'd been Grant's instructor at West Point, asked permission from Grant to take his division and attack on the left. Rebel forces were concentrated on our right wing and would be weak on the left.

"Our position of attack was nearly barren of trees. We formed position of attack with the Second Iowa in front. This regiment was in disgrace for some of its boys had destroyed property in the St. Louis library and the boys just longed for a chance to wipe out the disgrace. Behind them came the Seventh Iowa, the Twenty-Fifth and then our regiment.

"Away the column went with guns at right shoulder shift. Up and up and faster and faster. Before we advanced with the column, a leaden hail began to drop among us and faster and faster came the bullets. On went the boys in our lead. Not a gun was fired from our side but on and on we ran. I think we gained on those in front of us for I know that when we went over the breastworks, we were close on their heels. Some of the rebels waited until our men sprang over the works, but most of them were seen running toward the next works sixty rods away. Some men were killed with bayonet and some shot and some captured, but most of them escaped.

"We were masters of the outer works. The rebels had a battery on the next works and at once they began shelling us. Some of our men had followed them half way across the next works. There is no doubt if General Smith had had all of his division here at this time we easily could have captured the next line of works that evening.

"When they began shelling our men, the officers ordered us back outside the works to the protection of the embankment. The rebels had gunners with this battery, for after we were outside the works, they threw their shells so they passed about two feet above the works we were behind, and shell after shell burst as they passed the works. We lay very close to the ground while this lasted, and it continued until dark.

"Snow had melted and mud was ankle deep... As soon as it was dark some of us made a raid over to the abandoned rebel tents just inside the works. We were in search of provisions. We found quantities of cornbread which was quite a treat to us... At midnight our camp cook brought two camp kettles of hot coffee. We had had no supper and could have no fires.

"Sunday, Feb. 16, 1862, Before daybreak we heard a bugle sound in the enemy's ranks. We supposed he was forming to make a charge. Again and again it sounded till it become light enough for us to see the works. There was a man standing on their works waving a white flag, and a bugler beside him blowing the bugle. One of our lieutenants and the color sergeant took our flag and went out to meet them. The rebel emissary had a message for General Grant... Not until noon did the Union men learn that the fort had surrendered.

"Oh, how we cheered! We were not hungry, nor tired nor anything but just anxious to get into the fort as soon as our legs would carry us there. Immediately the order was given to countermarch. Back to the breastwork and over them again; then on to the next line of march and over them. Here we came upon the first rebels. They were drawn up in line and as we approached they laid their guns on the ground in front of them.

"Just as our regiment was at the entrance of the fort, an orderly came riding up and stated that the rebels were destroying public property at Dover two miles up the river. Our regiment was ordered to stop this... There we found several wagonloads of flint lock guns, some ammunition and a large amount of flour and meat but saw no evidence of an attempt to destroy it. There were broken vehicles and crippled horses scattered about the streets. In many of the houses were dead men who had been carried in from the battlefield by their friends. Some wounded men and many prisoners. Nearly all of the houses were abandoned by their owners. No law. No order... Many of our boys gathered up what they thought would be useful in camp. STOAKES and I thought that some of the flour that was so plentiful would come good, but as it was in barrels, we were not able to carry a barrel, we knew not what to do. By chance we saw a trunk. We quickly emptied the clothing out and opened a barrel of flour and from its contents filled our trunk. This was the foundation of slapjacks for many a day... We arrived at the fort after dark, wet, muddy, hungry and tired... Had not eaten much for 24 hours... Cabins sufficient for our use had been reserved for us. Rain began to pour down. We sank down onto the cabin floor and slept. If we awoke to consciousness during the night it was merely to murmur to ourselves, 'Victory, victory' and sleep again.

"The whole North went wild over the victory at Donnelson. The Iowa legislature adjourned after voting to suspend the statutory liquor laws for 24 hours. There was the sound of revelry in Des Moines that night."

Next morning the soldiers made slapjacks out of their flour and some water and cooked them on the bottom of a broken kettle. Some other boys had a quantity of brown sugar and it was melted into syrup.

"The gathering of arms and army stores and guarding prisoners and marching them to boats busied us for several days.

"Mar. 7, Left Donnelson for the Tennessee river. Came to the river at dark and went directly aboard our boat the 'Autocrat.' Next morning steamed south on the old Tennessee but had not the least idea where we were going.

"Arrived at Savannah, Tenn. March 16. Peach trees were plentiful here and in bloom. I sent peach blossoms in a letter to Miss Stoakes.

"We frequently heard the name of Coring, Miss. as the next place we might expect battle. It was 15 or 20 miles from the river. Corinth was claimed to be a much stronger place than Donnelson but we felt sure we would be able to capture it when the time came.

"March 19, Started on south and passed other boats. Arrived at Pittsburg Landing and found all hurry and bustle. Bank or bluff there was probably 50 feet high and very steep. Many boats were tied up there." The 14th unloaded wagons and mules and other goods up a steep zig zag road that had just been built and made camp a mile and a half from the river. The whole country was covered with a heavy growth of timber. "Buds of the trees were swelling and bursting. Among the beauties of nature was congregated a large army fitted and equipped for a bloody contest.

"April 4, We were told that one of our regiments had gone some distance from camp and was attacked by the enemy. After a sharp fight, the regiment fell back within our lines. Two days rations were issued us that evening with orders to cook it and be ready to march in the morning.

"April 5, Everything quiet."

Shiloh

"Early the morning of April 6 we heard firing far distant on our right. For some time we thought it was one of our divisions on review. The fire increased and seemed to come nearer. STOAKES and I were washing dishes. We joked about the rebs coming in on us and wondered if they would let us alone until we got the dishes dried. We did not believe we were attacked.

But before we finished the dishes the long roll sounded in the Second Iowa and the doleful sound was re-echoed by our drums. Everything was hurry then. We began faintly to realize the rebels were upon us. We were soon in our accoutrements and took our haversacks and canteens with us but left everything else. Our knapsacks and blankets were left in our tents. The regiment was formed... joined the brigade... and marched toward the horrible roar in front. Soon we began to meet stragglers and wounded men hastening toward the river. They told us all was lost, that a large rebel army had attacked us and was driving everything before it... On we went and faster and faster. Still far in front we heard the terrible roar of infantry firing interspersed with the heavier discharge of cannon. When we approached as near as we thought wise, we formed line of battle and awaited the enemy's approach. Our ground was clear of underbrush and near the top of a slight ridge. On the other side the ground was covered with underbrush. On our right is open timber and facing an open field was the 12th Iowa. The 7th Iowa was beyond them. The 8th Iowa was on our left.

"Very soon the 21st Missouri appeared before us, looking frightened, and scattering like skirmishers and said the rebels were coming in heavy columns. We could hear the rebels coming. Our colonel asked the Missourians to lie down so we could fire over them, but they came right on. He ordered us to lie down and the Missourians went over us to the rear. When the rebels were quite close we plunged forward into the bushes after them our guns loaded and our bayonets set. But only the dead and wounded were there. Their flag was captured. We retired to our position... Again we heard them coming. This time they knew where we were. The battle raged for a long time but we held our ground and finally they were again put to rout.

"A battery was brought to our support. A rebel battery in front got the range and throwing a stream of shells compelled our battery to leave the field. The rebels now come in force and we were ordered to lie down. Our other battery poured its grape and cannister into them with all of its power. When the enemy was so close it could almost have laid hands on our cannon, it gave way and soon was in full retreat. Our colonel had two horses killed under him directly in front of us.

"During all this time both wings of our army had been driven back. Steadily the noise of battle swung back on either side of us and still we held our ground. During the lull of battle we discussed the situation: we thought our wings would fall back until the enemy formed a V cap outside our lines, then we would be reinforced and pierce their center.

"Our wings went farther back and we became anxious... a wide gap opened and a large body of enemy threw themselves through... We saw the 2nd Iowa and the 7th Iowa far away going from us at a double quick toward the landing. We had no orders to retreat and we poured a heavy fire into the rebels. Bullets reached us from several directions. We were ordered to the right. A few of us were among fallen trees and in easy firing distance of the rebels, so we kept firing as fast as we could load. Our major rode back and called to us to come on... We gained the top of the ridge and saw many rebel batteries but not firing. When we got back where our regiment was formed, they had their guns stacked. We had surrendered. A solid column of rebels stood beside us. Two of the rebel cavalry got the 12th Iowa's flag and banner and dragged them through a puddle of water. Our own old cotton flag was torn to pieces and tramped in the mud. The 14th's Col. William T. Shaw of Anamosa was the officer who had to hand his sword to the rebel commander and gave the final order of surrender to his men, 'Right dress. Shoulder arms. Stack arms.'

"We were formed into lines and started off the field. Our men were camped for the night in an old cotton field surrounded by guards. We built fires and prepared coffee, laid down to sleep, nothing under us but the ground and nothing over us but the sky. A heavy rain accompanied by hail filled the furrows of the cotton rows. After the rain, the rebel guard carried in rails for us to build a fire. We stood around the fire. Not over a thousand of us were prisoners. Next day we were hurried along the road to Corinth which was literally covered with wounded rebels, one of the most gruesome sights I ever saw. We were marched down the streets of Corinth, halted and we sat on the ground. We sat there until after dark and those in front were loaded into boxcars and sent south. Rain began to fall. Peter Wilson (a Tama man) was very sick and STOAKES and I took the best care of him we could, and that was but little. We were moved to the railroad tracks under a roof built on posts. There was a floor too small for all of the men to get on. Wilson begged so hard to lie down, I got down and held him in a sitting position. I knew nothing more until I awoke cramped with bodies of men lying piled together, so we slept until roused near morning and marched into boxcars. This was more comfortable.

"Arrived at Memphis after dark. Thousands of citizens gathered, some to comfort and cheer us, others to chafe and revile us. We were marched through the rain and slush. Wilson begged to let him lie down, but STOAKES and I supported him between us as best we could. We were ushered to the third floor of a large warehouse on the wharf. We sank to the floor and were asleep at once. No furniture, no conveniences, but plenty of room. The surgeons came and sent Wilson to a hospital. The commissioned officers were taken from us. A surgeon came into our room, told us he was going through the lines and would carry short letters for us. I wrote home. It didn't reach home for nearly two months.

"We fell into lines four times that day to go farther south. Each time we were dismissed and sent back. Rain was pouring. We had thin blouses and no overcoats. Some large tarpaulins in our room seemed especially for our benefit, so we cut them into five and six foot squares to use as blankets. A man came looking for the tarpaulins insisted we must pay or he'd compel the United States government to pay him and we laughed. He then insisted that if we attempted to carry off the pieces he'd have those taking them separated from the others and punished. The next day most of the boys left their tarpaulins behind. It was raining hard and some of us could not resist spreading them over our shoulders as we went out. We saw nothing of the owner nor did we abandon the blankets till we got to Nashville two months later and drew wool blankets.

"Many visitors came to see us. Frequently they whispered, so the guard could not see them, that they were Union men and gave us the news. Some slipped us the daily paper. Guards were about the room to keep order and at the stairs to keep us from passing up and down. About three boys at a time were permitted to take a number of canteens and go down to a hydrant for water. A line of guard around the lot prevented prisoners leaving. One of the prisoners discovered a hogshead of molasses stored in a shed, cut a hole, filled his canteen and plugged the hole. The news spread through the building and molasses flowed freely. Nearly all of the canteens were filled with it.

"A rope doubled over a large pulley near our ceiling passed down through a trap door in each floor to the basement. Our boys managed to raise the trap door and began an exchange of prisoners. If a boy on one floor belonged to a regiment on another floor, he grasped the rope and the boys passed him down to the proper floor. By this means many of the boys were placed with their friends. By this means some of the boys went to the basement to explore, found quantities of cigars and soon the prisoners had cigars to smoke. This was all done on the sly when the guards weren't looking.

"April 13, Taken by flat cars to Canton, Miss. Talked with citizens who came to the cars. All seemed to be strong Secesh. On to Jackson in tight boxcars. Arrived Mobile April 16. Marched through the streets to a large cotton shed, 150 by 90 with 12 foot brick walls, roofed except the center. We were guarded by Prussian soldiers hired for the job. There were probably a thousand prisoners.

"The first morning there, a large hogshead of crackers was rolled into the pen and left with us to divide. The boys made a rush, some were trampled underfoot. We had a small boy with us, and we worked our way to near the hogshead as possible, then tossed him over the men's heads into the hogshead. Instantly he was tossing handsful of crackers to every Company G man within reach. After this we appointed officers to divide the rations as should be done... The sunshine poured through the open roof space, and there was no means of getting circulation. The prisoners divested themselves of all but their scantiest raiment and lay panting in the shady side of the pen. The water from an inside hydrant was pure but warm.

"April 19, We were ordered to bake our meal into johnnycake and nearly 400 of us were taken out of the pen that evening and placed aboard the steamer, St. Charles, and started up the Alabama river. Morning came upon us in a dense fog and we saw the trees covered with trailing grey moss, a somber sight.

"April 21, Arrived at Cahaba, Alabama. Marched to a partially finished brick warehouse with walls and partial floor and roof. Space for the windows was high up from the ground. This was our prison for nearly two weeks. Rained. Next day the rest of the prisoners from Mobile arrived. We were sent in haste out of Mobile because Union gunboats were near there and might attack at any time... No provisions were made for rations here. What we were given was entirely insufficient. Cahaba was a town of 600 or 800. The citizens learned of our condition and sent in some provisions. One good old lady came to the door with a plate of beans for us. A plate of beans to feed a thousand men! Think of it. But she did what she could. Barrels of cornbeef came from Mobile but when opened stank so, they had to be removed. Finally a good barrel was opened. We boiled the meat in iron kettles and with cornbread lived fairly well. Water from an artesian well, too warm to drink, was brought by gutter and trough through the prison and ran into a barrel we sank into the ground, and from that barrel ran into a barrel a little lower, and into a third one flush with the ground. We used the last barrel for a bathtub and it had customers nearly all of the time. We filled our canteens out of the top barrel, wetted the cloth that covered them hung them in the air to dry and the water soon cooled to drink. Many of the men got sore eyes from the pitch pine given us for cooking fires. We discussed the chances of getting to our lines if we cut out of the prison; discovered there were eight revolvers among our men; decided we could overpower our guards but had little chance of getting to our own lines; so abandoned the idea of escape.

"May 2, Put aboard boat at sunrise, arrived at Montgomery in evening. Taken to amphitheater at the fairgrounds to sleep. May 3, Put in boxcars and started east. Guards wanted us to believe we were going to our own lines. Changed cars at Columbus, Georgia. May 4, arrived in Macon, Georgia, four weeks from day we were captured. It being Sunday many idlers were about. Many questions were asked us, some wise, some silly, some kindly, some bitter. Marched to border of city and put in fairgrounds, Camp Oglethorpe. Grounds closed with tight eight foot board fence. Several buildings. Long row of cattle and hog sheds- these we occupied as sleeping quarters. Many men had to sleep on open ground, no coats just thin blouses and no blankets except the tarpaulins some of us brought from Memphis. A small stream gave us plenty of pretty good water. At noon we received a loaf of bread, the first white bread we struck in the confederacy. Two crackers for supper, one for breakfast had been furnished us up to this time. We received the lower jowls of the hog pickled and smoked, the first smoked meat we'd seen in the South. They also gave us soap, candles, sugar, etc. Well, this was a change. Lots of open air, clear water and a variety to eat if not in very large quantity. Succeeded in getting the first paper in a long time. It gave a terrible account of a battle below New Orleans, whole rebel fleet lost, and claimed great barbarity by our officers. Roll call and inspection each morning and evening with orders that all equipment, hands and face bright and clean and hair combed.

"The orders were that no outsiders could converse with prisoners, no papers or books for the prisoners. We were the first prisoners brought here and during the novelty we were treated very well and fed pretty well, but the novelty wore off and we fared pretty hard for rations, and practically no beds, not even straw to lie on... Where the confederacy got all of the jowls they fed us was a mystery. Many were spoiled and wormy. We did get some meal, some cabbage and some milk by exchanging the rotten meat with the civilians.

"One evening some straw was brought in and Southwick secured a large armful which he kindly divided with us. Southwick and STOAKES bunked together and Felter and I (all Tama men.) The straw made quite an improvement in sleeping, but a few evening later a candle was knocked over and instantly the straw was in blaze. The shed caught fire but the blaze was extinguished.

"Every day the boys played baseball, an exciting game and plenty of exercise. Some pitched quoits, and some marked checkerboards on the ground and played checkers.

"We overheard the quartermaster contracting for wood to be delivered along all summer. I lost the last spark of hope that we'd be paroled or exchanged."

While ELEAZER STOAKES was being held a war prisoner in Macon, Georgia, a nineteen year old girl back home in Tama county, (who would become his wife), received her certificate to teach. On May 5, 1862, the county superintendent of the Common Schools in and for the County of Tama and the State of Iowa certified that he had "this day examined Miss E.A. GRANGER in orthography, reading, writing, arithmetic, geography and English grammar and found her competent to teach the same, and being fully satisfied that she possesses a good moral character, and the essential qualifications for the government and instruction of children and youth," authorized her to teach in the public schools of that county for one year.

Prison life continued for the men at Macon. "May 14, The rebels urged the prisoners to take an oath never to bear arms against the confederacy, and told us our government had abandoned us and refused to exchange for us. Our men were dying nightly in the hospital.

"May 18, We were told that our government absolutely refused to exchange prisoners, and we were asked to sign a paper stating that if it were impossible to get us a parole, we'd take an oath not to bear arms against the confederacy. Some boys were willing to do this arguing we'd soon be dead here, and better to be back home and help in the civilian life. A majority of the boys were firm in refusing to take the oath, and unless all took the oath, it would be given to none.

"May 20, This morning we were called into line to listen to orders. The major read the following order: 'All prisoners captured at Shiloh, except commissioned and noncommissioned officers, shall be at once paroled not to bear arms against the confederacy until legally exchanged. The officers to be held as hostages for the fulfillment of the parole by the privates. By order of General G.T. Beauregard.'

"May 22, Yesterday evening we drew a loaf of bread to seven men to last 24 hours. We had a little rice upon which to make one meal.

"May 24, At six in the morning we approached the gate, halted in squads of ten and twelve, raised our right hand and repeated after the officer, "You and each of you do solemnly swear that you will not take up arms against the Confederate States of America nor aid in conspiring against them in any manner until you are exchanged or otherwise honorably discharged from this obligation.'

"Soon we were in boxcars speeding north. Passed through Jonesborough and to Atlanta. Left Atlanta in evening, cars so crowded no room to lie down.

"Sunday, May 25, Still among the mountains, saw some vineyards on the steep hillsides, also orchards of peaches, apples and pears. Arrived Chattanooga at night. Disembarked at a cotton shed.

"May 26, Drew a half ration, marched through city and put on a steamer, Point Rock. We swung around the foot of Lookout Mountain. The Tennessee is a beautiful river and the mountain scenery is grand. Oak, ash, hickory, male, pine, and sycamore gave the landscape a variety of color. Not far from Bellefont, we went ashore to sleep. Some of us found an old wagon box and slept in it. It was a very comfortable bed after what we had been having.

"Next morning ran upstream about three miles and landed on an island. There was some corn in a rail pen which the boys parched. In three days we had only a half day's ration.

"Some men came to the north side of the river and called to us. They were some men who had left us the day before and a lieutenant of General Mitchell. To say we were glad to see this lieutenant put it mildly. Everyone wanted to shake his hand and ask a hundred questions. He said that General Mitchell knew we were here and would send cars. He had a squad of men on the railroad six miles away. Six mile and we would be with our own men! Many men wanted to go at once but our guard would not permit it until our officers were there to receive us. Next morning McClaury had some hardtack and STOAKES some cornbread upon which we made our breakfast. Soon the boys started to strike out for Bellefont. At first a few, then more and more. Some of the rebel officers and a few guards went with us to transfer us. Bellefont was three mile from the river and it was three more miles to the railroad station.

"The people of the town heard we were coming and in a starving condition. Word had been sent into the country for available eatables and many of the town citizens were up all night preparing and cooking for us. The first boys into town found plenty of eatables, but by the time we arrived the place was pretty well cleaned out. One lady gave us her last cup of coffee and a small piece of brad and pork. An ordinary hungry man could have eaten what they gave to 10 or 15 of us. The people of the town were rank Secesh but did what they could for us. No train. Depot had been burned. Waiting was monotonous. Shoats weighing 60 to 70 pounds were running around. One of the boys caught one and killed it. In a few minutes it was dressed, the boys built a fire, found a large sheet of crinkled iron that had been burned in the depot. Soon every depression in this iron became a little frying pan containing a fresh piece of pork being browned in its own grease. Frying and eating did not cease until several pigs had been yielded up to the Union cause.

"Near evening we heard the low rumble of the approaching train and after awhile a far distant whistle. Again the noise of the train coming nearer. Among the hills and valleys the sound would sometimes seem so near and again die away until you heard nothing. Again a sharp whistle near the headland of the valley and every voice was hushed and every eye strained on the point where the rails turned about the jutting hill and were lost to view. The locomotive burst into view. The sun was low in the west, the locomotive a half mile away. On one bow floated a small white flag; on the other, the beautiful stars and stripes. The sunlight brought all the beauty of the flag to view. The boys made no sound of joy. Then a might shout of joy from every throat. Shout on shout and cheer on cheer. Men hugged each other, pounded each other, wrestled with each other, turned summersets and handsprings and in every conceivable way manifest their joy. The last American flag we had seen the rebels were dragging in the mud at Shiloh two months before this."

With the prisoners onboard "the train was heavily loaded and frequently came to grades where the locomotive failed to pull it. Then we on the flatcars would get off and push the train over the grade. We crawled along so slowly and were in such a hurry!

"Arrived at Huntsville, back of the Union lines the evening of May 28. Marched and countermarched so much looking for an empty building for us to sleep in, we were tired. When we came to a smooth flagstone paving beside a house and sheltered by large catalpa trees we laid down on the smooth stones and slept until morning. We were somewhat disturbed by citizens awaking us and admonishing us to get in someplace or we'd catch our death of cold sleeping in the open air. Little they knew that this was the most comfortable place we'd slept in two months.

"May 29, Collected in the courthouse square, full rations were set before us and each one helped himself to what he wanted. Just think of it: all we could eat and all we could carry away.

About this time we missed STOAKES. He had gone no one knew where. Our squad was sent quite a distance from the city to dwell with the Third Ohio regiment. When we arrived at their camp, there sat STOAKES among them. One company of the Third Ohio was raised in STOAKES' old home in Ohio. He chanced to meet one of the boys he knew in the city and went to camp with him. Chance sent us to the same camp to tarry. They received us very kindly and made everything pleasant for us as best they could.

"The Third Ohio boys cooked our food that night so we might be prepared to go in the morning. They were splendid fellows. They had entered the service before we did, marched about 2,000 miles, never been in battle. We had scarcely marched any, been in two battles and spent two months in prison.

"Next morning, we were at the depot early, thought we were going on the cars and then were started on foot to Nashville. We now learned very sad news. When we had come to Chattanooga, General Mitchell was at Nashville. The rebels sent word to Huntsville that we were there and wished to be received into Union lines. The officer in charge ordered that we be received. But General Mitchell had come back to Huntsville before all our men were transferred and immediately rejected the order. So the rest of the paroled men were returned to Macon, Georgia. The excuse he gave was that he was about to make an advance upon Chattanooga and if he received the paroled prisoners, they would consume his supplies and thereby frustrate his plans. It was an act of kindness by the rebel general, Beauregard, to parole us when his government would not release us. It was most heartless act by General Mitchell to reject the men when they were at his own lines to be received. One Tama man died after being returned to Macon, but such also would have been our fate if General Mitchell had been in Huntsville one day sooner.

"Now we were on a long tramp across the state from Huntsville to Nashville. We were not alone. The Tenth Ohio was with us and guarding a long wagon train, 186 wagons of cotton bales. The sick and starved boys walked and the cotton was hauled. General Mitchell boasted that he captured enough cotton to pay the expenses of his command.

"My eyes had been sore for some time. One of the boys always walked with me to guide me as I could hardly see. The first day we marched 17 miles, and started marching at three-thirty next morning fearing attack at the crossing of the Elk river. Passed safely, and struck an excellent gravel pike. Marched until eight in the evening and camped three miles from Pulaski, 17 hours of marching. Our boys were not used to this and got very tired and sore. Rained some during the night. STOAKES, Felter and I started ahead of the column. After we had left, the order was given for all sick and unable to walk to get into the wagons. The soldiers at Pulaski gave us a hearty welcome and their and played patriotic airs. When we learned that many of the boys were riding, STOAKES asked the wagon master if I might ride. He said if I did not avail myself of the opportunity when the order was given, it was now too late. I trudged two or three miles more and told the boys I could go no farther, for them to go on and I'd go back to Pulaski until my eyes were better. As we were talking, a teamster stopped and asked what the matter was. He said to get right into his wagon. I told him that I might get him into trouble. He said to get right in and be still and the wagon master would not know but what I got on in the morning. The boys helped me into the big wagon and I rode the rest of the day. In the evening they came for me and took me where they had camped. Rained. We built a fire to dry our clothes and warm our bodies. After breakfast, we marched to Columbia, 8 miles.

"In evening, took the cars to Nashville. Quartered in the fairgrounds amphitheater, only a roof and a floor, plenty of spring water and good rations. Remained several days.

"STOAKES, Felter and I got a pass to the city and went sightseeing. Saw the house of President James K. Polk... Visited the state house and saw Governor Andrew Johnson, afterward U.S. president. Met an old man on the street. He said, 'The day will come when Lincoln's name will be held in equal reverence with tht of Washington.' It did us good to hear the old man talk so loyally. A large majority of the people here were Secesh.

"June 19, Felter and I in city again, went to a wharf to see what chances were of getting away on a boat unobserved by guards. The Hazel Dill was to start down river next day, but the captain was not interested in taking our silver watch to take three of us to Smithland, at the mouth of the Cumberland. We had not a cent of money. We turned away, another man proposed to take our watch and pay our way to Smithland. We got back to camp full of joy at the prospects of going home. STOAKES refused to go. He thought we better wait until they sent us home. After much coaxing he finally concluded to go with us for we would not go without him. We slipped away from camp the next morning, concealed ourselves on the boat. At noon the boat started down river. We came out to see the sights. We passed the city limits and came to where a river bridge had been destroyed. The prow of our boat struck a sunken pier with full force. The shock nearly threw us off our feet. All the power of reversed wheels and prod poles would not start her off. A large rope was fastened to a tree on the north bank of the river, and the captain of the boat driven by a donkey engine tried to pull her off. At ten the boat still lay on the rocks. We went to bed and the next morning awoke and the boat was tied up at the wharf we'd left the day before. We kept ourselves in close quarters until the boat was repaired and finally started about evening. Our plan was to land at Smithland, cross to the Illinois side of the Ohio, walk to the Illinois Central, an estimated 20 miles. There we expected to sell our other watch and get enough money to travel to Clinton, to General Baker's presence. We understood that soldiers traveled at half fare. Our little boat drew about 26 inches of water but she was on the sandbar more than half of the time. One day when the boat was stuck near the bank, we left her in search of blackberries knowing if she got off the bar, she'd soon be stuck again.

"One of the passengers, who knew some of my relatives in Ohio, asked how we were off for money. I told him the whole story. He asked how much we needed. I thought ten dollars with the watch. He gave me twenty-five and thought we should take more.

"We took three days to make the one day trip to Smithland. The stream was very low. We passed Fort Donnelson and were surprised to see everything in such good repair. At Smithland we employed a man with a skiff to carry us across to the Illinois side. We had drawn extra clothing at Nashville and gave him an extra pair of pants to carry us across to the other side. We learned we were sixty miles from the railroad and should have stayed on the boat until Golconda.

Felter was sick and grew worse. We were obliged to employ a man to take his team and wagon and carry us to the railroad. We gave him our watch and he was to give us ten dollars to boot. He left the watch at home and had no money to pay us the boot. At the station we learned no agent north of Cairo had the power to sell us tickets at half price. We were 40 miles from Cairo. We decided that we'd save money by buying tickets back to Cairo. There was a chance, too, of getting a boat there up the Mississippi much cheaper.

"There was no boat the next day and probably would not be for a week or more. Notices were posted everywhere that no person was allowed to leave the city without a pass from the provost marshall. So we went to the provost for passes. We intended telling the provost our whole story and take our chances on being detained because we had no furloughs. But he was writing and without looking up wrote, 'Pass Corporal B.F. Thomas and two men to Toledo, Iowa.' At the station we learned that if we'd gotten a pass with transportation, we wouldn't have to pay. Back to the provost we went. He said 'If you want a pass with transportation, we must charge your transportation to your furlough and you will pay it next time you draw pay. It will make you bother and save you nothing.' As soon as he mentioned furlough I knew all about it and thanking him, bade him goodbye. We went to the ticket window, laid out our money and asked for tickets up the road as far as that would take us. Enroute, Felter said if our tickets had taken us one station more we would be at Sublette where Dr. Adams lived, an associate of Felter's father. We told the conductor and he told us to stay on the train until we reached Sublette. The doctor was glad to see us, had us take dinner with him, and furnished us plenty of money to carry us home.

"Arrived at Clinton at sunrise June 29, 1862. Went to General Baker's residence. Saluted him and told our story, talked an hour or more. He gave us a note for hotel lodging and meals until Monday (no trains on Sunday), and free passage home. He told us to go home and stay there until he sent us word to come back.

"The North Western railroad was finished only to Otter Creek. We stayed overnight there with a farmer and next day went to Toledo. The same evening arrived home and were joyously received. There was little sleep that night; there was too much to talk about. Oh how glad we were to be at home once more."

Not only the shadow of the Civil War was hanging over all America, but in western Iowa, the Indians were causing trouble again. They had been stealing horses, had shot a couple of farmers over near Sioux City, and put the areas of Sioux City and Council Bluffs in panic.

On August 1, 1862, President Lincoln issued a proclamation ordering all the paroled Civil War prisoners who had gone home without leave to return to Benton Barracks on or before August 20. B.F. Thomas wrote in his diary, "In obeyance, STOAKES, Felter and I started for St. Louis August 10 and arrived August 17."

The Northern cause needed men and on August 20, 1862, WILLIAM POLLOCK, age 35, native of Scotland, enlisted at Fort Dodge. He became a member of Company I, Thirty-Second Regiment Iowa Volunteer Infantry. The history of this regiment says, "The average age of the officers and men was greater than that of earlier regiments, and there was a proportionally larger number of married men among them." Now both of the men who would become our grandfathers, ELEAZER STOAKES and WILLIAM POLLOCK, were a part of the war.

POLLOCK was not called up right away, but soon after he enlisted alarming news reached Fort Dodge of the terrible slaughter by Indians of white people 125 miles to the north in Minnesota. News of the Spirit Lake massacre, five years earlier, had taken 14 days to reach Fort Dodge. How soon the news of the Minnesota massacre reached Fort Dodge we do not know. The Spirit Lake massacre had taken the lives of 32 settlers. The Minnesota slaughter took the lives of 650 or more. This was the worst Indian massacre in American history.

The Sioux of Minnesota and Dakota, led by 60-year-old Little Crow, had taken up the tomahawk and gone on the warpath! Why?

In 1850, the Santee branch of the Sioux had regretfully and under pressure sold to the U.S. government the southern half of Minnesota. Now, 12 years later, the white man was engaged in his own war and payments to the Indians for their land were inadequate and tardy this year. Money and goods promised to the Indians "by the time the grass turned green" were months overdue. The Indians were bitter and they regretted the loss of their loved land. August 17, 1862, some young, daring braves murdered five white settlers. The Sioux nation of 7,000 immediately feared retaliation from the whites and so they decided to rise in a giant gamble to try to get their lands back while the whites were preoccupied with their own war. At New Ulm, Minn. and other places, the Indians in hideous war paint fell upon the whites and killed without mercy. White men, women and children tried to flee but few escaped with their lives. Killing continued for several days. One hundred soldiers lost their lives. The rest were settlers.

Panic reached into Iowa. Killings were confined to Minnesota but terror filled northwest Iowa and isolated settlers quit whatever they were doing and ran.

Iowa's governor acted quickly. Full companies of mounted men were stationed at Estherville and the Chain Lakes and part of a company was sent to Spirit Lake. Other companies were divided and stationed at Ocheyedan, Peterson, Cherokee, Ida Grove, Sac City, Correctionville, Little Sioux, West Fork, Melbourne and Sioux City, a chain of troops across the northwest border of Iowa.

By early October the white man was in control in Minnesota again. Iowa had ordered and was building forts at Correctionville, Cherokee, Peterson, Estherville, Spirit Lake and Iowa Lake. The largest was Fort Defiance at Estherville.

The white men had captured 300 Indians and condemned them to death. Lincoln, however, busy as he was with the Civil War, studied the cases and commuted the sentences of all except 38. They were hung in a mass hanging at Mankato, Minn. Little Crow escaped for awhile, but one day while foraging for berries, was shot by a farm youth.

POLLOCK was still at home with his wife MARY MARGARET and their little ones, Will and Jennie, when this uprising took place. But the brother-in-law Jared Fuller had already gone to war leaving Sarah and her small sons behind. Now with peace barely restored in Minnesota

POLLOCK was called to service on October 7 and was sent to Camp Franklin at Dubuque. Years later Jared Fuller's obituary would say that he and POLLOCK "united their families under one roof and both enlisted to serve their country." Under which roof the two sisters, MARY'S or Sarah's, lived we do not know. This was the last of the Indian trouble in Iowa and southern Minnesota, but, of course, the settlers couldn't foresee this then, and fear huddled over them for a considerable time.

Meanwhile back at Benton Barracks, STOAKES, Felter and Thomas had received their back pay of five months. Thomas wrote, "We were on parole and therefore did not do any guard duty nor drill. All we did was draw rations, eat and sleep. We frequently got passes for a day in St. Louis. During September we lived the laziest life possible. In St. Louis we attended the theater, visited the public libraries, the parks and gardens. The Mercantile library was an especially pleasant resort. It had the most extensive collection of books I ever saw, besides much fine statuary. The librarian was always very courteous to us. In the barracks we wrote letters, poetry, history and fiction, sometimes several writing at once on some given subject. Again we taught each other in branches of learning wherein we may have been deficient. Many of the boys received great benefit from the studies pursued by lying at Benton Barracks. Most of them, however, spent their whole time in playing cards.

"Nov. 1, STOAKES had been sick for sometime. We urged him to ask for a discharge but he still thought he would get well. We had been quite uneasy about him but finally he concluded to apply for a discharge.

"Nov. 8, 1862, STOAKES got word that his discharge had been sent to the commander for signature. And one week later it was returned duly signed. He now drew his pay and prepared to start home. Felter and I concluded to go with him, so we went, STOAKES with his discharge and Felter and I on what is called 'French leave,' that is an imaginary furlough. We took passage on a steamboat to Davenport, and from there to Marengo by rail. Arrived at Marengo a little after noon and ordered dinner at the hotel. The stage, outside of the hotel, waited to take us to Blairstown. From Blairstown we took the cars to Toledo and the next day drove home.

"Do you know what the word means? If you have always lived in the best home on earth you can not realize its meaning. It is necessary to bear some of the crosses, some of the trials, some of the hardships and deceptions, some of the ingratitude and some of the false friendships of the world before you fully appreciate what home, with parents, brothers, sisters and true friendship is. If you have borne only a part of these trials you may appreciate something of our feeling at this homecoming.

"Before the war began Felter was engaged to my youngest sister Rebecca, and I was engaged to STOAKES' sister Sarah, so our homecoming was something of a general rejoicing throughout all three families. During our stay this time, John (Felter) and Rebecca (Thomas) concluded they would consummate their engagement by getting married. Dec. 10, 1862, they were married. My Sarah thought she would prefer to wait till the war closed or my enlistment expired. If it were not for STOAKES' ill health this would have been a very happy time, I assure you.

"Only a little more than a year ago we had gone to Davenport with ten able men in our mess; now but two of us were returning to duty. Five dead, one discharged and still sick, another at home sick and one at St. Louis."

STOAKES was given care by his family. When his health permitted, he began farming again.

WILLIAM POLLOCK'S brother-in-law, Jared Fuller, had gone into the army before POLLOCK and had written home in three sections from Dubuque (in a letter now preserved by his granddaughter Marie Baumchen, daughter of Ed Fuller):

"Sept. 26, 1862, Dear Sarah Still hare to day has ben a very exciting day in this plase. First it has ben the national fort______ and two the departure of Col. Vandever regement for St. Louis to reinforce Gen. Freemont the fact of 100 men leaving all they hold dear would I think awaken the fire of patriotism in the hearts of any. I have heard two sermons to day they were patriotic and had the song of the right mettle. I see by the conference appointments that G.W. Prindle of Port Richmond is stationed here. he used to board at Dulouise before you lived theare we are doing nothing by driling and preparing for the field.

"30th Dear Wife and Children I cannot but think of one year ago tonight you know what I mean. I wonder how little Edy will look when I see him again but the uncertainty of return but we must not despair. I think you have the qualities which will carry you through these trying times I trust mutch to the courage and Iron will of your race and above all the sacred nature of the couse in which we are engaged. there never was a time so important to the wellfare of our race as the present. it calls for great sacrifices on the part of all.

"I think often of you in your lonely home almost a widow (solitary and weeping?) I have not failed to visit nightly. Oh such dreams of love home and kincher those little arms that I feel about my neck every night and the little stories that I listen to but it is all a dream but I must not talk thus the Father and husband must be in a mesure forgot in the soldier and the prattle of children given way to the din of war and write often no more this time from your Jarod.

"Tuesday Oct. 1 Dearest Not gone yet there is sompthing about the railroad companies that has delayed us til now but the thing is all straight now and to morrow is set for the day of departure that there is so mutch delay about these army movements that it is hard to tell when we shal start. I have just learned from the Capt. that Prushia and Blinedot was here and they told him that POLLOCK was getting ready to come on and go with us I shall like to have him do so if he thought best (this is the hour of heros) the company now had over 80 men.

"I will send you some more papers I wish you would get the Independent I see it is the best paper yet how I do want to heare from you. if you could have known that we would have ben till now you could have written befor this. Take good care of youself and all the boys has tow head got over his poor spell yet. tell Markie to be a good boy and help his mother does Edy get in the dishpans any more forgive this light talk so good bye for this time kiss all the little ones for me."

On November 16, 1862, the Thirty-Second regiment of which WILLIAM POLLOCK was a member of Company I (according to his discharge paper) left Camp Franklin at Dubuque, embarked on transports and were conveyed to St. Louis, Mo. and went into quarters at Benton Barracks. On Nov. 25 the major part of the regiment including Company I left St. Louis and was conveyed to New Madrid, Mo. The colonel, Col. John Scott, soon discovered that prior to his arrival, large quantities of merchandise of all descriptions had been distributed at New Madrid and had gone beyond the Union lines into the possession of those engaged in the Rebellion. Negroes who had escaped and sought protection of Union soldiers had been returned to slavery.

The history of the regiment continues with this information: Dec. 17, A detachment, including Company I, made a reconnaissance into the country west of New Madrid; gone five days, marched about 100 miles, captured eight prisoners, and a quantity of arms and stock. The march proved false the report that a large force was moving against New Madrid.

Dec. 23, Col. Scott embarked on the steamer, Davenport, to examine points along the river where goods were being smuggled into enemy lines with a view to preventing it.

Dec. 27, The Thirty-second received orders to burn the gun carriages and wooden platforms at New Madrid, and spike the guns and destroy the ammunition totally, take the boat and proceed to Fort Pillow in Tennessee on the Mississippi under convoy of gunboat. The headquarters of the regiment remained at Fort Pillow for nearly six months, until June 18, 1863. Garrison duty and daily drill was the principal duty while the regiment was stationed there.

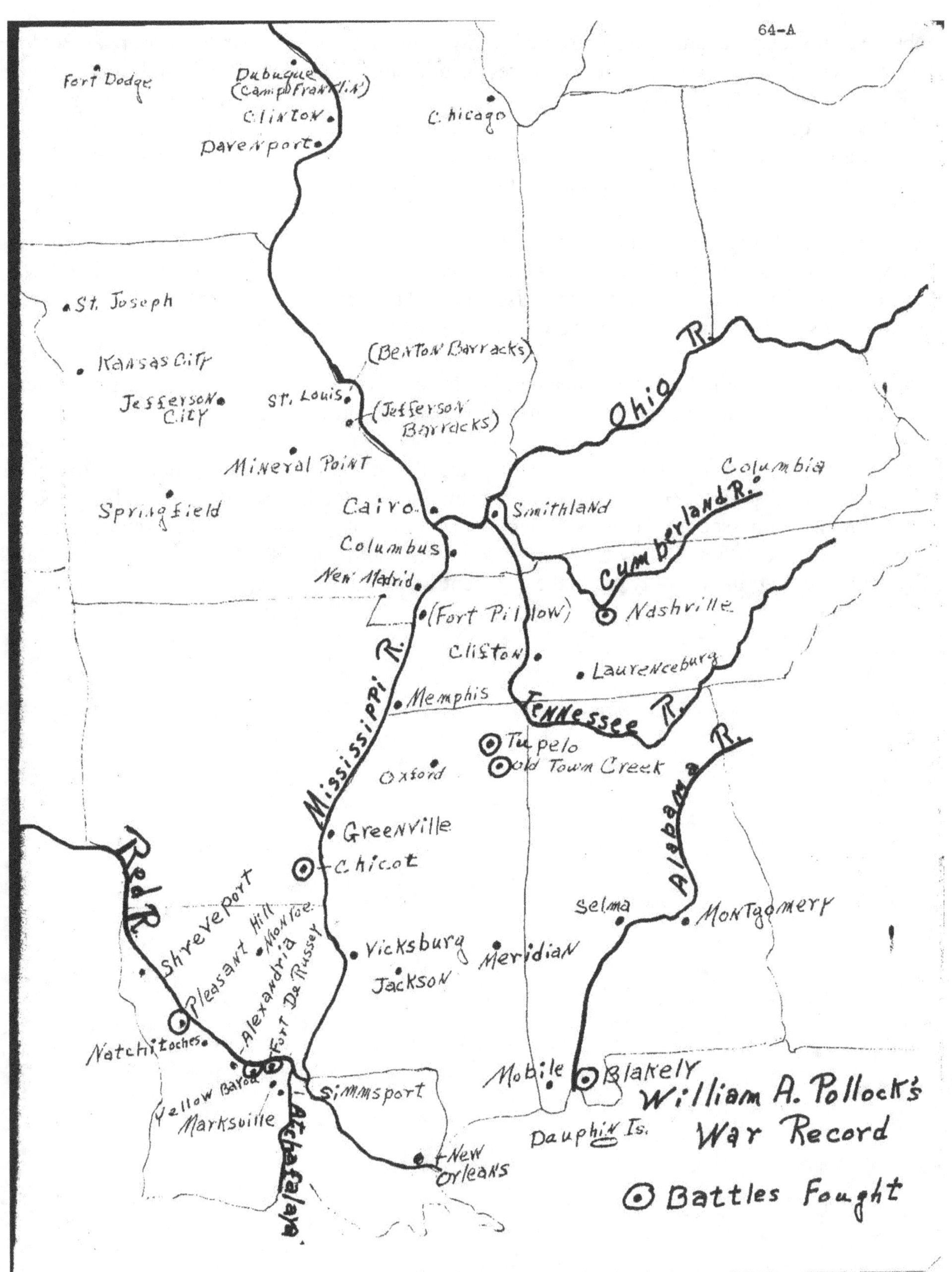

Fort Dodge
Dubuque (Camp Franklin)
Clinton
Davenport
Chicago
St. Joseph
Kansas City
Jefferson City
St. Louis
(Benton Barracks)
(Jefferson Barracks)
Mineral Point
Springfield
Cairo
Columbus
New Madrid
Smithland
Ohio R.
Cumberland R.
Columbia
Nashville
(Fort Pillow)
Clifton
Laurenceburg
Memphis
Mississippi R.
Tennessee R.
Tupelo
Old Town Creek
Oxford
Alabama R.
Greenville
Chicot
Red R.
Shreveport
Pleasant Hill
Monroe
Alexandria
Fort De Russey
Selma
Montgomery
Vicksburg
Meridian
Jackson
Natchitoches
Yellow Bayou
Marksville
Atchafalaya
Simmsport
Mobile
Blakely
Dauphin Is.
New Orleans
William A. Pollock's
War Record
⊙ Battles Fought

Whether Jared Fuller and WILLIAM POLLOCK actually were in the same outfit we are not sure. The exchange of letters between Jared and Sarah show conditions and the spirit of the day. Sarah in her two room cabin with her three little sons, James, Mark and Eddy, not only took in a couple (the Lovejoys) to room and board, but some of the time she taught school in this limited space. On Jan. 26th, 1863, Sarah wrote:

"My Own Dear Husband- The little ones are asleep and my boarders are retired and so I sit to have a little chat with you. The last letter I received from you was mailed Jan. the 1st but I think it must be the fault of the mails I have not heard from the P.O. since Thursday. I heard indirectly yesterday that the package you sent to Des Moines is at the P.O. I got Mr. Coffin to send for it to Des Moines.

"I have delayed to write to you till I should hear from the money again. I thought it might be necessary to send for the receipt that the express company gave you for the money.

"You said you thought I must be in wont of money but I have not felt the need of it much. What Lovejoy pays for their board helps very much. he has got my wood since I used that Scott delivered for the pigs...

"The children are all well at present. Eddy's fever I spoke of in my last was nothing serious. it came I think from cutting teeth he has three double teeth through now. He begins to say little words. The other children are well. The worst is Marcus is not so interested in his book as I could wish.

"I feel it is not pleasant living without you but I trust you will return and then we shall be so happy. I cannot help thinking about you this cold weather. I fear you must be suffering. I feel almost impatient to hear from the P.O. again. I think there must be a letter there from you and suppose you will be anxious before you get this... it is quite too bad that I have not written before."

The above letter seems to indicate that Sarah Fuller and MARY MARGARET POLLOCK, sisters, were not living under the same roof while their husbands were away at war. But the following letter might indicate they were together for Jared speaks to James of his AUNT MARY and of her son Willie. The Fuller and Pollock cabins were several miles apart.

On February 3, 1863, Jared wrote from Suffolk to his oldest son: "James B., Dear Son I received your kind letter and was glad to hear you was well and was a good boy and helpt Mother and AUNT MARY and had got a new coat with soldier botons on... I would like to come home and work the little oxen... make a sled for you and Markie and Willie and Edie could ride on it... but you must be a good boy always and then you will go to heaven when you die whear all good men and boys go when they die, you must write me another letter. I sent you and Markie som money to by candis with. Jared Fuller to his Dear Boy."

In Tama county, the ROBERT GRANGER daughters were telling each other of their activities in little letters. Lizzie, now Mrs. Kober, lived near her parents' home and had several little children. ELIZA was teaching near home at Wolf Creek. Mary, 18, had gone to Waterloo to school, the first of the Grangers to go away to seminary to study. Alice was still going to school near home, as was their your brother George, 13. George had golden blonde hair, a ringlet of his hair is tucked away in one of these century old letters.

Mary wrote from Waterloo to ELIZA at Wolfe Creek on Jan. 20, 1863, "I came back to town the next Wednesday after I was home... I rode up with Mr. Daniel Seadd. Fanny and Mary Beales rode with him too. When we got within half a mile of Mr. Millers the wagon wheel came off and we had to walk to Millers and stay about three hours until Mr. Seadd could get another wagon so that we did not get to town until after dark. It snowed yesterday and it is now about four inches deep on the ground so that we have to go through the snow to get to school. I am studying Arithmetic Grammar and Astronomy. I read in the history class and spell in the dictionary... We are going to have another party at the seminary something similar to the one we had on thanksgiving evening. It is to be a Washington's birthday... we have all got to write a very patriotic composition and I wish you would send me a subject to write upon... love to all and write as soon as you get this so good bye... I remain your affectionate sister Mary Granger P.S. tell Alice and George to write too."

The little letters that ELIZA treasured through the years were, of course, ones written to her. The correspondence lacked ones she herself had written. However, her nieces, Ermina Kober and Emma Endicott, found one in their things that   Eliza   had   written   in   precise,   beautiful penmanship.   The letter was written Jan. 30th, 1863 from Buckingham in reply to Mary's above letter. ELIZA wrote: "Dear Sister Mary, I now take my pen in hand to inform you that I received your kind letter yesterday. We were all glad to hear from you to hear that you was well. We are all well and hope these lines will find you the same. I received a letter from Mary Damon yesterday they are all well except Johns wife but she is recovering. Henry is at home on furlough and expects his discharge every day (Mary, John and Henry are cousins in Ohio.) We have not seen any of M. Reads folks since you was home. Mr. Ames and Emma were over to the corners to a lecture delivered by Mr. Roberts last Wednesday evening she says they were all well. We expect to go to a donation party at Mr. Wilburs for Mr. Taucett next Tuesday evening the old and the young folks are all going in the evening we expect to have a good time. We went to Hartshorns as we intended... it was Delbert Greens and Judson Wilburs party... Wright P. Sherman is married to Miss Lizzie G. Huntley of Elmira... It took him about three weeks to go to York state and get married... Hattie can talk quite well... Elizabeth and George are well. Amelia did not go to school today... Deb, Cass and Lib went. Amelia went to Mr. Copes today to a turkey roast... Ellen Ried is well... We have sent you a subject redy writin as you will preceive. Alice and I did the best we could... You must copy it for her pen was poor. I hope you will have a pleasant time at the party... Please excuse me this time I cannot think of any more now... We all send our love to you... write soon... Good bye. I remain your affection sister ELIZA A. GRANGER."

On the same sheet young George had written: "Dear sister Mary I now take the opportunity to send you a few lines to inform you that I am well but have been some sick. I donot know what ELIZA has wrote and donot care... there has been about 2 inches of snow... we had a good spelling school the other night Mr. Slades folks were up and Buckingham school was over and we spelled them down... five of them went down on alscision... I cant think of any more this time excuse all bad spelling and writing... so Goodbye... I remain your affectionate brother... George G. Granger

On Feb. 19, 1863, Mary again wrote from Waterloo because it was storming and she could not go to school... "I received your first letter the next Monday after father was here the first time. The subject you sent was very acceptable and I am very much obliged to you and Alice... I hope you will succeed with your exhibition for I know it will be real pleasant. I have been to one surprise party and got home by ten o'clock which I don't believe you can say about either of the parties you wrote about... John is going the rounds spelling the schools down I hear for I have not been to one this winter. I think Buckingham school was real mean to spell down but I am glad you spelled them down when they came over to the corners. I should like to have been there to have helped you."

On the same page, Mary wrote to George, "Dear Brother George... I am very sorry to hear that you had been sick but am glad you are better you take care of yourself and not get sick again... I can't think of anything by nonsense..."

Back in the South, POLLOCK'S regiment had been stationed at Fort Pillow in Tennessee doing nothing except garrison duty and daily drill for six months, was embarked on transports and conveyed up the Mississippi river to Columbus, Kentucky on June 17. The regiment, the Thirty-second Iowa, went into camp at Columbus and remained for another six months, until Jan. 20, 1864. Some of the companies were sent on short missions out of headquarters, but POLLOCK'S company, I, remained at headquarters all of the time.

While the Thirty-second was at Columbus, two of the major battles of the war were fought. The northern forces under the command of General Grant and Rear Admiral Porter took Vicksburg on July 3. Vicksburg had been the one prime obstacle to complete command of the Mississippi river by the federal forces. At the same time, July 1-4, the Battle of Gettysburg was fought, now famed not only for the battle itself but for President Lincoln's Gettysburg address.

While his company was relatively inactive at Columbus, Kentucky, WILLIAM POLLOCK took this opportunity to go home to Webster county, Iowa to check on his family and farm. How long he was there is not known. Was he there long enough to help with the harvest? Undoubtedly food for his family and a well stocked woodpile to last through the winter would have been of prime concern. Webster county history tells of men who remained at home during the war forming into wood chopping gangs going from house to house restocking woodpiles where the man of the house was fighting in the war.

In August of this same year, up in Pocahontas county, three men from the little village on the Des Moines river, known then as Rolfe but later as Old Rolfe, engaged in the last buffalo hunt in the county. The animal was spotted near the courthouse. The men armed themselves with a revolver and two old muskets and gave chase on horseback. After shooting the buffalo repeatedly, skirmishing with him in many sloughs, and after three hours they finally felled him in some tall prairie grass five miles northwest of the courthouse. They skinned him, established his weight at 1400 pounds, and divided the meat with the settlers.

ELIZA'S COUSIN, J.B. Porter, wrote from Hinckley, Ohio, this summer of 1863, "I was glad to get your picture but I had rather see the original."

That winter ELIZA enrolled in the seminary at Waterloo, as her next younger sister Mary had done the winter before. ON January 17, 1864, the youngest sister Alice wrote from home at Buckingham to ELIZA in Waterloo, "Dear sister, ELIZA, As we have your drawers done after so long a time and have a chance to send them to you I thought I would write a few lines to you to let you know we are all well and hoped these few lines will find you the same. I suppose you have needed them and wondered why we did not send them before but father forgot to get any thread with them and we could not make them until we could get some then we made them just as quick as we could. We did not have any New Years as we expected because it was so cold and stormy. Now ELIZA when you get this do write and tell us what kind of a place you have got to board and how you are getting along and all about it I did not know but you had forgoten us living in town and having so much to take up your mind but if you have forgoten me... I have not you for I do miss you... Write as soon as you get this and if the cars have not got there yet send it by some one that is up to town and we will get it so good bye... your loving sister, Alice"

Alice, 17, did miss her sister ELIZA, 21, up in Waterloo for Alice wrote again on Jan. 26, 1864, "Last Saturday George and Lizzie (the oldest sister- almost 23 now) came over and I went with them to Mr. Sprolls and we had a very good evening visiting and we did not get home until 11 o'clock... As you wanted to know how we got along during the storm I tell you we had a very bad time. Father did not get home until Sunday and George had all of the work to do. I could not help him because I had the ague for a New Years present and shook about an hour and a half. I thought it pretty hard to have the ague... such a cold day as that was but we got along very well considering everything... Father spoke to us about your aprons but there was not any calico sent home and we thought as you did not go to school that week and did not send them home but was going to make them yourself not knowing wither you would get them or not on account of the stormy weather but pa went up town and got some and we have them made and will send them to you as soon as we can get a chance. I don't know when that will be for the roads are very bad. Mary has not been home yet but we are looking for her every day. I do wish she would for it seems very lonesome here. When you write do tell me if you have heard anything about a school or not for I think it is time we were looking out for one... If you get one out there father says he would like to have me teach out there if you could have success in getting one... Mr. Messer is having a protracted meeting at West Union... There has been pretty near all of the girls forward to the anxious seat and some of the young men. It commenced two weeks ago last night and Mr. and Mrs. Cope have met with us every night but one. You wanted to know how my hood suited me. I think it is very pretty... Mrs. Cope said it was about as pretty a one as she had seen."

Mary did get home and on Jan. 31, 1864, she wrote from Buckingham to ELIZA up in Waterloo... "I came home yesterday and intend to stay two or three weeks. I am very glad that you like the school. I was almost sure that you would... They did not draft any here but got three volunteers. Frank Thomas is at home on a furlough has been at home almost three weeks and is recruiting for the 14th regiment. I went up to the Honkerson School house to a spelling school and spelled them down... Alice and I are going to see John and some of the neighbors while I am home for I do not get here very often. I won't get here very soon to stay so long for I shall be a woman of business and more cares on me. You know what I mean. ELIZA I dreamed of seeing you last night and you were just the same as ever but there is no danger of that being realized for I expect you will be very proper and so nice that we can hardly understand you... what has become of that young Mr. St. John... you did not say anything about him... please tell me what time school is out... I think I shall be up to town sometime next month and perhaps I shall come to the seminary and get you to go down town with me so you must be ready. Father, Mother and Alice all send love." On the same sheet you George writes, "Deare Sister... I am going to school. We have got over to divisions of fractions. We had a snow storm last night and we had quite a nice little storm when Pa was to Waterloo. I remain your kind Brother George Granger."

WILLIAM POLLOCK was back South on duty in time to be conveyed with his regiment from Columbus to Vicksburg, Miss. on Jan. 20, 1864. The regiment went into camp there. General Sherman was there preparing for an expedition into the heart of the state of Mississippi. Part of the Thirty-Second, including POLLOCK'S company, I, was to go with Sherman. In the same brigade was ELEAZER STOAKES' old regiment, the Fourteenth Iowa Infantry but STOAKES was no longer with it having been discharged because of ill health.

The army left Vicksburg on Feb. 3 and returned to that place on Mar. 4, 1864, having marched 328 miles. The troops had been supplied with but ten days rations when the march began. After that supply was exhausted, the troops lived upon such food as could be obtained in the country through which they passed. This necessitated the sending out of forage trains every day, with large details to guard them, as the enemy's cavalry in large forces hovered in front and upon the flanks of General Sherman's army. There was more or less fighting every day, mainly done by the cavalry which lead the advance and the infantry which constituted the guard to the forage trains. The troops had no tents on this expedition and suffered much from the inclemency of the weather. The Thirty-second performed its share of duty on this long and arduous march but did not come in contact with any considerable body of the enemy. One man from Company I was captured. The march took them as far east as Meridian.

Up in Tama county, the Grangers are writing frequently and affectionately to ELIZA in seminary in Waterloo. Lizzie wrote Feb. 14, 1864, "Dear Sister,---Father, Mother and Mary were here last Monday and made a visit. We was all at home las thirsday but you... We had a very pleasant time and wished that you was there. Mr. Messor has been holding protracted meting at west union nearly five weeks and about forty converts... I have the girls red dresses dun and they halv worn them several times. john lives with us this winter... he is ahelping George get out fencing. Fathers health has not been very good for two weeks back. they halv not herd from Ohio since you left home. Mary is just beginning to walk alone... she can walk about half way across the room a lone. Hattie says she would like to see AUNT ELIZA and have a frolic with her... Mary is macking her weding clothes now her dress is morrenow i expect she and Elias will be married next month and then we will have another brother... Mary has been home two weeks... I do not know how long she will stay. Alice sayes it is not so loansome now Mary is there... your loving sister Elizabeth J. Kober. There has not been any drafting here yet. Three volunteered."

Feb. 17, 1864, gay young Alice again writes to ELIZA at seminary... "It is Wednesday evening and we are all home... Father and Mother are sitting by the fire talking... George is standing by me cutting paper and talking about bringing in his wood... Mary is sitting by the table reading...

She has been at home over two weeks and we have a very gay time and we have thought and talked about you a great deal and wished you were here. Elias was here last Sunday and stayed to supper and about an hour afterwards and just before he started home he asked Father and Mother what they thought of his and Mary's arrangements and of course you know they said yes. O, ELIZA, I wish you could have been here... Now I must tell you about school. I have got over to profit and loss in my Arithmetic and I think I understand what I have gone over and I have got over to Synthesis in my grammar and I analyze every day... Mary and Mother were up to Lizzie's the other day and read your letter... It is very bad roads... it is neither sleighing or wagoning... You said your shimey was to pieces. We have one to send you if we ever get a chance... we are calculate to attend a donation party tomorrow for Mr. Messer... Tell me if you have heard anything about a school."

On the same date, enclosed in the same envelope, George writes, "I am going to school every day... We had one spelling school last thursday. We spelled them all down. A whole load of them came from West Union to spell against us but Alice spelled them all down... I should like to have been out to the concert you spoke about in your last letter and heard the soldiers funeral song. Hattie (Lizzie's oldest child) says AUNT ELIZA has gone to Waterloo to school and she says she would like to see AUNT ELIZA first rate. We all send our love to you."

Ten days later Alice writes to ELIZA again, "I am enjoying myself very well. I am attending school every day and getting along very well in my studies. I have got over to exchange and currency. I thank you for the good encouragement you gave me in your last letter. I was so rejoiced to hear of the good success you had had about a school. I should of liked to have come over to the examination today. I thought of it a good many times but I could not for it is such bad roads that all the creeks are overflowed with water that we could not get there but I will try to study all I can and get ready for another day. Mary is at home yet. It is four weeks today since she came. We have had some very good times since she has been with us. We went out to a spelling school at John Hopkins school but we did not spell them down... We had a very good time. I wish you could have been with us. Mary and I went down to Mr. Greens a week ago this afternoon... We all went to singing school in the evening... it was the first singing school I have ever been to... George Stoakes (ELEAZER'S youngest brother) goes with Alice Barbour... we went to the donation party... Father, Mother, Mary and myself went in the afternoon and stayed the evening but they did not stay up late... we got home at ten o'clock but if we did get home early we had a very pleasant time. Mr. Messer got about $40... I got a letter from Cousin Henry... they did not say anything about coming out."

In the same letter Mary writes, "It is four weeks today since I came home but I think about going back on Monday... Elias was here tonight... he said he had taken a farm ten miles beyond Cedar Falls... it has a good log cabin on it and there are 54 acres under cultivation so you can see I will have a log house to live in and be quite a distance from home. I am very sorry but I am afraid we will have to go away before you come home. I am very sorry. I did not want to go without seeing you but Elias says he thinks of starting about the first of the week with a load of things and then come back and take William's horses and buggy and take his Mother and me up there... if we go by Waterloo I will stop and see you if it is nothing than just to say how do you do and good bye... Now ELIZA you must not feel hard toward me if I get married before you get home... you must come make us a good long visit to pay for it... we are not going to make any wedding at all... I remain your loving sister Mary G."

Not long after that, Alice writes from Buckingham to ELIZA, "Dear Sister I suppose you will come home with John Hopkins Friday... Father wants you to get two of those trunks that you saw at Mr. Gilbert's store... Here is 50 cents and Mr. Healess told father that he would leave $6 at Mr. Hungerfords for him... you get that and father said that will pay for them for Mr. Gilbert told him that they were three dollars and a quarter apiece... pa says get them if you can get them as cheap as you can... Speak to Mr. Hungerford about the school because I do not want him to neglect it... Father and I would have come out for you but it is not very good roads and John was coming so pa made arrangements for him to bring you home which he said he would do willingly... I suppose for the sake of your company... I hope he get carried away riding with a city lady."

By March 23, 1864, Mary was located in her own home and ELIZA was back home with her parents at Buckingham, Tama county. In a little letter from Union, Iowa addressed to Miss ELIZA GRANGER, Mary writes, "Dear Father, Mother, brother and sisters... I received you letter today for George got here about noon and I was glad to hear from home and that you are all enjoying yourselves so well... So there have been two more weddings since I came away from there... I am sure I wish them well and hope they enjoy themselves as well as I have since I was married... the Methodists are having a protracted meeting at the school house... it commenced on Sunday evening... we have been every evening until tonight. I have enjoyed the meetings first rate. Elias said he would write some in this letter so he will have to make his own excuses for not coming to see you when he took the team back... You must all come out and make us a good long visit this summer just as soon as you can. The neighbors say that there are a great many plums all kinds of berries, walnuts and butternuts in the woods. I am anticipating taking a great deal of comfort going into the woods for it is but a little ways from the house. Alice, Mother (apparently speaking here of her mother-in-law) says she often thinks of you and would like to see you. She says I must tell you all that she is enjoying herself first rate... Mary Wightman."

WILLIAM POLLOCK with the Thirty-second Iowa was in the division under General A.J. Smith that embarked March 9, 1864 in nineteen transports on the Red River Expedition in Louisiana. The division consisted of about 10,000 infantry and three batteries of artillery. A fleet of eleven gunboats accompanied the transports. This formidable naval force was under the command of Admiral Porter who was to act in conjunction with all land forces under the command of Major General Banks. History books say that General Banks was trying to move through Louisiana and into Texas, partly for the sake of cotton that could be picked up along the way, and partly because the government believed that Napolean III would give up his Mexican adventure if a Northern army occupied Texas and went to the Rio Grande.

The fleet on March 12 entered the cut-off into which the Red river empties, and into which the Atchafalaya flows, and passed down the latter river to Simmsport where the troops disembarked. The Thirty-second was in the Second Brigade as was ELEAZER STOAKES' old Fourteenth Iowa, plus the Twenty-seventh Iowa, and the Twenty-fourth Missouri's Infantry and the Third Indiana Battery.

March 14, 1864 at 6am the soldiers, with the Second Brigade in advance, began marching rapidly in the direction of Fort DeRussey, the first object of the expedition. The march was conducted with great vigor, and late in the afternoon, the brigade reached the village of Marksville, two and a half miles from the fort. The Twenty-seventh was detailed to act as rear guard for the division. The rest of the brigade moved forward and was soon within range of the enemy guns in Fort DeRussey.

The Thirty-second Iowa was assigned to the right side in support of the skirmishers of the Fourteenth Iowa... The battery was returning the fire of the enemy's guns from the fort, and the Fourteenth and Thirty-second took possession of a line of rifle pits from which the enemy skirmishers had been driven, and from which an incessant musketry fire was kept up making it difficult for the enemy gunners to serve their artillery. The Fourteenth Iowa had exhausted its ammunition and was relieved. An immediate assault upon the fort was ordered. All regiments advanced promptly. At 6pm the Union was in possession of the fort consisting of a garrison of 350 men.

In twelve hours, the Union soldiers had marched 28 miles, fought two hours and captured Fort DeRussey. The entire loss of the two brigades under General Smith was three killed and two severely wounded. WILLIAM POLLOCK'S discharge paper lists Fort DeRussey and all the other battles in which he fought.

The troops dismantled Fort DeRussey and moved forward to Alexandria, La. There General Smith and his men waited for an order from General Banks who was moving up with other troops under his command.

Col. William T. Shaw of the Fourteenth Iowa Regiment commanded the Second Brigade and it is through his written account that we go on this Red River Expedition paying special attention to the Thirty-second in which POLLOCK fought. This is the same Col. Shaw who surrendered ELEAZER STOAKES' regiment, the Fourteenth, after Shiloh. The Fourteenth was now back in action but without STOAKES.

"Went into camp near Alexandria March 16th, and remained until the morning of the 28th when we started up the bayou road with rations for three days to meet the transport at Bayou Cotile Landing above the rapids. March 18 miles the 28th, and nine on April 2nd when we embarked on transports and landed at Grand Ecore. Remained in camp on the bank of Red rive a mile above Grand Ecore until April 7th.

"On the morning of April 7th the Thirty-second regiment with 469 field, staff and line men armed with 420 rifled muskets moved from Grand Encore in the rear of the brigade. Everything progressed satisfactory until two o'clock when we encountered the headquarter train of Major General Banks entirely blocking the way. In this manner two brigades, including artillery, were delayed more than four hours in the midst of a heavy rain storm. Our troops failed to make the assigned camping grounds and camped two miles short of the proper position. Subsistence and camp equipment did not arrive until the night was well advanced.

"April 8th- moved forward 20 miles and camped near Pleasant Hill at sunset. For hours we had heard heavy artillery firing some miles in advance. During the night our camp was overrun with stragglers from the front, who circulated the wildest stories of disaster and loss of men, artillery and trains.

"April 9th- These stories were repeated and exaggerated. The road was crowded with teams crowding to the rear. Evidence of past defeat and prospective retreat were everywhere visible. These were the moral surroundings as we moved to the extreme front and took position in line of battle at 10 a.m. We were supported on the right but our left, for some unknown reason, was without support. We rested in the edge of a woods in the rear of an old field across which our skirmishers occasionally exchanged shots with the enemy pickets throughout the day, but without casualty to us.

"About four o'clock p.m. enemy skirmishing increased and advanced in heavy force across the open space in our front, moving in a column by battalion, reploying with the advance... Our skirmishers were recalled and our left company which had been guarding our exposed flank were forced back with some loss. Our fire was reserved until the enemy was within easy range. Then our fire was so destructive the enemy faltered, passed left through the open space and to the rear losing heavily by our fire but threatening to cut us off from our main forces. Word of our peril was sent to a superior officer but no orders came back. We kept up firing and kept the enemy at bay, but the enemy was steadily pouring past the left to the rear. In short time, the battle was in full force at our rear. In this state, we discovered all the troops to our right had withdrawn. The timber and undergrowth was so thick, we could not observe our whole line. Firing upon us started from the right. Now we were being fired upon from three directions. This was our position until sunset. The enemy had been forced back some on the left and we were able to meet and join our most advanced troops. Our men were nearly out of ammunition, exhausted but not dismayed. We could not pass the picket line in the night to reach our wounded still on the field. Our position was such that many of the wounded passing to the rear must have fallen into the hands of the enemy. Thirty-eight were killed 116 wounded and 56 missing, total 210, or about 50 percent of the Thirty-second Iowa. Total loss for the entire brigade was 483."

General Banks was severely criticized for using only a portion of his available army at Pleasant Hill and thus suffering this costly defeat.

"Early on the morning of April 10, General Banks ordered a retreat of the entire army to Grand Ecore, during which the Thirty-second Iowa with its brigade was assigned to the position of the rear guard. From Grand Ecore the retreat was continued to Matchitoches and thence to Alexandria. The enemy followed closely and our brigade occupied the post of greatest danger. From Alexandria the brigade was sent below town and occupied a position near Governor Moore's plantation, where it had frequent skirmishes with the enemy. On May 13th Alexandria was evacuated and the army began its retreat down the Red river with the rebel army following closely. There were frequent skirmishes.

While WILLIAM POLLOCK was with his regiment in retreat down the Red river of Louisiana, a baby boy was born back in Webster County, Iowa. He may have been born in his parents' log cabin near Lizard Creek, or he may have been born in the log cabin home of his mother's sister

Sarah Fuller, five miles distance. He was welcomed by a five year old brother Will and a three year old sister Jennie, and by three little boy cousins, James, Markus and Eddy Fuller. The birth date was May 14, 1864.

The mother named the new baby Grant Robert. Ulysses S. Grant was the man of the hour. On March 12, 1864, he had been named commander-in-chief of all of the Union forces. He had been in command at the victories at Fort Henry and Fort Donnelson. At Fort Donnelson he had been nicknamed "Unconditional Surrender Grant." His command had been successful at Corinth, Miss. and in the big fete of capturing Vicksburg. The mother was probably thinking of her oldest brother back in Delaware county, New York when she gave the baby the second name of Robert, a name the baby never used in his adult life preferring to sign his name just GRANT POLLOCK. The little baby would know only the love of his mother, his Aunt Sarah and the five little folk until he was nearly a year and a half old, when the war would end and his father would come home.

On May 18th , the Thirty-second Iowa bore a prominent part in a severe engagement at Bayour Gaize. "Owing to the intense heat and necessary rapidity of our movements, many of the men were exhausted and had to be carried from the field. On May 19th, the brigade lay in line of battle all day. On May 22, it reached the mouth of the Red river and embarked on transports and was conveyed to Vicksburg arriving there May 24th." The above is all from Col. Shaw's account of the Red River Expedition.

Another historian says that Banks's retreat on the Red river was in such panicky haste that Admiral Porter's accompanying fleet of gunboats narrowly escaped complete destruction. The water level in the Red river was falling and for awhile it seemed as though the gunboats would never get out. They were saved at the last when a backwoods colonel in the Union army took a regiment of lumbermen and built dams that temporarily made the water deep enough for escape.

POLLOCK and his regiment had only eleven days in Vicksburg. On June 5 they embarked and went up the Mississippi river to Greenville, Miss. at which place and at Point Chicot, Ark. the enemy was endeavoring to blockade the river. The regiment disembarked on the Arkansas side of the river and moved rapidly against the main force of the enemy. The enemy had heavy losses and the Union brigade lost eight men. The Union troops marched to Columbia, Ark. and were conveyed on transports to Memphis arriving June 10th and remained until June 24th.

On June 24th, the Thirty-second Iowa with its brigade and division departed on the expedition to Tupelo, Miss. where it sustained its full share of hard service in the battles of Tupelo and Old Town Creek, both of which are mentioned on POLLOCK'S discharge paper as engagements he took part in. Owing to the brigade's position in line, its losses were light. (General Sherman at this time was marching to the sea.) POLLOCK'S regiment returned to Memphis and remained there until Aug. 4th. On that date it left on a march in pursuit of an elusive enemy with whom it did not come in contact, and after reaching Oxford, Miss. returned to Memphis.

While the business of fighting continued in the war areas, the raising of crops, teaching of schools and the pursuit of day-by-day living had to continue on the home fronts. The Grangers kept each other informed with letters.

On Aug. 27, 1864, Mary Granger Wightman wrote from Beaver to Sister ELIZA and Brother George at Buckingham, "I received your letter three weeks ago today but have not found time to answer it for we have just moved and I have been busy getting things straightened around. I have more to do than I did the fore part of the summer for we milk five cows now and that makes considerable work. I have half of the butter I make from them and I have sold ten pounds of butter for 36 cents a pound. We have moved about three-fourths mile up the West Fork so when you come to see us instead of going past the schoolhouse at the right after you cross the bridge on the West Fork you must take the left hand road and go up the river to the second house. It is a white house with a grove around it. It is a real pretty place just the place to take comfort and I do take a great deal every day... Aug. 31, ELIZA you spoke about a school... we will do the best we can for you and try to have it all arranged by the time you come up here to see us... Well George... I will try to think of something to write you. You say the chintz bugs injured your wheat some. They are pretty bad here on some pieces but oats did pretty well and corn looks good. Elias has about thirteen tons of hay in stack and wants to get enough more to make twenty... today I went out where the bees are and they got mad and took after me. One of them stung me on the forehead."

On Oct. 16, 1864 in a letter written from Beaver and postmarked Cedar Falls, Mary Wightman wrote, "Dear friends at home... we were very sorry to hear that Lizzie had such bad luck to get her hand hurt so badly but glad she did not have to have her fingers amputated... there is to be a draft this week... there has got to be three men drafted out of thirty and Elias has got to stand his chances with the rest. We heard today that William Read had been drafted and hired a substitute... when you write please let me know if it is so and who he hired to go in his place. We went to meeting today and heard Mr. Fawcett preach for he is on this circuit this year. He preaches here once in two weeks. He wanted to know if I wouldn't write and have you all come up here so as to stay over Sunday and go the meeting. I wish you could. I should have written before but have been waiting to find out for certain whether we could get ELIZA a school up here or not. We have tried every schoolhouse that we know of but nearly every one they appear to be in favor of getting a man teacher for the winter term. There is but one chance left that is about three miles and a half from here. Elias is going to the Falls tomorrow and he will stop and find out about it."

Then Elias wrote on the rest of the sheet. "Dear Friends one and all- I wish to forward the thought, although absent, you are by no means forgotten your kindness to me is deeply engraved on hearts memory... We are all very sorry to hear of Lizzie's bad luck... I have tried to get a school for you ELIZA but have not been very successful... if I don't succeed tomorrow as I go to the Falls, we shall have to give it up. If I fail on this one last chance, we shall feel sorry for it would be pleasant to have your society here this winter... Yours Truly, Elias Wightman. P.S. I could not get the school. The Director had obtained a teacher. I will make farther inquiries but think it will be doubtful whether I shall be successful."

POLLOCK'S regiment was now back in Memphis, Tennessee after two long marches of the summer, already told about above: the first across the top of the state of Mississippi from Memphis to Tupelo in which vicinity two major battles had been fought; and the second from

Memphis southeast to Oxford in pursuit of an elusive enemy with whom contact was never made.

Now after a very short rest in Memphis, the regiment with its brigade and division embarked Sept. 5 on the Mississippi river to Cairo, Ill., thence to Jefferson Barracks, just south of St. Louis, and thence were sent by rail to Mineral Point, Missouri. They returned to Jefferson Barracks on Sept. 29th.

A longer-than-ever trying march began Oct. 2 when this army, under General A.J. Smith, started in pursuit of a rebel army. The march took the union men across Missouri to the Kansas line without record of having come in contact with the enemy. POLLOCK'S regiment marched 700 miles and upon its return to St. Louis Nov. 18th, many of the men were almost barefoot. They were given only a single week to recuperate before entering another campaign. During their march across Missouri, Abraham Lincoln had been reelected president on Nov. 8, 1864.

On Nov. 25th, the Thirty-second Iowa was embarked upon transports and sent to Smithland, Kentucky and thus up the Cumberland river to Nashville, Tenn. where the troops landed Dec. 1, marched three miles south of the city and went into camp. On the 15th and 16th, the regiment advanced with the army to attack the rebels, and on the first day remained in the reserve line, and the next day took the advance and soon came within range of the enemy's artillery. Here the regiment was halted and waited five hours for orders. At 3:30 the men moved forward at a double quick over the open field, under severe fire from the artillery and musketry, and in a few minutes gained the entrenchment, captured 50 prisoners and five pieces of artillery. At dark the Union men were ordered into camp near the mountain. The loss of the Thirty-second Iowa in the Battle of Nashville was three killed and fifteen wounded. "Nashville" went on POLLOCK'S discharge paper as one of his engagements.

From the 17th to the 30th of December, the Thirty-second was engaged together with other troops in the pursuit of the defeated and demoralized rebel army. The pursuit was abandoned at Lawrenceburg, Tenn. On Jan. 1, 1865, the regiment marched to Clifton on the Tennessee river and embarked there on a steamer, proceeded to Eastport, Miss. where it landed Jan. 5th and went into camp for a period of rest.

On Feb. 9, 1865, the regiment again embarked on a steamer, was conveyed to Cairo, Ill. and thence to New Orleans where it disembarked on the 21st and went into camp near the city. On March 7, 1865 the regiment was taken aboard an ocean steamship and conveyed to Dauphin Island, where it remained a short time, going thence to Donnelly's Landing, from which it again took up the line of march and arrived at Sibley's Mills near Mobile, Alabama on March 26th.

On April 3rd the regiment advanced with its brigade and took part in the siege of Fort Blakely. The Thirty-second performed its full share of duty in the trenches during the siege, but was so well protected that it had but one man wounded. The fort surrendered on April 9th, 1865. The date marks the last conflict of the regiment and "Blakely" became the final engagement marked on POLLOCK'S discharge paper.

The Civil War officially ended that same day, April 9th, 1865 when General Robert E. Lee surrendered the Army of Northern Virginia to General U.S. Grant at the McLean house in Appomattox village, 20 miles east of Lynchburg, Va. Grant wrote out the conditions of surrender, which were accepted. Officers and men were to be paroled and not to fight again until exchanged, in consideration of which they were not to be disturbed by the federal government as long as they observed the law. Officers were to retain their side arms and their private baggage and officers also were to retain their horses. Lee, after a moment's hesitation, said that many of this cavalrymen and artillerist owned their own horses, and Grant agreed that they might keep them for "spring ploughing."

To all intents and purposes Lee's surrender was the end. Johnston had fought his last fight- a valiant but unavailable blow at Sherman's Army at Bentonville, North Carolina late in March... A ponderous federal cavalry force was sweeping through Alabama taking the last war production center at Selma, and going on to occupy the onetime Confederate capital, Montgomery. On the Gulf Coast, the city of Mobile was forced to surrender.

President Lincoln was immediately concerned about restoration. To those who said that Jefferson Davis, president of the Confederacy, must be hanged, Lincoln said, "Judge not, that ye be not judged". Five days later the president met with his cabinet and said, "We must extinguish our resentments if we expect harmony and union". That night he was assassinated at Ford's Theater. It was April 14, 1865.

On that historic night, the Thirty-second Iowa was on its last long march from Fort Blakely toward Montgomery, the march having started April 13. The troops arrived in Montgomery on April 27 and remained there until July 15. Thus, WILLIAM POLLOCK was in the capitulated capital of the Confederacy when the little son he had never seen (son GRANT) marked his first birthday near Fort Dodge, May 14.

The Thirty-second remained in Montgomery until July 15 when they embarked on the Alabama river for Selma, from there they were conveyed by rail to Jackson, Miss., from there to Vicksburg where they embarked on a steamer for Clinton, Iowa. On August 24th, WILLAIM POLLOCK and his regiment were mustered out of service at Clinton.

His discharge paper says he had enrolled in the army Aug 20, 1862 for three years. In that time the war had ended and his discharge came three years and four days after his induction. He is officially listed as having taken part in engagements at Ft. DeRussey, La., Pleasant Hill, La., Yellow Bayou, La., Lake Chicot, Ark., Tupelo, Miss., Old Town Creek, Miss., Nashville, Tenn. And Blakely, Ala. This five foot eleven inch stonecutter with dark complexion and dark hair and blue eyes was ready to go home. He had marched more than 1633 miles while he was in the service.

When POLLOCK, returning from the war, came trudging unannounced down the long lane toward his cabin home, his year and a half old son came toddling to meet him and was willingly picked up and carried in the big strong arms of his father whom he had never seen. This little scene of GRANT's welcoming his father home was described down through the years and wondered at, for the children growing up in the woods away from people were as shy as little wild animals. Did the child instinctively know his father and go to him? This is the question always asked.

Now both of our ancestors were home from the war. Donnelson, Pittsburg Landing, Shiloh were marked sharply in the memory of ELEAZER STOAKES and would be passed down through the family as full of meaning. Pleasant Hill was the indelible battle for WILLIAM POLLOCK. But POLLOCK came out of the war and its horror with a love for the beauty of the State of Mississippi, so much so that his son GRANT grew up with a desire to see that beautiful state. This ambition was realized when GRANT himself was well advanced in years. He, too, loved Mississippi and its natural beauty.

B. F. Thomas, who kept the diary of STOAKES' regiment through the war, arrived home himself on Nov. 20, 1865. On the closing pages he wrote, "I went to the Stoakes home where I received the kindest welcome by one who had been my guiding star though all these three years of war. A thousand things I had to tell STOAKES of our comrades and our ventures, though I had but one story to tell Sarah – the old, old story that is ever new".

"Of the ten of us who first messed together, five died before we'd served ten months. ELEAZER STOAKES had been discharged for disability when in the service one year. One was in prison yet, and three Mat Clark, J. R. Felton and I had just been discharged".

"I urged Sarah to name the earliest day possible for our marriage. She said December 22......There were present at the ceremony only the bride's family".

Letters – Marriage – New Cabin

During 1865, while the war was drawing to a close and the soldiers were returning home, other events of family interest were taking place.

POLLOCK'S brother-in-law, Jared Fuller, was elected treasurer of Webster County.

ELEAZER STOAKES was selling his original Tama County farm of 80 acres in Perry township and looking around for a larger farm to buy.

The railroad had pushed west into Iowa as far as Iowa Falls which is fifty miles west of Waterloo. Services were being held in the new Little Brown Church in the Vale which had been completed and dedicated as the year 1864 ended, a little church to become famed by song. It is at Nashua, 30 miles north of Waterloo.

And the Grangers were still keeping in touch with each other through the charming little letters preserved now for a century.

Alice, 17, had finished her common school education, had gone to visit her sister and brother-in-law, Mary and Elias Wightman, and was looking for a school to teach in their vicinity of Beaver. In her gay way, she wrote from there March 1, 1865:

"Dear Sister ELIZA......That day when we came away from Georges we went to Mr. Ames and took tea then we went to Mrs. Reads and stayed all night they all appeared very glad to have us stay with them we started from there the next morning about seven o'clock. It rained when we started and the snow was going very fast we had good sleighing until we got to the falls then from the falls up we had a mud ride for there was no snow at all we got home about six o'clock. I have got my garabaldi done and wore it to a donation party last evening at Mr. Churchills the donation was for a Methodist minister by the name of Dawson. O, ELIZA, I cannot tell you how I enjoyed my-self for I felt like a stranger in a strange land I was introduced to so many that I could not remember half of the names but I got along better than I expected to Mary and Elias was on the committee there was a great many young gentlemen and ladies there more than you can scare up at Buckingham if you try ever so hard. I did wish that I was acquainted with them I should have enjoyed myself so well. I have heard nothing satisfactory about a school yet Elias spoke to Mr. Churchill last evening about that one but he said he could not do anything until after the election which comes up next Monday then I shall see who ever is elected right off I shall try to get a school if I possibly can O, ELIZA hope with me that I may be successful. I got me a skeleton that day when we came through the falls and a net like those silk nets at Cornells I went into three different stores but they all said they wore these more than any kind so I got one. Libbie and George has been down twice since I have been here (this Libbie is Elias' sister). The water has been very high in the Beaver the day after we got here it almost swam a horse so we were lucky in getting home the day we did......Your loving sister
Alice Granger

Ten days later, March 10, 1865, Alice wrote again from Beaver to ELIZA at Buckingham: Dear Sister, I was very glad to hear that George felt so much better for I have thought so much about him since I have been up here and wished I could hear from him. (This is just one of many references to their young brother's ill health.)......Elias attended the school meeting last Monday evening and applied for the school. He wanted to know what recommend Elias could give   he told him that I had passed two examinations but had never taught school he said he had known new beginners teach as good a school as those who have taught several years I thought that was quite encouraging Elias said he should not wonder that I got the school. I am ahead of everyone else any way......George Wightman's children are anxious that I should teach their school but I should rather get this one by Mary's if I possibly could. A week ago tonight Mr. Churchills young people came along and wanted us to go up to Mr. Woods for an evening visit Elias had just got home from Waverly but we went   we did not get home until twelve o'clock we had a very pleasant time the next evening we went to singing school. I dare not describe it for I am afraid I should make it worse than what it really is   to tell the truth their singing teacher does not understand singing him-self   there was not more than half a dozen sung and the rest talked and laughed all of the time I am getting acquainted with some of the young folks now when I meet with some of them I can speak without being introduced. Grandma (apparently Elias's mother) says she thinks we are counting the days more than you are until your school will be out then we shall look for you and George up here if the going will possibly admit it. I think you must have been taken by surprise when the county superintendent came to visit your school if it had been me I donot know how I could have got along   It was very kind in you to think about my clothes and if I needed any money   I am getting along pretty well for clothes and have a little money yet I shall try to prepare myself as well as I possibly can for examination when you write tell me all of the news......Tell me how George and Libbie and the children are......From your loving sister Alice"

In the same letter from Beaver on March 10, Mary wrote: "Dear Sister......As Alice was writing to you......We got home on Tuesday night but we had a pretty stormy day it rained almost all of the forenoon but the snow stayed so it was pretty good sleighing until we got to the Falls then from there home we had what you might call a mud ride for it seemed as though the snow all went at once when it got started......Elias Alice and I went to Georges last Sunday......We went to a donation party at Mr. Churchills for Eldon Dawson (a Methodist man) the next week after we got home   they had Elias and I on the committee and that was what I did not like for I had to work nearly all of the time. It was not a very large donation. they got in all about twenty-six or seven dollars. ELEAZER STOAKES has been up here looking at the country to see if he could find anything that suited him for a farm. he came here night before last and staid until this morning for it was so cold and stormy yesterday that he did not hardly dare to venture out or else it was the company I don't know which that made him stay but I think it is a pity that some of the girls don't take pity on the poor fellow for I expect he will have a farm and a nice house and then he will wont somebody to keep house for him. When your school is out if weather and roads will permit you and George must certainly come up and see us I believe I left my belt at home if I did please bring it when you come......your affectionate sister Mary Wightman".

The little letters are self explanatory and vivacious Alice, bubbling with enthusiasm, wrote again from Beaver on March 29, 1865, "Dear Sister ELIZA......As we are alone again I thought I would try and answer your kind letter. we had company all day Mrs. Churchill and Mrs. Newel Mrs. Wood and Libbie and George Emma and Frank have been here to day   we got the work done up this morning and put on Mary's comforter and we quilted it off in about four and a half hours now I dont believe you can beat that   We are all well as usual and hope these few lines will find you the same and enjoying your-self as they leave us at this time I suppose you will soon be free again but perhaps you will not be glad but I suppose ma will be glad for I presume she had to work pretty hard since I came away   I received a letter from home yesterday   pa wrote some and it seemed so good to have him write I suppose you will not like it because I did not write to you as soon as I got a school but I wrote home about it so I suppose you will not care so long as I have got one When you send me my trunk please send that black braid of that traveling goods dress I want to put it on my purple dress Also send me those old morocco shoes I think I can patch them so they will do to teach in this summer Also those little scissors if you can spare them just as well as not and if it would not be asking to much of you please send me your little knife for I do not feel able to buy one I will be very careful of it What kind of shoes do you think I better get for nice shoes these that I have got are getting very bad they are not fit to go any where in When you get you a nice dress and bonnet or hat please get one just like it and send it up when you can keep count how much it is and I will pay you in the fall Now do not send so many things you rob your self if you do I shall not like it if you do not need the mental Arithmetic please send it to me   also send me a testament Now I think I am about through begging I am very sorry to hear about Loisa Shiners death I was not expecting any such thing I think she must have died very sudden Mr. Hard and his daughter and her husband from the army was down on a visit they came last Friday night and stayed until Tuesday morning we all went to meeting Sunday Elder Dawson preached and we had a very good meeting I am trying to prepare myself for examination as much as I can. I cannot be examined until the last Saturday in April for the water was so high in the Beaver and West Fork that I could not get there but Elias will take me down the last Saturday in April. When you see Ellen Reid tell her if she will write to me I will be very glad to hear from her I send my love to Amelia and all the rest of the family I can not think of anymore at this time Write as soon as you get this good bye From you loving sister Alice Granger.”

Added to the bottom of the letter was: “Oh yes I understand all about the circle around the moon just as well as you do or George W either……If it would not be to much trouble will you fix a bottle of that hair oil such as we fixed before you went to your school and send it up when you send my trunk. Alice”

On April 9th, 1865, Alice wrote again from Beaver to ELIZA at home: Dear Sister   This is Sabbath evening we have not been to meeting to day and I have got tired of reading so I thought I would answer your kind letter which I received last Tuesday We are all well at present and hope these few lines will find you enjoying the same great blessing health I am very sorry to hear that George is so poorly How much I have thought about him and wished I could see him since receiving your letter that I hope and trust that he will get well soon I went up to George Wightmans last Tuesday and stayed until yesterday as you can see I had a good long visit It stormed nearly all of the time I was there if it had not been such bad weather I should have had a much pleasanter visit. Libbie’s brothers have not been here yet she is looking for them every day now their time was up six weeks ago she does not hear anything from them either so she thinks they must be on the way I was glad to hear that you was getting along so well with your school I hope that I shall have such good success next summer I guess we are going to have winter all summer for it is snowing now and is very cold. Elias has sowed some wheat about an acre and 70 rods he sowed that last Monday then went to the Falls on Tuesday with a hog and got twenty two dollars for it ever since then it has been such bad weather he has not been able to do much of anything I have tat considerable tatting since I have been up here I made two yards and gave it to Grandma then I made two yards for myself. Mrs. Wood thought it was so pretty that she wanted me to make her some I made three yards like I was making at home and one yard of wheels I am getting considerably acquainted with her and she is one of the best of women Elias had a letter from Clara stating that they had sold their place I suppose they think they are independently rich now she said they were coming up in a day or two to make a good visit I suppose you are at home again now you and ma are having good times working and talking together once again Now Ma you see that ELIZA writes good long letters to me and tells me all the news what you are doing and what you are going to do and how you are going to do it and all about it ELIZA when you write me send me that ten cent silver piece and I will send you back a pretty silver ring. Grandma had a ten cent piece and George made two rings out of it and he said he could make two for me if you wanted to have it made into rings send it and I will keep one and one for you I send my love to George and Libbie and kiss all the children twice yes three times for me and tell them I should like to see them Does Hattie talk yet? I will have to close for I can not think of any more this time Grandpa and Grandma send their love to Pa and Ma I send my love to you all and all inquiring friends good bye Ever your loving sister Alice R. Granger I send my love to Amelia and Deb and all the rest of the young folks.

Besides the letters from immediate family, ELIZA often received letters from cousins in Ohio which we omit, but on April 20, 1865 a letter was written from Diamond Lake, Ill. Saluting her as "Dear Friend". After telling detailed news of friends and soldiers, the letter concluded, "We have had very bad news from the seat of Government Our President being assassinated I felt so bad I could not do anything after I heard it. The Nation mourns the loss of a great man. I hope that Andy Johnson may be a second Lincoln. I think he will be more severe on the Rebels   As Every Your Friend E. Wenban"

Another look at Alice comes in her letter written from Beaver April 26th, 1865: "Dear Sister and All   It is with pleasure that I sit down to write those that I know will be glad to hear from me……we were all very glad to hear that George was getting so much better I long for the time to come when he will come up here for I want to see him so bad that I can hardly wait so long……I presume you have got your brown dress fixed over so nice that I shall hardly know it again when I see it……I have turned my blue dress skirt up side down I did not have a pattern to make the sleeves over so the waist is just as it was I will have my belmorral stockings done some time In reference to my hat I do not what to tell you I do not like the shapes of the hats they wear this spring very well. I had given up having a bonnet as nice as we had talked about having. A straw bonnet would be nice enough for me but I do not know what would be for the best you and ma know best do just what you think would be right and I will be satisfied I calculate to attend the examination next Saturday. Mary is going with us if she can. Mrs. Allbright and Mrs. Wood are going with us to the Falls. If there does nothing happen to prevent it I commence my school next Monday it seems quite an undertaking to me but I shall strive to do my every known duty. Every one that I have spoke with thinks I will have quite a full school. The Buckingham girls are quite unfortunate about getting their certificates. I hope that I shall be more fortunate. We have had another winter up here (as you say) it snowed Thursday night and all day Friday……Elias finished sewing this morning and has commenced ploughing for corn. Mary and I went visiting yesterday up to Mrs. Woods and we are going to Mrs. Hantses to day but we have got disappointed for Mrs. Churchill and Mrs. Goings the directors wife came here on a visit……Now Ma when George and ELIZA come up you must come to if you possibly can for I do want to see you awfully bad (as Hattie says) Now Pa you must not be jealous and think that I think more of Ma than I do of you for I do not I hope that George and Libbie do not think that I have forgotten them because I have not written, for I will write to them soon give my love to them and kiss all of the children for me when you write tell me what they have named the baby As ever your true and loving sister Alice Granger Tell George to write or has he forgotten his sister Alice."

On May 11th, 1865, Alice (still 17 – not 18 until June) writes from Beaver to ELIZA at Buckingham: Dear Sister Is it possible that I have taught school three days and one half O dear sister it does not seem like a reality it seems like a dream when I get to thinking about it   I received your kind and loving letter this morning after I came to school and it is now noon I thought I would answer it the children are all out doors playing except one girl she is older than I am she is nineteen I have twenty scholars and am getting along first rate I have mental arithmetic twice a day have two practical Arithmetic classes four Geography classes and one history class but I am getting along well I have not come to any-thing but what I understand perfectly, and I have one class in Analytical Grammar I expect I shall have some more scholars next week We are all well as usual and enjoying myself well and hope these few lines will find you all enjoying the time as it flies and in good health as it leaves us at this time We came home that night from Waterloo it rained pretty hard soon after we got half way to the Falls and we drove a pretty good jog and it soon slacked up and then did not rain any. When we got to the Falls, Mrs. Wood and Mrs. Albright was waiting for us and we all thought we better try and get home so we come along and got over the Beaver bridge before dark we had good roads from there home so we did not care so much about the dark In reference about my hat it was so late when we got to the Falls that I did not have time to do anything with it I have not had an opportunity to go to the Falls since I think that I can go with Mrs. Wood she is going down after planting is over and if they go on Saturday, I think that I can go with them. I do not know what shape I shall have it nor I have not made up what trimming I shall have for it I am wearing your felt hat yet George Wightman's folks are all well her brothers have got home from the army They got here Monday night and Tuesday evening when I came from school they were here When you come up bring Hattie with you for I want to see the little dear so bad Elias is getting along with his spring work pretty well he commenced to plant corn today When you write tell me wither you found that young man or not. I think your cloak would be full as pretty to make a military jacket of it (especially if you bring it up to me) I think you must be very entertaining if you write letters every time you have company I send my love to Amelia and De and tell her that I should be very glad to receive a letter from her I suppose you have forgotten all about me though by this time I send my love to all the loved ones at home and to all inquiring friends Ever your true and loving Sister   Alice R. Granger"

News of the family and manner of living in that day continue to be woven into Alice's epistles. She wrote from Beaver Aug. 6th, 1865 to "Dear Father Mother Brother and Sister……It is Sabbath evening I have been to Sabbath school and meeting and have just got home and as I have been thinking a great deal about you all day I thought I would write a few lines to you I do not know wither you will get it before you come after me or not My school closed last Tuesday nearly all of the scholars were sorry school was out there were eight come in to visit school the last day it seemed hard to part with the scholars   the inhabitance seemed well pleased with the school I did not hear of a complaint during the term I have taken the school for the coming winter I can board close to the school house I do not know what the wages will be yet the director does not know yet but will find out as soon as he can I was very surprised to hear that Hattie Coon was married I can say with George that I hope she will make a better wife than she did a school teacher if she does not I pity her husband.

I have my blue dress skirt done and wore it to Waverly the fourth I shall not make the waist until I come home I must close for to night for they are all gone to bed but me so good night As I have an opportunity to mail my letter I will not endeavor to finish it We are all well Elias is getting along very well with his harvesting He is about half through Mary does not have quite so much milk to take care of now they have had a division of the stock and Mr. Ward has sold some of the cows and his son-in-law has come down to night to take theirs home tomorrow so she will not have quite so much to do now and perhaps she will get more time to write oftener than here to fore. I was very glad to hear that George Kober was getting along so well with his corn house but tell him he must not work so hard as not to get to come up here for we have looked for them up here so much and we shall keep looking until we see them I will try and sell the collar ELIZA if I possibly can I am making up a spool of thread for a lady up here and have about four yards to make for Libbie Wightman I will have to be up and at it if I get it done before I come home I have sold two collars since you were up here......Well, Ma I begin to want to see you very much I send my love to you and Pa and hope it will not be long until I see all of you again   Give my love to George and Libbie and kiss all the children for me and tell them how much I should like to see them. Please excuse my poor pen and bad spelling They all join in sending their love to you al Every your loving sister and daughter   Alice R. Granger Good bye”

At the close of the summer session in August until school would open again for the winter term in November was apparently vacation time. ELIZA and Alice could be at home. They would enjoy the autumn together for school would not start until the corn was picked and the older boys free to go to school again.

In September 1865 a “Teacher’s Certificate – Second Grade – (was) issued by Tama County Superintendent of Common Schools to ELIZA A. GRANGER in Orthography, Reading, Writing, Arithmetic, Geography and English Grammar authorizing her to teach for nine months."

As school did begin again, ELIZA started a little diary: On Nov. 13, the “family arose at 3 o’clock. Pa and Ma went to Mary Wightman’s to visit and to take Alice to her school in Black Hawk county. I started at half past six. George and I both rode Molly and arrived in time......”Apparently, young brother George was delivering ELIZA to her school in Tama County via horseback. Five days later, ELIZA notes, “One week of school has passed in which I have tried to do my duty, and now I would like to see absent friends."
(ELIZA’S granddaughter Cora Belle Pollock now treasures a school bell which ELIZA used during her teaching days and which subsequently was used by ELIZA’S daughter BELLE, and then by BELLE’S daughter Cora Belle in their teaching days.)

ELIZA must have boarded near her school. She would get up and sew for an hour or two before breakfast and then go to her school, and often sewed again in the evening. She apparently sewed not only for herself and members of her family, but for other folks as well. When sewing, quilting or tatting for someone outside of the family, she kept account in her diary of time spent as though she might be doing it on a commercial basis. Of her 14 scholars, six were Scott children, and often her diary had an entry, "Sewed for Mrs. Scott."

The little diary was kept in pencil in minute writing and some of it has been obliterated in the passing of 100 years. On Nov. 17, she made the entry, "One week of school has passed……". Other subsequent entries included:

"Nov. 18 – Sewed all day, made two garments and finished another. Retired at half past ten o'clock tired enough to sleep sound."

"Nov. 19 – Arose at 8, read part of the history of 2 Greg. Went to church……disappointed the minister did not come. Friends arrived in the evening."

"Nov. 22nd Made tatting until 8. Went to school. Have not heard from home, wish I would. Tatting until……

"Nov. 23rd – Did up my chamber work and then made tatting until 8 then went to school

"Nov. 24th – Made the bed before breakfast, then sewed until 8. Made a fire while E and M gathered__________frightened so badly.

"Nov. 25th Finished a garment and washed then went to Clarks and got a pattern for ma would look pretty in a hood. In the evening E. came." (This "E" may be a modest reference to ELEAZER'S calling on her on a Saturday evening.)

"Nov. 26th – (Sunday, no doubt) – George and ________came in morning. We went home with them. Pa took me back to school in the evening.

"Nov. 27th……I knit until 8……finished a bed quilt.
"Nov. 29th – Arose at five……sewed until school time……Sewed a pair of pants in the evening. To bed at ten.

"Nov. 30th – Made my bed and sewed on those pants. Went to school alone. E and M came at 9, stopped at school and as they came from Waterloo at ¼ past 3. I rode home with them……in the evening J and I looked at the pictures in my history book. retired at 11."

ELIZA was busy with teaching and sewing and maybe in thinking about "E" for she neglected to send her customarily frequent letters to her loved little sister. Alice complains in a letter written Dec. 4, 1865 from Cedar Falls to ELIZA at Buckingham:

"Dear Sister I received your kind letter last Saturday evening and was very glad to hear that you had not forgotten me I had waited and looked with all the patience I could command for a letter from you and it was a very welcome visitor when it did come for I had been thinking all day that I should get a letter that night from you and when Mr. Churchill's people came home from the Falls they brought me a letter I was almost overjoyed when I got it. I am quite well and hope these few lines will find you the same you spoke in your letter of teaching with-out talking much I know dear Sister how to sympathize with you for I had a very bad cold for two days I could not talk above a whisper I tell you that is what I call hard work I am at school and the noon has expired and I must close......After the hurrah and bussle of comeing and going is over I will now endeavor to finish my long neglected letter for although absent you are not forgotten by me we are having winter weather up here it is pretty good sleighing at present there are a lot of young folks of us went on an evening visit eight in number went on Wednesday evening to some new commers to try and get acquainted with the young folks a young gentleman and lady we had a very pleasant time and the next evening we went to a candy pull at Mr. Hantses we did not stay very late but enjoyed it very much And the next evening which was last evening two couples of us went to Mr. Gibsons to a social party of young folks they had molasses candy to there were about thirty young folks and upward in attendance It was a very pleasant evening and the sleigh ride was as good as the party Sylvia was the other girl and my-self we did not stay late that was the best of it we were not up much later than if we had been at home for they sit up pretty late where I board Mrs. Churchill is weaving and she wants to get through as soon as she can O, ELIZA I have got my dress done and wore it once It is Friday evening and I feel as if my task was finished for another week I have taught three weeks and I am getting along well for ought I know I wish I could come home this evening and stay until Monday morning and have a taste of the apples I hardly know how to contain myself when I read what you wrote about them I wanted some so bad I have not been up to Marys since I started teaching I have wanted to go but have had no chance I hope I may happen on an opportunity tomorrow I heard last Wednesday evening that the teacher that teaches the school near there was boarding with them her name is Mifs White a lady from Waverly. O Sister they have got me coaxed up to having a spelling school it is to be next Wednesday evening O dear what shall I do how can I conduct a spelling school my-self I wish you and George would come When you write tell me that compliment for I am dying to know there is to be a debating school here to night and I must skedaddle before they come......Well I must commence again I went home and ate my supper and went back to the debating school and enjoyed it very much very sorry to hear that you had the hooping cough in your school for it must make it very disagreeable You spoke of putting tatting on your skirt I think it would be very pretty on the bottom but if you have not got time it would be very pretty without Please excuse my poor pen for it is so bad love to all loved ones at home Your loving sister in haste Alice Granger"

And now back to ELIZA'S little diary, thus keeping this account in chronological order:

"Dec. 7th It is thanksgiving. I feel almost guilty for teaching school......played games told stories.

"Dec. 17th Arose at 7 intended to go to church but was disappointed read my magazine it was very lonely took a walk with the girls. I felt almost homesick wanted to see my folks E"

"Dec 20th Awoke about daylight and heard it storming it was snowing very fast. Sewed until breakfast which was about 8 started for school and thought about E what would he say In the evening finished all I could do on my dress until I go home."

ELIZA did go home for Christmas vacation, but Alice taught too far from home to enjoy such a luxury in the winter. Only one section of land separated the home of ELIZA'S parents and the home of ELEAZER'S parents.

He was still living at home but had sold his own original 80 acres and had been looking around for a larger farm. He had found what he wanted in some wild prairie land in his own backyard almost……just a mile or two east of the Granger home and of his parents' home. He bought 217 acres in the southwest quarter of section 32 in Geneseo township and the north half of the northwest quarter of section 5 in Clark township.

News of a romance between ELIZA and ELEAZER had become known, and her sisters began giving advice and making comments in their letters to her. In a letter dated Jackson Dec. 21st, 1865, Mary W. wrote to Dear Sister ELIZA at Buckingham……"I have a good deal to do this fall and have yet for we have a boarder Mifs White that is teaching school in this district she is a real nice girl and we take a great deal of comfort with her. I have not seen Alice but once since she commenced her school Elias went down and got her last Friday and she stayed until Sunday afternoon and then he took her back again. We have moved about four miles of where we lived when you were up here. It is a log house that we live in now and it is not half as pretty a place as it was where we lived nor as convenient a house either but I mean to be contented and do the best I can for Elias and Father think they can do well and perhaps another year we can buy a place and have a home of our own not have to move every year……Dec. 22nd, I will try to finish my letter this morning for I had not much more than fairly got to writing when a sleigh load of young folks drove up to the door so that put an end to my writing. Alice was with them and I was glad to see her. She appears to be getting along with her school pretty well. We were sorry to hear so many had the whooping cough it must make it very disagreeable in school and then it makes the school so small. We have been having very cold weather here for a week or so past our house is pretty cold and it seems sometimes as though we should almost freeze but we have not yet there is a little snow on the ground but not enough for good sleighing you said you sometimes felt lonesome I should not think you would where there are so many but perhaps it is because they are not the right ones and that makes a difference sometimes. Now Eliza although I am younger than you are perhaps I have had a little more experience is some things than you have had and I am going to give you a little advice. If you want to get over being lonesome and take comfort get married for there is nothing I have found like good home enjoyment like having some one to sympathize with you in all your little troubles and to participate in all your joys and to look up to as a protector and tru friend.

"I can not think of anything more to write at this time so I will close by wishing you a merry Christmas please excuse all bad writing and spelling and write soon to your true sister Mary W. I forgot to say we are all well as usual and that I received your letter they all join in sending love to you remember me to the dear ones at home. I should like to see you all."

Marriage was in the near future and ELEAZER was building a little house on his newly acquired farm. ELIZA'S father, ROBERT GRANGER, had decided his family needed a new house, too. Alice refers to both houses in her letter under the date line Dec. 25, 1865, Cedar Falls, and asks ELIZA about her wedding dress:

"Dear Sister I have waited with all patience thinking that I should certainly hear from you I have not received but one letter from you since I have been up here I have almost come to the conclusion that you have forgotten me if you have I can assure you although absence you are not forgotten by me This is the way you write every week If you knew how much good it does me to get a letter you certainly would write oftener when I have been in the school room all day and night comes I think it would revive my drooping spirits so much I will promise you if you will write oftener I will I am well at present and hope these lines find you enjoying the same blessing. I am enjoying myself very much and you are doing the same......Dec. 25 I received your kind and loving letter to day one of my scholars brought it after school called this morning I could scarcely contain myself until recess and also one from home I was so glad to hear that Georges health was better and that Pas health was so good

"Now I must tell you how I am getting along I am prospering with my school for ought I know I have not heard any complaints yet I have twenty-nine names enrolled and that is enough to make me tired when night comes I had not whipped any yet I do not think any deserved it If they had I suppose they would have _______ it O dear Sister I must tell you about what nice spelling schools I have had but I believe though that self praise is no praise at all I appointed one about one week before the cold week and you know how cold it was that Wednesday night but we went and there was only fourteen of us but we had a very good one and Sunday evening after which was last Sunday evening I appointed another for the next Wednesday evening there was a load of young people went to the meeting and I promised them that I would have one and it came off last Wednesday evening there was a very large turn out The teacher and her school came down from where Mary lives and the house was almost full O if I could have been a scholar we chose up and spelled down twice and we had some declaiming there were five young men declaimed Joshua Churchill spoke first Then a young man by the name of Brown next then a Mr. A.L. Ferguson next then a Mr. J. Ferguson then a Mr. N. Churchill and Mrs. Brown spoke a gauntlet I think I hear you say what is that it is a piece where one gets up a speaks a piece and another gets up and trys to bother him by talking on different subjects I tell you it makes a lot of fun I wish you could have been here to have enjoyed it with us The next time I have one the boys are agoing to take down the drums and fife which they think will add much to the interest Last evening a load of young folks of us went up to Marys on an evening visit Last evening there was Hiram Churchill and his wife and Joe Whitney and Sylvia and the two Ferguson boys and Esther Bettleton Alice Tenim and my-self and we had a very pleasant time we had not gone a quarter of a mile before the sleigh turned over and every one of us landed in the snow we had lots of fun for it did not hurt any of us there has been several pieces of poetry made up about it and some that was quite comical to. This is Christmas morning and I wish you a merry Christmas from the appearance of things I shall for the first thing I heard this morning was gun fired real close to the house by window now Hiram and Joshua and Loren are playing the drums I can not tell you any more about Christmas this time I did not teach that cold Tuesday for most of the inhabitants did not think it would be prudent I think that was a very beautiful present that Ase (ELEAZER STOAKES) presented to you and presume you feel proud of it I wish I could have them to read after you get through with I presume the reading is a great deal better because he gave them to you. How is he getting along with his house and when are you going to be married or is this a pretty leading question you must take good care of him and not let his feet get cold Ever you loving sister Alice R. Granger"

Then she had some after thoughts and had written around the margin, "When you write tell me how Pa is getting along with his house I was glad he had got some one to work on it encourage him all you can I think about it so much Give my love to all inquiring friends and the loved ones at home Write as soon as you get this Have you got your wedding dress yet"

ELIZA did not keep up her little diary while she was home on vacation except for one day. This entry tells of going to a New Year Day party and of being sleepy the next day:

"Jan. 1st. Arose early did up the work prepared things for dinner then went 10 had dinner......1/2 past 3 went to a party at Mr. M......

"Jan. 2nd Began school after 1 ½ weeks of vacation. I came from home this morning. In the evening made tatting. Was so sleepy

"Jan. 5th Sewed on my poplin dress. Some sick pupils......I felt quite encouraged everything......

"Jan. 10th Arose quite early Cut a dress waist before school Sewed on it in the evening

"Jan. 12 Sewed until school time Tonight to make up for lost time made tatting. After school had a merry time with the scholars. Then went home feeling very happy and contented. Sewed until 12 in the night."

"Jan 19th Was quite disappointed because I could not go to church Read most of the day in the evening had popcorn and molasses candy had quite a candy pull retired at 10"

While ELEAZER was building his house and ELIZA was busy sewing, maybe on her bridal clothes, ELEAZER'S youngest brother was wed. George W. Stoakes, 23, married Alice Barbour, 22, on Jan. 11, 1866. He brought his bride to the farm home of his parents, JOHN and JANE (VANTILBURG) STOAKES, Sr., now 74 and 64 years of age, and subsequently reared nine children in that household. ELEAZER would be leaving his parent's home soon to establish his own home, but a sister, Californis, 25, continued to live at home. She never married and was fondly called Cally. Hers was the misfortune of not growing to full stature physically. She was always very small in size, but as years went by "Aunt Cally" became a specially loved person by her many nieces and nephews in the community. George W.'s bride Alice had come with her parents from Ohio in 1856 to settle in Tama County.

On Jan 11th 1866, Alice wrote from Cedar Falls again wishing she'd receive more letter from ELIZA: "Dear Sister......I have been up here for over three weeks and have not received but two letters from you......I do not know that it is to be wondered at for your mind is so taken up with the subject of matrimony that you can not think of me now I am pretty well now and hope these few lines find you enjoying the same great blessing health I presume you should be some what surprised if I should tell you that I have had the ague I had it the day before New Years I tell you I was pretty sick the chill came on about ten o'clock and lasted about one hour and a half then the fever came on and they would not let me stay up stairs any longer they made me go down stairs and lay on the bed down there I did wish I was home   they were very kind to me and nursed me up and the next day I took quinine enough to kill a horse and I have not had it since to give up I have felt like it quite a number of times This is Friday evening and my school is two thirds out Some of the inhabitants want me to teach another month there is no money in the treasury but they talk of raising it by subscription if they do do you think I had better teach it write me as soon as you get this and tell me what you think about it I think I am getting along with my school pretty well for some are very anxious that I should come back next summer I must next winter. How are you getting along with your school Have you had any spelling schools yet or have you attended any, if you have where were they. Do you attend singing schools any where this winter. Do you go home very often and how does Ma get along. Write and tell me all about it. Yours truly Alice"

ELIZA did not have time to receive the above letter from Alice before she was writing one to her from Buckingham Jan. 12, 1866, but the letter was never finished and was preserved among ELIZA'S keepsakes. It read:

"Dear Sister, I can not wait to go home to get a whole sheet of paper to tell you what a nice school I have now I have not heard any complaints and think I am getting along finely My school has increased to 18 pupils I have one of the best scholars he is just as good as good can be in school and he has built a fire and swept the schoolhouse floor as clean as the most exacting heart could wish for 2 mornings He is manly, quite good looking and is 18 just the right age for a beau for my baby sister but perhaps he is spoken for and perhaps you have as good scholars but I cannot think so But perhaps enough of this I have not had any reason to complain on the walking thus far this winter It has not been as bad as it was last March."

"Mrs. Corneleous Gay departed this life last Sabbath evening at 11 O'clock She was buried on Tuesday I went to the funeral there was a great many there considering what a storm day it was the services were at Buckingham She left three little children.

"Having got a fire built and the schoolhouse swept I thought I would try to finish this I am well as usual have not heard from home for nearly three weeks but expect to go home next Friday It seems the longest time I ever was away from home."

Alice in her letter from Cedar Falls on Jan. 14, 1866 was wanting to get in on the secrets of ELIZA'S wedding plans and wishing her well:

"This is not a very nice piece of paper but I know who it is going to so it does not make so much difference you know we have had some very stormy weather here this week it commenced raining on Tuesday morning and it has rained every day since it has stopped now and is quite cold It has been so icy that we could not get to school on foot they have taken us for three mornings and come after us in the evening it has been a week long to be remembered it has been so slippery horses could hardly stand up tonight one of them did fall down Mary Churchill is attending school now I have thirty-one names enrolled how many scholars have you I tell you it is all I want to do to get around and do each one justice when they are all here I find it harder to teach school in the winter than in the summer it is harder to keep order although I have done without any whippings thus far. have you whipped any yet? You said that John Scott was coming up this way. I have not seen anything of him

"How is Pa getting along with the house I was glad to hear that he had hired a man to work on it I do hope he will get it by spring for your sake if no one elses for I expect it will come off in March will it not How are you getting along with your work I wish I were there to help you on Saturdays When you write tell me all about how you are getting with your fixings and no one shall see it except me you need not be afraid to tell me about it for you know I can keep a secret. Now dear sister write as soon as you get this and tell me all of the news and tell me all about home for home is a dear place to me I am enjoying my-self tip top this winter I shall be sorry when school is out It seems as if I get more and more attached to the scholars every day. Elias was coming down after me tonight but the roads are so bad that he did not come they were all well the last time I heard from them When you write tell me how you spent your Christmas and New Years where you went who was there and all about it. Good bye until I hear from you again. I send my love to all the loved homes at home and all inquiring friends. Have you seen Frankies baby You must take good care of some body and not let him go out in the cold to much for you know the consequences Ever your true and loving sister
Alice K. Granger"

Alice was worried about loved ones at home but also filled with youthful enthusiasm for her own activities when she wrote from Cedar Falls, Jan. 26th, 1866

"Dear Sister, I seat myself to reply to your very welcome letter which I received about one week ago. I was very sorry to hear that Ma had been so sick do you think she worked to hard or what do you think brought it on I have thought so much this winter about dear Mother and was afraid the work would make her sick and when I received that letter from you I was almost homesick. And dear brother he is not off my mind hardly day or night. I have flattered myself with the hope that we shall see him live to be a man but O dear sister is it possible that I shall be disappointed. Is he actually failing It makes me cry as I write to think he has to suffer so much. O if I could only suffer some for him then it would not seem quite so hard but I still cling to the hope that Pa can get something to cure him. Libbie Wightman told me the other day that she thought some smart weed tea would be good for him but he must not have the cold air blow on him while he is taking it if it does he will catch cold very easy she said it would be for him to drink cold or warm. I received a letter from Frankie last week and was quite surprised to learn the George Stoakes and Alice Barber were married they have beat you now but suppose your intentions are good enough yet tell them that I wish them much happiness. Frankie seems to think a great deal of their boy have you seen it yet……You spoke in your letter about spelling schools being all the rage down there. They are becoming quite so here there was a sleigh load of young folks of us, eleven in all, went a week ago last Thursday evening to a spelling school they chose up and spelled down twice then they spoke pieces and read compositions and they did well they had some good compositions. I had a spelling school last Monday evening which some said was the best spelling school they had attended for two years the house was crowded we chose up and spelled down before recess and after I did all of the pronouncing my-self then we had some speaking and we had two musicians there they played on the fiddle they played some of the time two tunes and some of the time only one between the pieces we had some declamations and some gauntlets and some dialogues Mary Churchill and my-self had a dialogue and we had a very good spelling school in general a load of us went down to the Hacket's school house to a spelling school last Thursday evening they chose up and spelled down before recess and after recess they had kind of an exhibition and some of my scholars took a part they had some very good music a fiddler he had a daughter fourteen years of age she was a splendid singer She would sing and he would play and it sounded very nice. I pronounced half of the time and their teacher the other half and we had a very pleasant time take it all together. I have one appointed for tomorrow evening which I hope will pass satisfactory to all. I have only two weeks more school to teach if I do not teach another month I have not heard any complaints but some want me to come back next summer but I am afraid they will have to be disappointed I went and got twenty-five dollars more of my money and I can not get any more until April then he thinks I can get all of the remainder of last summers wages and this winters to. I was somewhat surprised to hear that Annie Torrence was married. Also to hear that Mary Slade was married have they come to Iowa to live. There is to be a donation party at Mr. Nettletons for Mr. Faucett next Thursday the old folks are going in the afternoon and the young folks in the evening if all is well I calculate to attend I was sorry to hear that you have not got anything done for the event which I suppose is not far distant I wish I was there to help you Give my love to all inquiring friends Please write as soon as you get this and write all of the news Give my love to all of the loving ones at home Every your loving sister Alice R. Granger To Miss ELIZA A. GRANGER STOAKES I mean"

In the next letter from Alice, she was still having fun with the young people, but part of her heart was at home with loved ones. She wrote, "Cedar Falls Feb. 4th 1866 Dear Sister……It is after school I am at the school house writing to one I wish was here just now so we could have a good old talk about matters and things that concern us most……I do not know that I have done right in teaching another month as I cannot be there to help you get ready to be married but I thought as they had raised the money and I was here and everything was agoing on so nicely and they all wanted me so bad I thought it over a great deal and at last made up my mind that I had better teach it……Thursday was the stormiest day that we have had this winter I did not teach school that day or the next one reason was because it was so stormy another great reason was because I was sick I had the hardest cold I ever had I think yesterday morning I thought I must try and teach although I could not speak above a whisper and so I went and built a fire and swept out and tried my best to teach but I could not because I could not make them hear me talk and my throat was so sore that I had to dismifs them at noon and come home. O Sister you do not know how bad I felt to come home at noon my throat is sore and I can not speak above a whisper now but I hope that I shall be better before Monday so that I can go to teaching......I have been enjoying myself very much lately I attended the donation I wrote about for Mr. Faucett I never heard exactly how much they got but it was over forty dollars they made Mrs. Faucett a present of a bed quilt I pieced one block for it it was a very pretty quilt there was a great many there and we had a very pleasant time. One week ago last Wednesday I attended a turkey roast at Mr. West's daughters there was eleven of us in one sleigh I tell you now we had a tip top sleigh ride and when we got there who should I find there but Mary and Elias and Grandma and Grandpa we had a very good supper and a very pleasant time I was very glad to hear that George was a little better I do hope that he will get better soon and be to us all that our hearts can wish but dear sister he is on my mind so much at nights after I go to bed I lay awake and think of him so much I want to yet I dread to get a letter from home because I am afraid it will contain some bad news about him yet I think I could not live if I did not hear from there pretty often......I have not been to Elias' to make a visit for some time......Why don't all of the young people down there get married if I stay away a while longer I expect they will all get married before I come back. there must be something nice about married life that I do not know any thing about or else they would not all want to get married it is a free country and everyone for themselves of course you do not think as I do now on the matrimony question so it is no use for me to talk to you now. Has Pa done anything toward a house yet He wrote to me some time ago that he thought he could get it up to live in next summer that was the best news that I have heard this winter. You wrote a good long letter last time......Ever your loving sister until death Alice R. Granger take good care of some body you know who STOAKES".

Apparently ELIZA worries about her gay young sister Alice and all of her sleigh rides, spelling schools, donation parties and turkey roasts. Both Elias and Mary try to assure ELIZA about Alice's well-being in a letter written Feb. 18, 1866. The Wightmans write from Jackson township indicating they may have moved again.

Elias writes, "I don't know that I have much news of importance to write to you – but will try to convey a few thoughts to you that you can have some idea how the time is passing with us and the vicinity of West Fork Alice was well the last time I saw her and that was at a school gathering at one of the neighbors in the vicinity of where we are living now. I think I ought to describe Alice's escort to you ELIZA for he has I think been very successful in obtaining Alice's company more than any other young man on West Fork he is not tall but rather short in stature light hair and about 20 years of age – and I think they make quite a good appearance in company. There how do you like my description - pretty good did you say......As to Mary and myself I think our cup of happiness as full as can be very well with man and wife and when we look back and think had it been different – our earthly ambition would have been nearly destroyed – that life would have been a desert while now with heart and hand united the desert is made to bloom like the rose while our hearts go out in thankfulness to him that doeth all things well – and feel that thare is no home like the home in the heart on earth......Give my best wishes to Pa and Ma and all inquiring friends Elias Wightman"

Mary wrote on the same page "Dear Sister Eliza....We received your much looked for and welcome letter about a week ago and were glad to hear from you and that you are getting along so well in your school but was sorry to hear that Ma had been sick and also that George's health is so poor this winter. I do sincerely hope that the medicine Pa has sent for will help him....The last time I saw Alice she was getting along very well in her school. I am not where I can watch her very close but I will try and not let any one run away with her. I believe the young folks don't do anything else but get married down that way but I suppose the fever is not contagious so of course it won't effect you any. My love to all the dear ones at home, George and Lizzie and all inquiring friends   Your sister Mary W"

ELIZA'S days of teaching school were drawing to a close. She had taught school for several years. The first record we have of her teaching career is a certificate to teach issued in May 1862 when she was 19 years old. Such a certificate was issued for a year, or even a period of months, and to be frequently renewed.

Whether she taught when she was 17 and 18 as Alice did, we have no record. Alice's little letters and ELIZA's own letters and little diary indicate that ELIZA enjoyed her teaching. Years later when she reached old age, she received a letter from a former scholar, "Dear Mrs. Stoakes – I have always entertained a very agreeable memory of what I believe to be my first teacher – MISS ELIZA GRANGER......This was a long time ago. I am now 67 years old. I saw by the Clipper that you are living in Traer and I thought I d like to tell you how pleasant a memory you left with me during a long and busy life. I have been quite a traveler having seen several European countries, China, Japan, Korea, India etc. I have seen our own country fairly well having visited nine of our national parks, Alaska etc. etc. I have about perfect health, am active in my clothing business etc. I hope you are growing old contentedly and are well and happy. Sincerely yours Lyman W. Felter. I am suppose to be the first person born in Crystal township April 13, 1856." The letter came from Canon City, Colo.

ELIZA GRANGER and ELEAZER STOAKES were married at her parents' residence March 1, 1866, we presume in the old house for Alice had said in one of her letters that the new house would not be finished until summer. ELIZA was 23 and ELEAZER 33. They made a handsome couple, she with her dark beauty, her hair pulled straight back in a classic style, and he with his curly reddish blonde hair and full beard. They had their wedding pictures taken to mount with their marriage certificate. The certificate and pictures are preserved along with the wedding dress. Her parents, ROBERT and EIZABETH GRANGER, signed the marriage certificate, as did the officiating minister, the Rev. Bennet Roberts.

ELIZA'S wedding gown was a blue light-weight wool, a lovely blue, the shade of an October sky. It was fashioned with full sleeves, a tight bodice, and a skirt measuring five and a half yards around the bottom which was pleated into a mass of tiny pleats at the 22 inch waist. A row of tiny black velvet buttons ran down the front of the bodice. At the neckline was a band of black velvet ribbon with a narrow fluting of white lace at the top. The ribbon was tied at the front into fashionable loops. An over-sleeve ended at a point at the elbow and was edged with black silk cord coming down to a black tassel at the point. She wore rather a wide belt with a buckle at the front.

Her bonnet was a matching blue created from ribbon. The bonnet was attractive with small pleated, flared loops of ribbon among which were nestled small blue flowers. Dainty silk lace circled the outer edge of the head piece. Two foot long, four inch wide blue ribbons fell from each side while narrow matching ribbons tied under the chin.

If ELIZA made her wedding dress, and we presume she did, hundreds of her expert stitches went into its creation. The bottom of the full skirt was edged with a black dust band. Every stitch is sewn by hand. The three undergarments and the night gown were daintily trimmed not only with tatted lace but with tatted insertion as well. Yards of this tatting must have been made on those winter evenings at her boarding house while she was still teaching. The lace and insertion made dainty the low boat neckline and the tiny puff sleeves of the muslin chemise. The petticoat, four yards around the bottom, was fashioned with horizontal pleats and the insertion. And under all were the pantaloons with fancy tatted insertion and lace. The garments are the keepsake of the writer and compiler of this account, granddaughter and namesake of ELIZA, Margaret Eliza Pollock Campbell. The groom wore a black suit with a double breasted vest and coat, the coat styled fashionably long.

The newlyweds moved into their own new little house on the 217 acre farm ELEAZER had purchased a mile and a half or two miles east of his parents and hers. Her married sister Lizzie Kober lived nearby, as did his married sisters Martha Jane Cope, Elizabeth Gaston, Sarah Thomas and brothers Henry, George W., William all of whom were married, and their young sister Cally. This, however, was the year the Copes moved to Waterloo and she started a millinery shop.

ELEAZER and ELIZA, not only had both sets of parents, and these many sisters and brothers living nearby, but there were 26 nieces and nephews to enliven family gatherings. ELEAZER had 23 on his side of the family in the county, and ELIZA'S sister Lizzie had three children.

On this farm, ELIZA and ELEAZER lived their entire married life and reared their family. When he died in 1911, he was described as a man "of gentleness, kindness, goodness, the salt of the earth." She was called a "loveable type of pioneer mother devoted to farm, home and church."

A little more than a month after the wedding, sorrow came to them. Her 16 year old brother George with the golden blonde hair, died at his parents' home. His poor health had been a deep concern to the family for many months. (Emma Endicott – Lizzie Kober's daughter – says he died of consumption, tuberculosis.) Death came April 9.

Word was sent to Sister Mary and her husband Elias. Elias wrote back from Jackson April the 18, 1866, "Sister ELIZA and Friends – Your letter of affliction reached us two days from the time it was mailed – and my pen failes to exprefs the feelings of sorrow it brought to our hearts – I endeavor to master the emmoritions of my own heart for the sad news took hold so hard upon Mary's feelings that I felt it my duty to comfort her as much as I could. How little I expected that one in our union was marked to fall so soon, but Death is on our track and we all must go, and how soon we know not and while God has come so near as to take one of our number let us all be Christians that we may in the future be an unbroken band in our Heavenly Father's Kingdom. Mary and I was thinking of writing you ELIZA a few days before we received your letter of sorrow – sending our congratulations in the object of your choice of a companion – and further sending our best wishes that your lives might be joyous in each others society – But as thare has a cloud of sorrow brought its shaddow as it was over your Bridal morn while you was in annimation to fulfill the duties of a wife – are thare not other duties for us as children to perform – while we mingle our sorrow for the departed let us try to be a comfort to a kind Father and Mother that their gray hairs may not come down with sorrow to the grave…..The present finds us all well as common. I am very happy now with my spring work. As the season is backward it seames all most impofsible for me as I am situated to come down thare until after planting corn is over   then providence permitting we shall endeavor to come. Mary ses pleas excuse her for this time and she will try to write the next opportunity.

"We would be very glad to receive a letter from you and AZE that we could know how you all git along more often   I remain with respect to all
Elias Wightman."

An insight into the day's mode of living is given by Mary Wightman a few months later as she writes from Shell Rock, Dec. 2, 1866, to "Dear Brother and Sister, It is with pleasure that I seat myself at this time to addrefs a few lines to you to let you know how we are getting along. We are all as well as usual and hope these few lines will find you enjoying that great blessing health. I suppose Alice has told you that we calculate to stay on this place another year so we shall not have to move this winter. O this moving I hate it. Elias has got along pretty well with his fall work   he has got his threshing done and his corn gathered and so forth, but the corn is not very good around here for that hard frost injured it very much but since that frost came we have had a very nice fall. I have made thirty yards of cloth his fall and have got it almost made up   I have made five blankets out of it and think a pair of them will be nice to sleep in these cold winter nights don't you. Elias has taken about two hundred sheep for the next year   Mr. Wests finds feed for them and Elias takes care of them and washes and shears them for one quarter of the wool and increase so I think I shall have all of the wool that I shall want to work but I like to spin and think I can spin considerably another year. When Alice wrote she said that Pa and Ma were coming up here before it got to be cold weather   we have been looking for them for a number of weeks past but they do not come and we do not hear anything from them only by way of others so I have almost concluded that Alice has forgotten us for I have had only one letter from her since she went home so I do not think she has kept her promise very well for she said that she would write often if I would not wait so long before I answered   Elias said that you must please excuse him this time   It has been such a rainy gloomy day that I could not more than half write and now it is almost nine o'clock so I guefs I will have to bring my letter to a close. Please accept it and write soon   they all join in sending love to you   From your loving sister Mary Wightman"

This was 1866 and the post-war development of the West was gaining momentum. The railroad had pushed westward and had reached Des Moines, the state capital.

Up at William and MARY POLLOCKS' log cabin on the Lizard in Webster county a new son, James Henry, had been born, June 9, 1866. GRANT was then past two and he and Jim were to be closely associated through long lives, Will was seven and Jennie five.

MARY'S sister Sarah and her husband Jared Fuller were looking forward to a new baby the following year, in 1867. The Fullers with their family of boys, now numbering four or five, had moved from west of Fort Dodge to the south part of the county, to a settlement called Holiday

Creek. It is tucked into the scenic, wooded hills of the coal mining area, a mile east of the present town of Coalville, on the Des Moines river.

A great tragedy struck. Sarah died in childbirth leaving her husband and five children behind: James B., approximately 11 years old; Marcus, about 9; Eddie, about 7; and two younger children J.F. and A.F. (probably Jared and Arthur.) Whether one of these was the new born baby we do not know. Sarah was 41 years old.

MARY POLLOCK must have grieved deeply for her sister. When Sarah and her new husband had come west from New York state to make their home near Fort Dodge, MARY had followed, had subsequently married and the POLLOCKS had established their home only a few miles away. The two sisters were left alone with little ones, dependant upon each other, while their husbands were away fighting in the Civil War. The two women were dear to each other and to each other's children. Now Sarah was gone.

Jared continued to maintain his Holiday Creek home, but the children turned toward "AUNT MARY" and she toward them. The children were frequent visitors in the POLLOCK home.

MARY had another sorrow come to her in 1867. Her father, JAMES BEATS, passed away back in New York state. He was 76 years old. Her mother had died 22 years earlier at the age of 45 leaving her family only partially grown. The father had remarried. Whether the second wife came west after her husband's death – maybe to help care for the Fuller children – no one left had ever heard mentioned. If she did she did not live long. There is a tombstone with her name on it the Fuller lot at Oakland cemetery in Fort Dodge. (Jared Fuller moved his wife's body from Holiday Creek cemetery to this Fort Dodge cemetery several years after her initial burial.) The lettering on the mystery tombstone is partially obliterated by time, but what is legible says, "Mary – wife of JAMES BEATS died Mar. 14 (maybe 19) – 1868 Age of (not legible) yrs 9 mos." At the bottom is a sentence or two starting "Dear Mother" and the rest can not be read. The "Dear Mother" adds to the mystery.

A mad race of railroad construction was underway. Iowa was being linked by gleaming rails from the Mississippi river on the east to the Missouri river on the west. At the same time, the Union Pacific had brought railroad construction materials up the Missouri river to Council Bluffs and tracks were stretching westward across the plains toward the setting sun. The Central Pacific was building from the West eastward and in a couple of years the tracks would meet at Salt Lake City with the driving of the golden spike and the nation could travel East to West on the iron horse.

ELIZA and ELEAZER welcomed their first child, a son Theodore, early in 1867.

Elias Wightman sent congratulations from Shell Rock, March 17th, 1867 to "Mr. AZE STOAKES – Dear Friend – I received your kind letter of Date Feb. 26 and we all were verry glad to hear from you for we was anxious to hear of you and ELIZAS health – we wish you much joy and happinefs in the future – with your son – for I think if life is permitted – it is in the reach of all children to be a blefsing to their parents   We was sorry to hear that ELIZAS health was so poor and that she had been sick so long – our desire and wish is that health may soon return for the comfort of your united hearts – I should like to be down there and have a good visit but I dont know that it would be best to come just now for it appears to be quite a time for Babes and I don't know that it might prove contageous and we dont see how we can afford it in our present circumstances – so when you think it is advisable for us to come please write and I will try to arrange businefs and come…..I think thare is going to be quite a lack of course feed in this vicinity and I guefs some teams and other stock will have to fare pretty hard. I think we have enough to do us verry well   I hear of some over on the Wapsy River hireing money and Mortgageing their farms to buy feed for there stock whitch seems rather hard   If I knew where thare was a healthy country South I think I would be in favor of going for I tell you AZE when a farmer looses his corn crop it is a great fall back – But I will never go south unlefs I know of a

Lee and Alice (Granger) Ferguson

country that is healthy   William Read has sold and is going to moove South some whare   they write that they are coming to visit us   before they moove and coax us to go with them, but they cant get me to move to a country that is feavery for I like the boiling springs of the North too well. I suppose William Read is now looking for a good country   He is going to look in Missouri and Kansas – I shall tray and come and visit you all as soon as I can arrange businefs   Mary and I wish to do all we can for the comfort of Father and Mother Granger in their lonelinefs for they have shown their love and kind regard for us in menny ways whitch had made them seam very near to us   But I will close for this time   Mary joins me in sending our best and good wishes for each and all   pleas write again   Yours with respect   Elias Wightman"

When Theodore was a baby, ELIZA received a scare from an Indian, as the story comes down to us by word of mouth. ELIZA was in the kitchen having just taken a batch of fresh bread out of the oven. She heard someone come in the door and turned to see to her great surprise and concern a large Indian man standing in the middle of the room. He was between her and her baby who was in the bedroom. She was immediately fearful that he might harm the baby. He apparently had been passing on the road and had been attracted by the smell of fresh bread. She gave him some bread and he left. The Indians at this time lived peacefully on their own land in the south part of the county at Tama, but Indian cruelties were too fresh in the memories of pioneers to make them feel safe especially when an Indian walked uninvited into a home.

Sometime in 1867 (or late the previous year), gay Alice and Lee Ferguson with whom she had been enjoying sleigh rides, spelling schools and candy pulls were married. She wrote from Shell Rock May 8th 1867 signing her name "Alice Ferguson" and addressing ELEAZER and ELIZA "Dear Brother and Sister……I am getting some better ELIZA so that I am able to teach school I am at the school house now writing, it is noon and I commenced teaching last Monday the 4th of May and intend to teach three months I get 23 ½ dollars per month pretty good wages I think as my board does not cost me anything The school house is a mile and a half from home but I have not walked it yet but a few times Lee takes and comes after me whenever he can I went to Butler Center and was examined the Saturday after Pa and Ma went home and I got my certificate the same day it was second grade My school is very large I have 14 scholars yet. Well I suppose I have written enough about school for I expect it will not be very interesting to you now……This is Sabbath evening this has been a pleasant day we have been to the Ford for meeting I was glad to hear Pa and Ma arrived safe at home all right I was so glad they came up to see us I enjoyed their visit so much. We have not seen Mary and Elias since they came up but I heard today they were well and intended to move next week.

"Tell Ma that I got my white quilt all pieced but have not got it set together yet but expect to before long Now tell her that I am feeling some better now than what I was when she was up here and that she must not worry about me. Well ELIZA I have at last succeeded in getting you tatting done I hope it will suit you I have got it pretty dirty you must not think it has been much trouble for me for it has not. Give our love to Pa and Ma and George and Lizzie and little ones and keep a large portion for yourselves. You must excuse Lee this time for he wants to be examined next July and is very busy reading all of his time nearly……write soon and often from your true sister Alice Ferguson"

ELIZA was still receiving little letters from back in Ohio thus receiving word of her mother's sister: "Hinckley Jun 3d 1867……I went to a dime party last Wednesday night and had a verry nice time they had an organ one from the citty there. They had had parties every Wednes or fryday night all winter to get an Organ for the church. They have the church enlarged. The Rhuematism troubles Mother a great deal this spring. I hope your little boy is better now Pleas tell Alice not to forget she has a cousin living down in Ohio……Hattie E. Porter" (age 16)

This cousin Hattie wrote again Jan 31st, 1868 from Hinckly and although many years had passed since ROBERT and ELIZABETH GRANGER and her sister and brother-in-law had left England for America, ELIZABETH'S sister (Hattie's mother) was still thinking longingly of dear old England. Hattie wrote "……this is a piece of Mother's and my dress……they have dime parties here every week……they are for the benefit of furnishing the church……Pleas try and have Aunt and Uncle come down here and see us we would be verry happy to have them come and we will try and make them happy……when you write tell us wheather Aunt and Uncle have had a letter from England or not……Mother says she would like to see you all but she don't like to travel or she would come up and see you……we have not had any letter from England for a long time……Hattie Porter"

Up in northwest Iowa, the first frame dwelling was being build, 1867, in Pocahontas County. It was on a high knoll overlooking the Des Moines river at a settlement then known as Highland City, later to be called Milton and finally Rolfe. For a short time it was known as Parvin, and then down through the years it was to become known as Old Rolfe. The frame house was being built by William H. Hait. He was sawing the frame lumber and sheathing on the site and was hauling the siding, flooring and shingles from Fort Dodge. The settlement had been founded a decade earlier by Hait, Robert Struthers, A. H. Malcolm and Guernsy Smith who had arrived by oxcart from Fort Dodge. The location had been first spotted when some of that foursome had gone with the Fort Dodge Expedition in March 1857 to the site of the Spirit Lake massacre planning to give aid to the settlers. Now when Mr. Hait was building his frame house at Highland City it had become a settlement of log cabins, a courthouse and a brick schoolhouse (both built in 1861), a general store (1860) and a blacksmith shop.

This same year in Webster County when GRANT POLLOCK was three years old (1867), his father WILLIAM was building the family a new cabin. There were four Pollock children and the new cabin probably was a larger one than the old. We do know it was a warmer one for it was insulated with brick.

When GRANT was well advanced in years, he built a miniature replica of the log cabin in which he was born and lived for three years on Lizard Creek. He spent many hours with his jackknife whittling and hewing tiny logs, fitting them into place and chinking them. He consulted with his oldest sister Jennie and their cousin Ed Fuller regarding some of the details, especially the location of one window. The cabin had a small window on the north, one on the south and a door on the east. He remembered best the doorway with its warm sunny doorstep, apparently a fine place to play.

In his later years, GRANT also used to recall one Christmas morning in the log cabin. His mother had pushed the children's beds near the stove for warmth. Grant was awakened that morning with someone putting something into his mouth. His eyes opened to see his mother standing there smiling. A stick of candy was in his mouth – "a real treat for us boys".

Another friendly little look at the Granger family comes in a letter from Alice written in Shell Rock April 8th 1868, "Dear Brother and Sister……I am getting better so that I am able to sit up most of the time all day. I was quite sick for awhile so that I had to lay in bed for nearly three weeks and the doctor came to see me four times. How I hate to be sick ELIZA and have to be waited upon so much. But Lee is so good I could not have had better care if I had been at home Lee tells me to tell you he is well and sitting by the stove reading and telling me what to write but I do not write the half of what he tells me to if I did I guess you would think it was a curious letter. Mary and Elias came over while I was sick and Mary stayed over night and until the next day about 3 o'clock. I enjoyed having her with me so well and they were over again a week ago Sunday. Mary says it seems as though she has little to do now to what she used to have to do. I intend to teach school again this summer if I get well enough to and if I can get a certificate I wanted to attend the examination the last of March but was not able. I intend to go the last of this month if I am able. I do hope that I will be for Lee's brother is director and he wants me to have the school. We talk now of agoing to keeping house next winter and if we do the money will come in play you know ELIZA as well as I do. And about making the tatting you did not tell me when you wanted me to have it done Me being sick my work has got behind so much that I cannot make it very soon perhaps though I can get it done by the first of June. I want to make it for you if I can. Write and tell me if it will do if I get it for you by that time. Well I must bring this to a close for Eugene is about ready to start for Shell Rock. You need not ask me in your next if we have no ink for we have a pint but the trouble is I have no pen that I can write with read what you can of this and guess at the rest Our love to Pa and Ma and keep a large portion for your-selves kiss Theodore for me Your true sister Alice Ferguson write soon".

ELIZA my have been wanting that tatting for baby clothes. She and ELEAZER had a new son, George E., born May, 1868.

At Fort Dodge, WILLIAM POLLOCK the stonecutter would have been interested in the two new quarries opened up in 1868, one in Gypsum Hollow and the other in Soldier Creek. Gypsum was easily quarried. The stone could be dressed into blocks of any size and shape with hatchets, axes or an ordinary wood saw and was commonly used for foundations, sidewalks, and recently for residences and business buildings. The two new quarries were opened because the railroad was approaching and a supply of rock was needed to build a station. The station was started before the railroad arrived.

That was the year a man, George Hull, arrived in Fort Dodge from Ackley, Iowa wanting a large block of gypsum. He finally found a man, Mike Foley, who would cut a block to the specified dimensions, 12 foot long, four feet wide and two feet thick. They loaded it onto a wagon and hitched four oxen to it and started the forty-five miles to Boone, the nearest railroad point. Enroute the wooden axle broke. Hull found another wagon but reluctantly had to have Foley cut two feet off of the end of the block to get it on the second wagon. Folks around Fort Dodge, including WILLIAM POLLOCK, wanted to know what the block of gypsum was to be used for, but Hull was evasive.

In October of the following year, 1869, well diggers came upon a "petrified giant" on the farm of Hull's cousin, Stub Newell, at Cardith, N.Y. Newspaper men came flocking, as did scientists, ministers, and the general public. The road to the Newell place was crowded with buggies and lumber wagons. Soon Newell was charging four bits a person to see the ten foot long stone man with the large stately head and calm smile. Indians claimed he was one of their old prophets. Hull appeared at the Newell place and the price of admission went up to one dollar. Scientists came and studied and developed theories. The president of Cornell University said it was just a piece of gypsum, but a New York geologist called it "The most remarkable archeological discovery ever made, clearly of great antiquity." Another eminent authority wrote in the Scientific American, "It is a veritable petrification. There is not a chisel mark upon the entire image. Its perfection defies the artist. It is the most extraordinary and gigantic wonder ever presented to the eye of man." P. T. Barnum tried to buy it.

Skeptical reporters piecing small bits of information together finally located a stonecutter in Chicago, who fearing Hull had committed some crime, admitted that he had cut the giant for Hull. Then Hull admitted the whole hoax. He had bought the block of gypsum in Fort Dodge, shipped it by rail from Boone to Chicago, had it cut into the form of a giant, shipped the giant to New York state where he and Newell had buried it one dark night, and Newell had subsequently hired men to dig the well on the spot in order that they would chance upon it. Hull and Newell were some hundred thousand dollars richer. Proof of the hoax did not destroy its drawing power. It had been called the "eighth wonder of the world" and everyone wanted to see it. The giant was displayed over the country and people continued for years to pay money to see it. It was the last show at the 1935 Iowa State Fair and was shown some years after that at the Clay County Fair, Spencer, Iowa. It is now in the Farmers Museum in New York.

Through the years, the Cardith Giant had been an interesting topic of conversation around Fort Dodge and there has been a certain civic pride of having furnished the gypsum for "the eighth wonder of the world". The year the giant was discovered and dug up, the residents of Fort Dodge voted to incorporate their town. The town then had on schoolhouse with nine teachers and 350 scholars.

The WILLIAM POLLOCKS had a new daughter, Emma, in 1869. Through the years at least GRANT and Jim frequently called her by the affectionate name of "Em".

That was the year the whistle of the iron horse was heard in Fort Dodge for the first time. Aug. 16, 1869, railroad service between Fort Dodge and Chicago was inaugurated over the Dubuque and Sioux City railroad (predecessor of the Illinois Central). It was a day of rejoicing for the whole county. Freight rate for the county's markets was cut in half. Later in the year, the Des Moines Valley railroad, which became part of the Minneapolis and St. Louis, also reached Fort Dodge. The coming of the railroads brought a great rush of settlers willing to settle on the surrounding fertile prairies now that the rail connections with the older sections of the United States were a reality. The railroads spread rapidly linking up with even smaller settlements. The first rails were laid in the southern part of Pocahontas County that same year.

Settlers were still coming in covered wagons. The editor of the Fort Dodge paper wrote, "Our City for the past week has been filled with prairies schooners, laden with strong hearts and willing hands seeking homes in the West. Come on, there is yet room for more. Tuesday, Market Street was fairly blocked with emigrant teams".

Other excerpts from the paper described the times, "We have been informed the Webster City road two miles east of town is in very bad condition. The road that was formerly traveled has been fenced in by some persons owning the land, obliging travelers to go a different route, where, owning to sloughs and mud, it is almost impassable. Something must be done about this piece of road 'ere long we will have to chronicle the sinking of some emigrant through mud and water to regions below".

Webster County was making its first attempt to improve trails winding through the prairies, around the bogs, and marshes and ponds from town to town. A horse-drawn scraper blade was all the road equipment available and it merely cut off the turf between the wagon ruts. No attempt was made to grade the roads.

Farm machinery was improving. In the latter part of the sixties and early seventies Webster County farmers could purchase a combine reaper and mower in Fort Dodge. Of course, most farmers were still using the old reaper and even the cradle for their harvests, but times were changing. In the seventies, farmers started using the Marsh Harvester. This machine was built onto the reaper and used an elevator canvass to bring the cut grain up onto a table where it dropped to be bound by hand by two men who stood on the platform. This made the harvester a three-man outfit, but the two men standing at their work could bind more grain than two men walking around the field and stooping to pick up the loose grain.

The local editor bragged about prospective crops. "So far we have been able to ascertain, there never was a better prospect for crops of all kinds than there is this season. Wheat promises from 20 to 30 bushels per acre; corn 60 to 80; oats 50 to 70; barley 40 to 60; potatoes at least 150 bushels. We get these figures from farmers in all parts of the country."

"A number of deer have been brought to town that were killed about twelve miles southwest of Fort Dodge," the paper said. Other items in the seventies said, "Wild mallards are still found on the river.....Our German friend Bachring presented us with a very fat, nice brant, a fowl of the goose species and our better half says much better eating than a goose.....Sunday last was a good day to gather wild strawberries, and the time and the day were improved by some of the natives in the east part of town who could be seen in every direction upon their knees going for the berries."

Late in 1869, Elias Wightman had written from Janesville to AZE and ELIZA ".......We received a letter from Lee and Alice stateing that you, AZE, had a lame foot. We hope it has not hindered you from attending to your harvest. We have been troubled in secureing our grain on account of Rain. I have about one half of my stacking done and thare has been a number of days back that it has rained so hard that it has not dried enough to stack. I don't think thare is more than one fourth the grain in this vicinity stacked – My wheat is very good this year if I can secure it shall be able to make ends meet verry well this year in farming. It is on a small scale but it is an old saying and quite true that we must creep before we walk. It is my desire to feel thankful that it is as well with us as it is. I hear that you have been doing a considerable braking this year and making improvements on your farm – I guefs I must come down thare and see you before long as thare shall be so much of a change that I will not know where to find you, but I believe that you live in the second house East of William Stoakes on the same side of the road – no thare was some talk about living thare I believe but concluded to live on the opposite You have two children now I believe if we get started from home we shall have no difficulty finding you. We was some surprised to hear that George Kober wanted to sell and go to Kansas. I supposed that Missouri was the Elderado for him. I don't think I should ever want to go to Kansas In fact I don't know where to go to better Iowa for health and good farming country unlefs a person was to go to Oregon whare it is six months dry whitch would be verry nice to do stacking if nothing more.
"Sept. the 2nd. I am done stacking – and as I have an opportunity to send this to the PO will close pleas write soon. Your truly with Respect Elias Wightman"

A note was enclosed from Mary Wightman, too: "Dear Brother and Sister.......We was glad to hear that George and Lizzies little boy was getting better for I had thought a great deal about it since we heard he was sick how hard it would seem for them to part with him but I hope he is entirely well by this time and that he may still be spared to be a comfort to them. I am sorry to hear that Georgie still thinks of going to Kansas for we shall miss them so much when we come down thare visiting it will not seem right not to see them but I hope by this time that he has given up the idea of going. We would have liked very much to have gone home with Lee and Alice last spring but could not but we are going to make you all a visit as soon as we can. Kifs the children for me and give my love to all our folks with a large portion for yourselves. Please write soon from your true sister Mary Wightman."

Apparently George Kober wasn't thinking too seriously of selling and going to Kansas or else he changed his mind completely, for in 1870 he built a large two story frame house for Lizzie and himself and their growing family. The house was only a short distance from ELIZA and ELEAZER. The house was shuttered with many-paned windows, and was built with hewn logs for the sills and framework and was dowel pinned. The sills were made of oak, 8 by 8 inches. The large, beautiful, well built and well designed house must have been the envy of family and neighbors. It was set a considerable distance back from the road. Ninety years later the same house is still in good condition, a house of distinction, and still owned by the family.

ELIZA sometimes received a letter from the wife of ELEAZER'S brother John who stayed behind at Wellsville, Ohio although most of the Stoakes family had trekked to Iowa to buy land and live. This sister-in-law wrote from Wellsville Jany. 2nd, 1870, "I have no girl this winter and lots of work to do this Christmas and New Years time and we had a church festival and fair which took some two weeks time......letter from Iowa are few and far between We had one letter from Jane is all in a long time we have had no letter from Nancy Rider since she started home......Give my love to ELEAZER and Father and Mother STOAKES and all the rest John sends his love to all....from you sister E.A. Stoakes."

The bit of news that Nancy Rider had visited in Wellsville, Ohio is most interesting. Two decades earlier, in 1849, she and her husband and three small children had waved goodbye to her parents and brothers and sisters, all of whom still lived in Wellsville at the time, and the Riders headed West. They went first to Wisconsin and lived a few years, and then beckoned by the gold rush, went overland to Sacramento, Calif. where they lived the rest of their lives. In 1869, the Union Pacific and the Central Pacific railroads had come together with the driving of the golden spike at Salt Lake City linking the East with the far West by rail, making easy transcontinental travel possible for the first time in history. The western terminus was in Sacramento. It appears that ELEAZER'S oldest sister, Nancy, wasted no time in getting back to her old home town, Wellsville, for a visit. By then she was fifty years old and the mother of eight children. The Union Pacific ran from Chicago to Council Bluffs through Iowa. By that time her parents and most of her brothers and sisters were living in Tama county, Iowa. Chances are that she visited them, too. We have nothing that tells us she did. What a reunion that would have been!

The Grangers were still getting back and forth to visit each other and there was no lack of letters among them. Mary Wightman wrote from Jackson, Feb. 8th 1870 to ELIZA, "I expected to come out to your place again before we came home but we could not very well. We had a pretty cold ride coming home but did not care much for that we had such a good visit while we were down there."

Alice's husband, Lee Ferguson, was attending seminary in LeGrand, maybe studying for the ministry, for he became a minister. Alice wrote from LeGrand April 21, 1870, "Well ELIZA it seems odd enough to write you again but changes must come and friends must part but distance cannot change the heart I expect that Pa has told you what a time we had in getting here so it would be uselefs for me to write anything about it But I tell you we had a rather a dark time of it

We have finly got straightened around and fixed up comfortable I wish you could stop in and see us keep house all alone No one has eaten a meal with us yet but we have had quite a few callers I have got some acquainted with a few but being among all strangers is rather uphill businefs for me. I sometimes wish that I could see some of our own folks and have a good old fashioned talk But I shall get acquainted after a while and then I shall not feel lonely. Lee has been attending school nearly two weeks and likes it very well......We live in a pleasant part of town just across the street from the seminary It is pleasant to sit and watch the students come and go from school. I intend to commence to wean May next Saturday we have to buy milk for her five cents a quart for it we bought a cow soon after we came here for forty dollars but she has not come in yet and we do not know for certain when she will I do hope pretty soon for I am getting tired of doing without milk. May is beginning to talk. We heard from Pa last week. Give them our love We live very convenient to the church have sidewalks nearly all of the way I cannot tell you ELIZA how I like living in town sometimes I like it well and then again I think it is not so nice...when we got here baby needed a great deal of care she was so fretful I expect the little thing was lonesome. Lee has long lefsons to get and garden to make. Alice"

Days of GRANT'S Youth

The year 1870, Irish immigrants from Dubuque treked to Webster county, followed the Lizard Creek up to a site near the present town of Clare, and in 1871 completed a large church of worship, St. Patrick's Catholic Church, the first church built in Jackson township – where the POLLOCKS already lived.   Then the Irish built their homes around the church and the community became predominately Irish.

A protestant Sabbath School and Church had been organized in Jackson Center in 1870 and services conducted by the Rev. L. S. Coffin. Both Sabbath School and Church Services were held in the schoolhouse. Rev. Coffin had officiated at the marriage of WILLIAM and MARY POLLOCK and was a friend of the family.

With railroads taking over, the last Concord wagon stopped running in Iowa in 1870.

General Grant (military hero for whom GRANT POLLOCK was named) had become United States president and was occupying the Executive Mansion in the nation's capital. Under his predecessor, Johnson, the U.S. had purchased Alaska for seven million dollars, and in Mexico, Emperor Maximilian, abandoned by the French after a short reign, had been shot by the Mexicans. President Grant was not proving to be a brilliant administrator and spoilsmen were pressing in on him and his own cabinet of able men were dropping away. Gould and Fisk, financiers, had been trying to corner the gold market resulting in the disaster known in history as Black Friday.

A now faded sheet from ROBERT GRANGER'S farming accounts showed he was getting as high as 30 cents a pound for butter in 1869, but by 1871 was getting only 12 ½ cents and even as low as nine.

A third son was born to ELEAZER and ELIZA in 1870, Dewitt C.

An immigrant Danish couple, the Peter Jensens, living six miles northwest of the Rolfe settlement, became the parents of their first born, called Anna, in early August 1871. (She was to become the daughter-in-law of WILLIAM and MARY POLLOCK, and when past ninety years old was the person who suggested and inspired this Chronology of family history and charged, "Margaret, if you don't do it, much about the family members of the past will be lost." She has been a constant help in this compilation.)

Winter was drawing to a close, and spring was only a few weeks away, when the dread epidemic of membraneous croup hit the Jared Fuller home tucked among the wooded hills of Holiday Creek. That was a winter disease, Anna Pollock says, now known as diphtheria. Within nine days, three of the five sons were dead. To be seen today in the neatly kept little Holiday Creek cemetery are the three little Fuller headstones with the lettering partially obliterated by time but with the initials and dates clear: J.B.F. (James B.), J.F (young Jared) and A.F. (Arthur) and dates of death Mar. 11, 19 and 20, 1872.

Only Markie and Eddie survived, approximately 14 and 12 years old at the time. James was the oldest in the family, about 16. Jared and Arthur were the youngest. Their mother Sarah had died five years earlier. MARY POLLOCK had worried about these motherless sons of her sister Sarah. MARY feared "they were growing up wild down in the hills." The death of the three must have grieved her deeply. She had opened her heart and her home to all five boys. To them "AUNT MARY" was a very dear person, GRANT often said. The boys visited the Pollock home very often and stayed for periods of time.

In GRANT'S own advanced years, one of his great joys was to hear his own daughter Mary recite James Whitcomb Riley's "Out to Old Aunt Mary's." What memories it must have conjured up for him:

"Wasn't it pleasant, O brother mine.
In those old days of the lost sunshine
Of youth – when the Saturday's chores were through,
And the "Sunday's wood" in the kitchen, too.
And we went visiting, "me and you,"
Out to Old Aunt Mary's!

"It all comes back so clear today!
Though I am as bald as you are gray –
Out to the barn-lot, and down the lane,
We patter along in the dust again,
As light as the tips of the drops of the rain,
Out to Old Aunt Mary's!

"We cross the pasture, and through the wood
Where the old gray snag of the poplar stood,
Where the hammering red-heads hopped awry
And the buzzard "raised" in the clearing sky,
And lolled and circled, as we went by,
Out to Old Aunt Mary's

"And then in the dust of the road again;
And the teams we met, and the countrymen;
And the long highway, with sunshine spread
As thick as butter on country bread,
Our cares behind, and our hearts ahead
Out to Old Aunt Mary's.

"Why, I see her now in the open door,
Where the little gourds grew up the sides, and o'er
The clapboard roof! – ah, me!
Wasn't it good for a boy to be
Out to Old Aunt Mary's?

"The jelly – the jam and the marmalade,
And the cherry and quince 'preserves' she made!
And the sweet-sour pickles of peach and pear,
With cinnamon in 'em, and all things rare!-
And the more we ate was the more to spare,
Out to Old Aunt Mary's!

"And the old spring-house in the cool green gloom
Of the willow-trees, and the cooler room
Where the swinging-shelves and the crocks were kept –
Where the cream in a golden languor slept
While the waters gurgled and laughed and wept –
Out to Old Aunt Mary's!

"And as many a time have you and I –
Barefoot boys in the days gone by –
Knelt, and in tremulous ecstacies
Dipped out lips into sweets like these, -
Memory now is on her knees
Out to Old Aunt Mary's

"And O, my brother, so far away,
This is to tell you she waits today
To welcome us: -Aunt Mary fell
Asleep this morning, whispering "Tell
The boys to come!" And all is well
Out to Old Aunt's Mary's!

Now only Markie and Eddie were left to come visiting AUNT MARY'S and to enjoy the company of her own children: Will 13, Jennie 11, GRANT 8, Jim 5, Emma 3. And in the midst of this grief, a new daughter was born to the Pollocks and named Harriet Mae.

The Pollock household was soon to echo with the voices of a whole family of new cousins never seen before. Twenty years earlier, WILLIAM POLLOCK, his brother Thomas and two other young men had come to America from Scotland, had become lost from each other in New York City, and gone their separate ways. Thomas had settled in Canada, after a trip to the California gold rush, had married and become the father of a large family. Now in 1872 he moved this family to Webster county, Iowa and was reunited with his brother WILLIAM. Thomas' children ranging in age from 17 down to 5 years and in order of their birth were: Sarah, William, Elizabeth, David, Annabelle and Mary Jane. Two children, another David and Tennet, were deceased.

Thomas settled his family not many miles away from WILLIAM on a farm near Barnum. There was a stone quarry on that farm. WILLIAM taught Thomas some of the elemental skills of cutting stone and the two brothers worked together sometimes at this and sometimes at carpentry work. They built a large round barn for Rev. Coffin west of Fort Dodge which still stand, and cut stone and helped build the old A.B. White store building, and the old schoolhouse both in Humboldt. WILLIAM also did stone work on the A.B Symes building in Rolfe, and the courthouse in Fort Dodge.

By 1872 all of the four Granger sisters had become mothers. In the last one of the treasured letters, Mary Wightman writing from Janesville, April 14th of that year telling of her baby son and warning ELIZA not to work so hard: ".........we were sorry to hear of the bad luck you had in your horse getting kicked so badly.......Lee and Alice were here a week ago they were well and getting along quite well with their house   thought they might get moved into it the last of this last week. Alice seemed greatly animated with prospects of getting a home of their own on their own place. Our baby seems to be getting quite healthy now and is quite a tall child but not very fleshy. He is a great pet of all of us   his name is Lyman Granger Wightman.........we are having quite a cold wet spring here   there is but little wheat sown yet. Elias intends to commence this week if the weather is favorable and he gets a horse as he expects to now. One of our horses is sick and we expect to lose her. She is not very valuable but it will break up our team and we are obliged to buy one to get along with the work. I think ELIZA with your three children to take care of and the milk of seven cows you <u>will</u> have your hands <u>full</u> but if I were you I would not work so hard as to injure your health   it will not be much profit to you in the end."

The Wightmans through the years became the parents of two sons and three daughters, the youngest being twin girls.

The Iowa capitol building was begun in Des Moines in 1873 and was not completed until 1886. WILLIAM POLLOCK did much stone work on this historic building and of necessity was away from home for relatively long periods at a time. As years passed, his sons took over more and more of the farm work.

The financial panic of 1873 hit the nation hard and lasted for several years. Out West where the new settlers had shorted themselves on money in order to buy land and equipment, the panic pressed down hard upon them. POLLOCK, no doubt, was fortunate in having his old country skill of stonecutting and did not have to depend completely on the output of his farm to provide for his wife and six children. This, it is presumed, pushed his young sons into more of the farm work earlier than they otherwise would have been. President Grant was blamed for the panic and young GRANT POLLOCK at a sensitive age had to bear the load of carrying that name. Never throughout the rest of his life did he like the name very well.

With WILLIAM away from home so much of the time, the Pollock children grew up extra ordinarily close to their mother. When work was first begun on this family history and most of the and most of the grandchildren were contacted to see what memories or knowledge they had of her, everyone came back with the same initial statement, "She was much loved by all of her children."

Following this came other information, "She had a great gentleness and warmth, was quiet and mild." "She made wonderful bread and was a fine butter maker." "She had a hearty laugh." "Her children took their problems, their sorrows and their joys to her knowing they would find understanding." "She was a fleshy person, carried quite a bit of weight. She liked to serve cheese – her own homemade pressed cheese."

Money might be hard to get then but the Pollock family never lacked for love or food. WILLIAM'S timberland was full of things to eat: fish to catch; rabbits, doves, prairie chickens and waterfowl to shoot; hickory nuts, butternuts and walnuts to gather; wild plum, grapes, gooseberries and strawberries to pick. These combined with meat (home butchered), milk, eggs, vegetables, cane sorghum and dried apples from the farm made an abundant and healthy diet for the growing family. Meat was usually smoked or put down in brine.

Prairie fires were dreaded. Anna Jensen Pollock has written of her experience with one when she was only a little past two years old: "We lived in a two room log house with an attic above and a dirt cellar beneath on section 8, Des Moines township, Pocahontas county in northern Iowa....One day my father took a load of wheat to Springvale (now called Humboldt) to have it ground into flour for our winter use. It took two or three days for he had to wait his turn at the grist mill. He paid the miller with a toll of flour, shorts and bran.

"My mother, with an infant child three weeks old and with me who was a little more than two years old, of course, stayed home. All went well with the chores, milking and household duties until the afternoon of the third day when the wind arose to a great velocity. With it came the roaring prairie fire from the vast uncultivated region northwest of us. The tall slough grass was easily kindled, the tumble weeds as large as bushel baskets flew over the firebreaks.

"These firebreaks were made by plowing several rows of furrows around the haystacks which were out in the open. Around this circle of plowing was left an open space and then another circle of rows of plowing of great circumference was made. The space between them was burned off. This sort of firebreak was also made around farm homes and buildings.

"The fire came with a great roar and the flames leaped as high as the tree tops, burning off the leaves and small branches. My mother ran into the cow yard, opened the bars and let the cattle and hogs out. Fortunately the horses, the wheat and the wagon had gone to the mill. Then she dragged us children out into the middle of the plowed field where she left us and gave me strict orders to stay there and mind the baby. She rushed back to the log house and carried clothing, bedding and whatever else her strength enabled her to bring to this place of safety.

"My father, coming home with the grist of wheat products, could see, hear and smell the fire when he was still miles away. Fearing the worst had happened to his family and possessions, he urged the team of horses on at a terrible rate of speed and yet he said 'It seemed as if they were not moving and that I could jump out and run faster.'

"When he reached home some of the neighbors who had saved some of their own belongings were on hand and were using buckets of water, wet sacks, mops and old brooms in trying to save the log house, our home.

"Anyway we had the house and its contents, even if all the other buildings, the rail fences, hay stacks and winter quarters for the animals were gone. We still had the potatoes which had not been dug, the flour from the load of wheat, and could milk the cows and thus be assured of bread and milk diet. Many other pioneers hardships can be enumerated but we never went hungry.

"Even though I was very young at that time, my memory shows me a picture of the log house surrounded by blackness and cinders which occasionally showed a gleam of red in the darkness. And of my father sitting at the northwest corner of the log house with buckets of water, soaked grain sacks, the wet mop and broom. He was one man fire department to quench the first red cinder, flame or spark of fire that might develop."

The panic of 1873 would bring the booming railroad construction almost to a standstill for a period of years. Not, however, before the rails of the Burlington, Cedar Rapids and Northern were laid in Tama county. When the railroad did come to the county, the rails didn't pass through either of the rival towns of Buckingham or West Union but went exactly between the two where the Eldora Trail crossed Wolf Creek. That was at the southwest corner of the cluster of Stoakes and Granger farms. There the town of Traer grew. A Tama county history says, "On July 28, 1873, a work train whistled with certain officials and their wives sitting in state on the platform built in front of the cow catcher. The mayor was wearing a tall silk hat and a large crowd was on hand to meet them. It was a great day for the new town as the disappointed businessmen of Buckingham began preparations to move. Their shops, homes and churches all were moved to the new town of Traer on the railroad. Soon nothing was left but a few houses and the two story school building. Old Buckingham became a ghost town. Both villages, the West Union settlement like Old Buckingham, vanished."

Today there really is a small town of Buckingham north of Traer and a neatly kept Buckingham cemetery. All that is left of West Union is a cemetery.

The history continues, "Traer became a boom town, the terminus of the railroad for four years.....There was no railroad extending on west or northwest, and wheat, the main crop, was hauled here to market from a distance of 30 or 40 miles. The new town had four elevators within a few months......Traer's population grew to 800 in two years......By this time 17 places in Traer sold liquor with brisk business when the railroad men drew their pay."

ELEAZER'S sister, Martha Jane Cope, became a widow for the second time when her husband, L.S. Cope, with whom she had moved from Tama county to Waterloo seven years earlier, died. She had opened a millinery store there. After his death she moved to Traer and opened the shop there. By then she was a grandmother. Her only living child, John S. Hopkins was married and the father of several children.

That same year, ELIZA'S sister, Lizzie Kober, was left a widow. The Kober farm with the big house was close to ELEAZER and ELIZA. There were six little Kober children.

The book "They Came to North Tama" says: "In 1873, George Kober and John Axon plowed up wild parsnips. They looked good. Axon peeled some and they both ate. On the way to dinner Axon felt the results. He was helped to bed by Kober who also said he would lie down as he was not feeling well. In a short time both men were dead. Doctors do not know to this day the antidote for the poison of wild parsnip."

The Kober children, Hattie, Mary, John, Sarah and Ermina ranged in age from 13 years to a baby. A son Samuel had died in infancy.

But Lizzie did not remain a widow long. The following May, 1874, she married her late husband's brother John who had worked for them and he became a kindly father to the children. He was a German immigrant who had lived in North Tama for a dozen years. He and Lizzie became the parents of five more children namely Theodore, Amelia, Frank, Katie and Emma.

ELIZA and ELEAZER, parents of three sons Theodore, George and Dewitt, became the parents of their first daughter in 1874. ELIZA named the baby after her own joyous, gay young sister, Alice. This is the same year a boy with a great destiny was born at West Branch, Iowa – Herbert Hoover.

A few months later ELIZA'S parents, MR. and MRS. ROBERT GRANGER decided to retire from their farm and moved into a modest home at Traer. He was 67. She was 65. Part of the time while they lived in Traer he was street commissioner. Their daughter Mary Granger Wightman and her husband, who had lived on so many different rented farms, came back to Tama county to farm the Granger land. Now three of the four sisters, who long ago as little girls had driven their father's cattle cross country when the family moved by covered wagon from Illinois to Tama county, were living side by side again: Lizzie Kober, Mary Wightman, and ELIZA STOAKES. Only their youngest sister, Alice Ferguson, was living at a distance.

Up at the WILLIAM and MARY POLLOCK home, the last of their seven children was born in 1875 and WILLIAM named her Exie. Anna Pollock says, "He got the name from Scotland. He may have had a sister by that name."

The official registry in Edinburgh, Scotland records one sister's full name as "Elizabeth Leckie Pollock born 1841" – so she would have been about ten years old when WILLIAM left Scotland. The spelling probably was changed from Leckie to Exie.

Sometime during the years the children were growing up, WILLIAM cut stone and built the family a two story stone house. He located it on a little tributary of Lizard Creek where the land was rolling and wooded and scenic. A big fireplace was part of the interior. Outside he planted pine trees, which grow tall, at the two corners of the house on the east side. Anna Pollock says that it looked like it was patterned after some old castle he might have remembered in Scotland. From the road, one had to cross a little bridge over the little stream to reach the house. Some of his children, partially grown and probably at a criticizing stage, wished he had built the house up along side of the road "like other people" and put two doors in the house instead of one.

Jared Fuller and Markie and Eddie had moved from Holiday Creek back to Fort Dodge and Jared had been elected county clerk in which office he served two years – two terms.

Through the years when the Pollock boys were small, the Indians from Tama county came along the streams of northwest Iowa to hunt and trap and fish. GRANT, when he had children of his own, told tales about these Indians: how he and Jim would daringly examine the muskrats in the

Indian traps, and how one day he and an Indian boy had even removed some of the muskrats. Another memory included the time GRANT was working alone in a field and heard someone give a grunt behind him. He looked around into the face of an Indian boy his own age. To his children, "Daddy had lived a long time ago and his stories were wonderfully fascinating and frightening." He was asked repeatedly to tell them again. History says that the last Indians from Tama came through Webster county in 1875. Webster was a populated county by then: 13,114 people. By the following year, there were three schools in Jackson township with a total enrollment of 141 scholars.

The Pollock children attended the one room Preston school walking the mile and a half southwest of their home through the woods and along Lizard Creek. What a magnificent route to school in good weather! A child could hop back and forth on stepping stones across the creek. The majestic elms, the maples, the basswood and the nut trees towered overhead. In the spring, the woods was fragrant with wild plum blossoms, purple violets and dozens of other flowers. The many gooseberry bushes dotting the woods were emerald green.

GRANT used to tell of his and Jim's coming upon a pond of water lilies in bloom enroute home one day. He said, "It didn't take us long to skin out of our clothes and wade in to pick a bouquet for mother," and his account always ended, "My, oh, my, how she loved them!"

The site of the Preston school is something to remember. GRANT took some of his children there one time when only the foundation was left. The school nestled in the woods on a hill looking down on a loop of Lizard Creek meandering through the woods below.

The school accommodated all eight grades with just one teacher. The children sat in double seats. GRANT often shared a seat with his Irish friend Mike Conlon. There was a heating stove, a blackboard and a pail of water which had to be carried fresh each day.

Here the children learned their lessons from the old McGuffey books. Long passages of the readers were committed to memory. In their later years, Jennie and GRANT used to vie good naturedly with each other to see who could recite the most by memory.

The poem GRANT'S children liked best was the one he'd shout from the bottom of the stairs to awaken them on the first snowy morning in the winter. Or maybe it would come when he arrived home from work in the early darkness, and open the door, stomp the snow from his feet and sing out:

"'It snows!' cries the school boy
Hurrah and his shout are ringing
Through parlour and hall,
While swift as the wings of
The swallow, he's out
And his playmates have
Answered his call.

"It makes the heart leap

To witness such joy.
Proud wealth has no
Pleasure I trove
As the rapture that thrills
In the pulse of a boy
As he gathers his treasure
Of snow."

Singing out that poem became a ritual each year with him and his children at the first sight of snowflakes. His youngest daughter Jean especially loved the merry ritual.

Rolfe ceased to be the county seat in 1876. County offices and records were moved to the center of the county to the town of Pocahontas.

Fort Dodge business firms in 1876 were advertising: Pianos, organs and other musical instruments; Gentlemen's Parlor – shaving, hair dressing, hair dying done in the highest styles of art; Patterson House with excellent table, good rooms and clean beds; Western House – first class accommodations to man and beast; Bakery and Confectionary with oysters and ice cream in season; Photography gallery; Book seller; staple and fancy groceries; suits made to order.

Indian battles were still being fought on the western plains – in Montana, Colorado, Wyoming, Oklahoma. A transcontinental railroad had pushed through this area, game had been ruthlessly killed off by the Whites, and settlers were continuing to push westward looking for land. Indians were fighting to retain some small part of the vast land they had once owned.

The Whites were handed a humiliating defeat in the Battle of the Little Big Horns, news of which reached the Eastern papers July 6, 1876 as the country was in the act of congratulating itself on its first 100 years. Two years earlier gold had been found in the Black Hills. Although the Hills had been guaranteed to the Indians by treaty, the discovery of gold put a different value on the Hills for the white man. With the use of troops they "persuaded" the Indians to sell. Now two years later some of the Indians were still "unpersuaded." Crazy Horse and Sitting Bull had gathered Indians – some say up to 6,000 – on the Little Big Horn river. General George Custer with a force of 264 men moved against the Indians, not knowing how many Indians there were and not waiting for other army troops to move up. Custer and all his men were surrounded by the Indians and annihilated. This news reached the East July 6. Then the army in great numbers moved against the Indians hunting them down and driving others into Canada. It was the end for the red man but the dying wail went on for years even as late as 1890.

As the years rolled along, births and deaths were noted in the families. Another daughter, Ella Mae, came to ELEAZER and ELIZA in 1877. Thomas Pollock's oldest daughter, Sarah,, died.

The oldest WILLIAM POLLOCK daughter, the pretty one with the dark hair, beautiful eyes and queenly carriage, Jennie, started teaching. She was just 16 and did her first teaching in country school in 1877. Such a young girl and no doubt some of her scholars big boys larger than she and maybe older. This was the beginning of a long teaching career, a profession she thoroughly loved. She taught 55 years, 45 years of which were spent in the Fort Dodge schools. She first taught in town in the grade school called Lincoln; then went as principal to Wahkonsa school, and in 1901 returned to Lincoln as principal, a post she held for 31 years.

 With the beginning of a new decade, on Feb. 11, 1880, the old gentleman JOHN STOAKES passed away at the age of 87 and was buried in Tama county. He had come as a young boy from England with his older brother, their little sister (who died before completing the journey) and their mother to join the father who had come to America two years earlier to carve out a home in the wilderness of Ohio. When JOHN'S children were mostly grown, he and their mother (JANE VANTILBURG STOAKES) had come West with most of the children to buy land and make their homes in Iowa. JOHN and JANE were the parents of 11 children, grandparents to 63, and are the ancestors of all the many Stoakes living in Tama county today. JANE, who had been born in a government fort, died at 72 seven years ahead of her husband. ELEAZER and the other children highly respected their parents and had always lived in close association with them. The deaths of the old couple undoubtedly was felt deeply by all of them. Time was marching on.

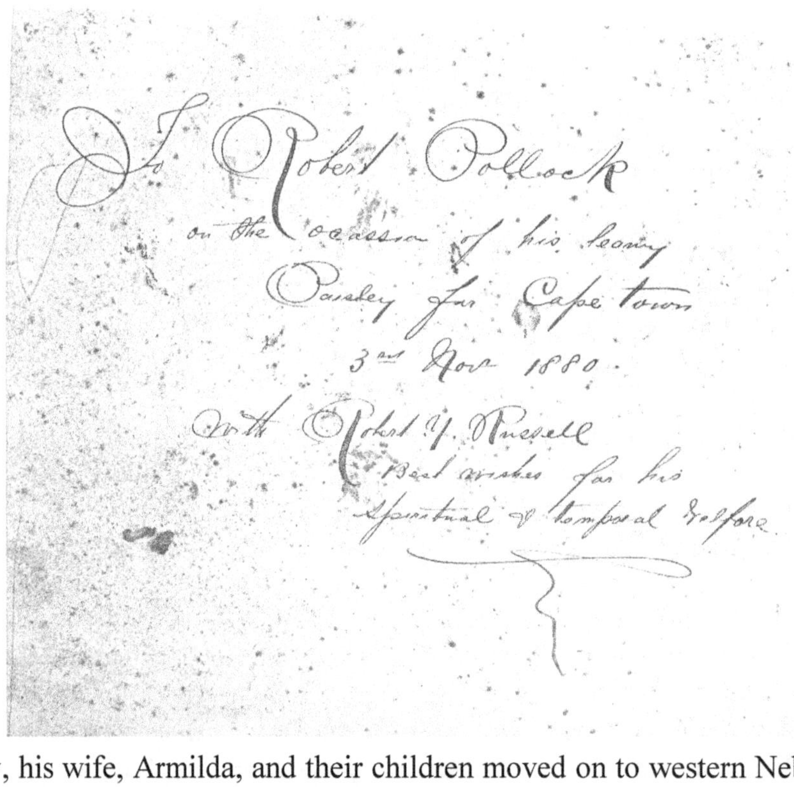

The son Henry Stoakes, who had come with the parents, brothers and sisters in the caravan into Tama county in 1855, now in 1880 moved still farther west to O'Brien county, Iowa. Later Henry, his wife, Armilda, and their children moved on to western Nebraska and subsequently to southern Missouri. There were eleven children.

Events of interest to WILLIAM and MARY POLLOCK were occurring overseas and in eastern United States.

When WILLIAM and Thomas Pollock, nearly thirty years ago he left their boyhood home in Scotland to come to America, a little brother had followed them down the lane crying to go along. Presumably that was Robert who would have been eight then. Now in 1880 Robert was leaving Scotland for Capetown, South Africa.

A large book, yellowed with age, "The Sunday Magazine for Family Living," still in the family, has this written inside the front cover, "To Robert Pollock on the occasion of his leaving Paisley for Cape town 3rd Nov., 1880 with Robert Y. Russell Best wishes for his spiritual and temporal welfare." No one now knows anything about Robert Y. Russell. Robert Pollock was 36 years old then.

Word of mouth stories down through the years say the Robert was attracted by the Kimberley diamond mines. Working of these renowned mines had started nine years earlier when the British flag was first raised there. How long Robert stayed no one seems to know. He did go to Australia later to see if that would be a country he would like. How long he stayed or whether he went back to Scotland, we do not know, but years later he did come to America, but that will fit into the chronology as time unfolds.

MARY POLLOCK'S oldest brother, Robert Beates, of who she was very fond and very proud, was elected to the New York State Legislature in 1880. Years ago he had bought their father's farm – their childhood home – and expanded it. He was a successful farmer, a lumberman, and a Sunday school superintendent. (These two "Uncle Roberts" may have been the reason GRANT'S own son was later names Robert.)

The same year, Robert Beates' and MARY POLLOCK'S youngest sister died at the age of 45. Mrs. Bolivar (Harriet) Horton had lived all of her life in the East, was the mother of nine children. The youngest was Walter. When this chronology was started, Walter was still living (in Florida) and when asked about memories of his mother, he wrote that he really didn't remember her for he was only two and a half when she died.

Of course this death would grieve MARY POLLOCK and it had an added significance for her. Her own mother and now both of her sisters had died when their big families were only partially reared. MARY had seven children of her own, and now she worried that she might not live to rear all of her own children. (MARY'S granddaughter and namesake, Mary Pollock, says, "Dad told me that he (GRANT) used to wish passionately with all of his heart that his mother would live forever. When she did go – at age 85 – Dad was satisfied knowing that his mother had lived as long as she wanted to live.")

When GRANT was 17 years old, he and Jim and "some of the boys" were riding horseback to Manson for the Fourth of July Celebration. Enroute, a man came hurrying down his farm lane and stopped them, "Boys, I have just heard that our president has been assassinated. Will you try to find out something about it in town and stop on your way home and tell me?"

News moved by telegraph service to towns and then spread into the country by word of mouth. Garfield had just been inaugurated that year, 1881, on March 4. He identified himself with the cause of civil service reform irritating some folks. On the morning of July 2 he was about to leave Washington for an appointed function when he was shot by a disappointed office-seeker. He lingered between life and death for weeks and died in September.

The boys were able to confirm the shooting of Garfield and get a few details and stopped enroute home to tell the farmer.

Maybe this was the Fourth of July GRANT remembered as having spent his money for lemons. The lemons were a novelty to the boys and they bit off the ends and gradually sucked out the juice savoring it as one would a confectionary.

Two days after this Fourth of July, a 15 year old girl – not many miles from Fort Dodge – was to receive nation-wide acclaim for her brave deed in saving a train with hundreds of passengers from a serious wreck. Kate Shelley lived with her widowed mother near the Chicago and Northwestern tracks between Boone and Ogden where Honey Creek empties into the Des Moines River.

It was a dark rainy night and the water was rising in both the creek and the river. A gale was blowing. From the window of her home, during a flash of lightning, she saw the pusher – an engine used to push trains up grades – and she saw it break through the creek bridge. She grabbed a lantern and rushed out into the wild night. She could see the two men from the pusher clinging to a tree down stream but could do nothing to help them. Her thoughts were with the Midnight Express with its hundreds of passengers hurtling through the night toward death. She found she could get to the big high bridge – 600 feet long – and without hesitating began the perilous crossing. The terrific wind, the driving rain and the darkness with flashes of lightening forced her to crawl on her hands and knees even over spots where there were wide open spaces between the ties. Projecting spikes tore at her hands and knees. But she arrived safely at the far side, ran a quarter of a mile to the little Moingona station and alerted the trainmen. They flagged to a stop the Midnight Express and later rescued the two men from the raging creek. Her exploit became the subject of editorials, dramatic readings, poems, some of which even found their way into school readers. The Iowa Legislature gave Kate a medal and $200. The Chicago Tribune presented her with $500. (The Pollock school children memorized some of this poetry.) The long bridge across the river was officially named the Kate Shelley Bridge, and when the bridge was replaced with a fine new one three-quarters of a century later, it was rededicated with the same name, and her grandson, a well known Iowa radio broadcaster, Jack Shelley, was honored guest and speaker.

The laying of the Des Moines and Fort Dodge railroad tracks and those of the Toledo and Northwestern in 1882 brought them to a crossing point a few miles southwest of Rolfe. This was the age of railroads and the crossing of the lines started the immediate demise of the little Rolfe settlement on the Des Moines river. A new town was platted that autumn and a postoffice located at the crossing point. Residents of the old town moved to the new location bringing the town's name of "Rolfe" with them leaving the old town to be called for awhile "Parvin" and later just "Old Rolfe."

BELLE Born, Grows Up

In Tama county, a tiny daughter was born March 7, 1882 to ELEAZER and ELIZA STOAKES, just three days after her father's forty-eighth birthday. Her mother was thirty-eight. The wee one was named MARIE BELLE, to be known as BELLE. She was welcomed by three brothers and two sisters: Theodore 15, George 14, Dewitt 12, Alice 8 and Ella 5. Through the years the custom was that the father and this youngest child celebrate their birthdays together.

When BELLE was nearly five months old, she was still so tiny that she was carefully carried on a pillow when she was taken to the Golden Wedding of her maternal grandparents. ROBERT GRANGER and ELIZABETH NEWMAN had been married back in their hometown of Cambridgeshire, England July 29, 1832. Now their children and grandchildren gathered at their modest home in Traer to observe the passing of half a century. The living children were the four daughters who had driven the cattle from Lake county, Illinois to Tama county, Iowa – Lizzie, ELIZA, Mary and Alice. Four other children were deceased in childhood.

The home was too small to accommodate the family and friends, so the celebration to include the friends was held at the Congregational church. ROBERT GRANGER was presented with a gold headed cane engraved "R. GRANGER from his friends 1832-1882." What gift friends may have given MRS.

GRANGER, this writer does not know. The family presented each with a comfortable upholstered chair. The cane became a keepsake of Theodore Stoakes, and the chairs were handed down to Ermina Kober.

Martha Jane Stoakes Hopkins Cope, twice widowed, married John Wilson in 1882.

Some year, around this time, ELEAZER and ELIZA built themselves a fine new house on their farm. Harold Stoakes, who had lived all of his life near by, thinks the house was erected in 1879 when his father Theodore was 12 years old. Other sources say it was built a few years later. So BELLE was born in the new house or moved into it when she was a very young child. It would be the only childhood home she remembered. The new house was located close to the old which was later removed.

The two story frame house had at least five gables, the lines of which were softened with a modest bit of gingerbread. Gingerbread also ornamented the pillars of the front porch giving the house style. The house faced south. The horse barn was east of the house and northwest of the house was a large timber of trees that served as a wind break. The farm sometime grew from the initial 217 acres to 320 acres.

Harold Stoakes has drawn a floor plan as he remembers it and as he thinks I might remember it. I have no memories of the interior but pleasant memories of the surrounding yard: ants crawling around among the delicate petals of pink peonies when I was just tall enough to peer into them. Also white roses and the wonderful fragrance of honeysuckle. The tall white pines in the front yard dropped a soft carpet of needles which was fun to walk upon. Cora Belle Pollock remembers Grandfather's fine carriage with which he would meet us at the train when BELLE took her little children home for a visit.

Harold's drawings are as follows:

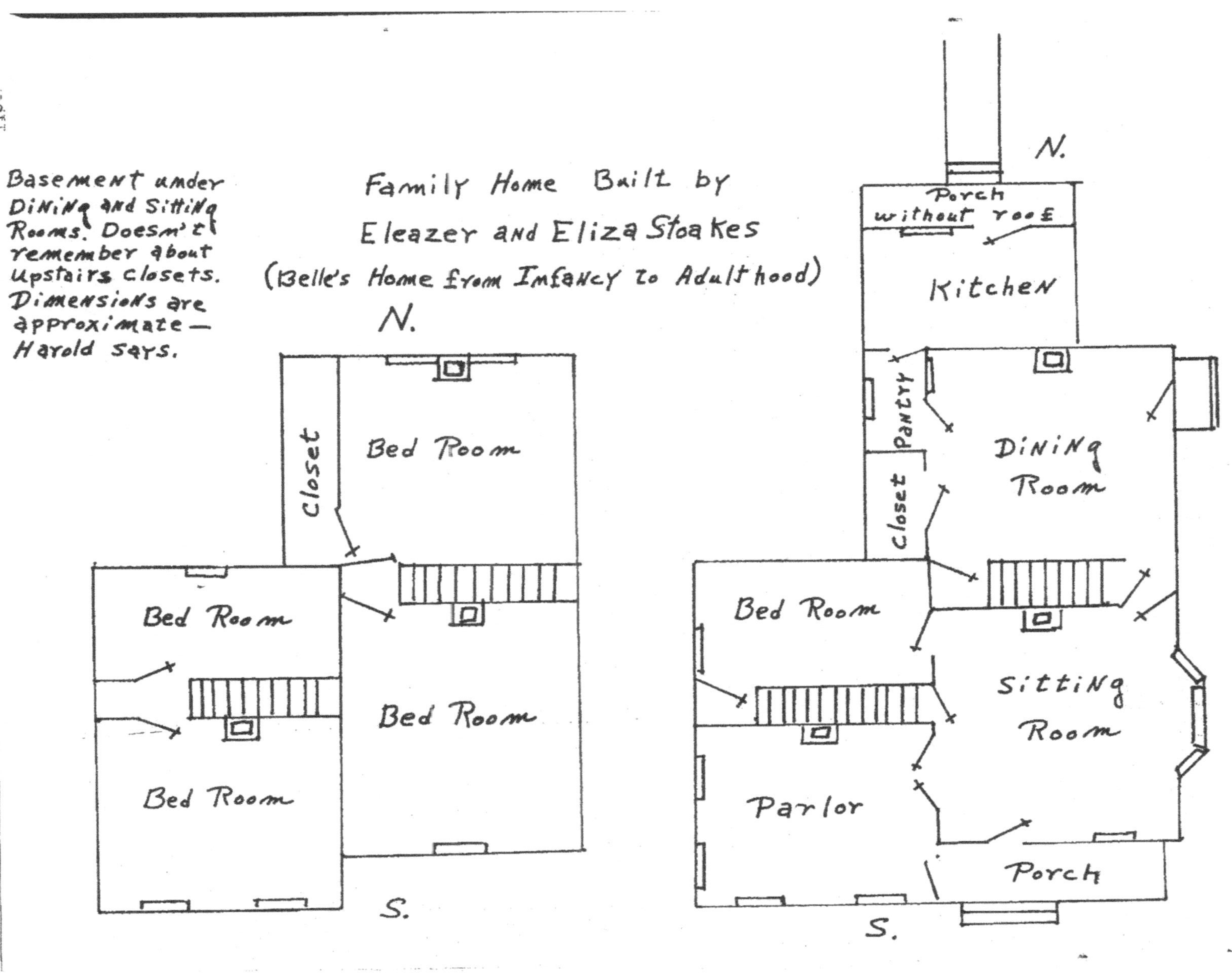

Basement under Dining and Sitting Rooms. Doesn't remember about Upstairs closets. Dimensions are approximate — Harold says.
Family Home Built by Eleazer and Eliza Stoakes
(Belle's Home from Infancy to Adulthood)
N.
Closet
Bed Room
Bed Room
Bed Room
Bed Room
S.
N.
Porch without roof
Kitchen
Closet
Pantry
Dining Room
Bed Room
Sitting Room
Parlor
Porch
S.
137

BELLE used to tell of helping, as a child, stretch the lace curtains on frames to dry at housecleaning time. She remembered the grograin carpeting being taken up in the summer, the old straw removed from under the carpeting and fresh straw being put down for padding. The carpet would be stretched and tacked down for another year. Large framed pictures of her father and mother hung on the walls. In the sitting room was a heavy, finely polished walnut secretary with a desk and a row of shelves above for books. This is now the property of a grandson, Fred V. Stoakes. The only interior picture BELLE had of this childhood home shows an upholstered rocker and settee, probably in the parlour.

When BELLE was a baby her father's sister Sarah and husband B. Frank Thomas (who had kept the Civil War diary) rented their farm and moved into Traer. They bought a hardware store. They moved to town to afford their sons better educational opportunities. Two became lawyers, one a physician, one later operated the store, and another ran a greenhouse.

BELLE had 75 first cousins! Many of them lived in the neighborhood but some were scattered as far away as California and Ohio. The oldest was 42 years old before BELLE was born. She was the youngest of all the Stoakes cousins living in Tama county. The Henry Stoakes in O'Brien county had one daughter younger. BELLE'S special Stoakes cousin was Esther, the youngest child of her father's youngest brother George. Esther was born a few months before BELLE and they went to school together and graduated high school in the same class.

When BELLE was a growing child, she knew well all of her father's brothers and sisters, and their spouses and children living nearby. Aunt Jane (Martha Jane Hopkins Cope Wilson) lived in Traer. Her only living child was grown with children of his own. Uncle John and Elizabeth Stoakes lived to the east 2 or 3 miles but of their five children, the youngest was 20 when BELLE was born. Uncle William and Aunt Caroline Stoakes lived southeast of Traer about 3 miles and of their 13 children, the oldest was 42 and the youngest was 12 when BELLE was born. Uncle B. Frank Thomas and Aunt Sarah Stoakes Thomas and their seven sons lived in town and the youngest was three years older than BELLE. Uncle Hugh Gaston and Aunt Elizabeth Stoakes Gaston and their nine children, the oldest 19 and the youngest three when BELLE was born, lived between BELLE'S home and Traer, a couple of three miles away. Uncle George and Aunt Alice Stoakes lived on the home place (FATHER JOHN'S original farm) close by with nine children, the oldest 15 years older than BELLE and the youngest Esther. Little Aunt Callie (California) Stoakes never married and was a frequent visitor in ELEAZER'S home, so much so that one bedroom was called Aunt Callie's room.

The Stoakes cousins were so numerous that in her adult life BELLE just referred to them as "the cousins." A few stand out in the minds of her children: Esther; John Hopkins who lived at Bradgate (who wrote the Stoakes Family History together with another cousin Arthur H. Thomas of Traer who compiled data); "Uncle Matt" a loved person 42 years BELLE'S senior who somehow was called "'uncle" rather than "cousin"; and the Thomas boys. To further complicate the situation, many of her cousin's children were her own age – and these were too, too, too numerous to even count. Two that stand out are: the grandsons of Uncle William and Aunt Caroline namely Ralph who lived in Fort Dodge and was the father of the triplets, and Howard who lived in Humboldt. Both men and their families frequently visited BELLE'S future home in Rolfe.

The cousins with whom BELLE and her sisters and brothers lived in even closer association were with her mother's sister, Aunt Lizzie Kober's eleven children. They were of an age span to fit with ELIZA'S and ELEAZER'S children and also lived close by. Eight were older that BELLE: Hattie, Mary, Elias, John, Sarah, Ermina, Theodore and Amelia. Younger than BELLE were: Frank, Kate, and Emma. And recently moved to the ROBERT GRANGER farm was Uncle Elias and Aunt Mary Wightman and their five children, the oldest being ten years BELLE'S senior. The seventy-fifth cousin was May, only child of Uncle Lee and Aunt Alice Granger Ferguson, and they lived at a distance.

BELLE was two when her brother Dewitt died at the age of 14 with measles, so through her life he was more of a name than a person to her. ELEAZER and ELIZA had lost another child in infancy.

WILLIAM POLLOCK added to the size of his farm in 1884. A deed from the Iowa Homestead Company of Dubuque conveyed 82 acres to him for the sum of $600.

That was the year a new boat called "The Queen" – built by the Dubuque Boat and Boiler Works – was hauled to Spirit Lake on a railroad flat car and launched. It plied the waters of the Iowa Great Lakes for 89 years, first on Spirit Lake and then on West Okoboji. As a child, BELLE once went with a Sunday School excursion to these lakes and always remembered with delight her ride on one of the big lake boats.

When BELLE was five years old, her grandfather, ROBERT GRANGER, died. He and Mrs. Granger had moved back to the farm from Traer and had been living with their son-in-law and daughter, Elias and Mary Wightman. Three rooms had been built onto the house so the GRANGERS could move back there and spend their last days. GRANGER was 80 years old when he died leaving his wife and four daughters. Born in England, he had arrived in Tama county in 1854 and since then had never left the state. His obituary says, "GRANGER is one of the men to whom we owe so much as a community. Coming here in an early day, entering land and erecting a cabin, he has been one of the active helpers in all of the better interests in the community for 30 years."

A newspaper clipping says, "The funeral service occurred from the residence, the old homestead, on Saturday at 10 a.m. The body was borne to the Buckingham Cemetery. It was a cold day but the attendance was quite large. But for the severe weather and the feebleness of MRS. GRANGER, the service would have been at the church. Father GRANGER had not been in good health for some years. He fell upon his head two years ago and received injuries from which he never recovered. His last severe sickness began a month or so ago. About two weeks ago he received a stroke of paralysis from which time the lamp of life grew dimmer until Friday morning last, when he dropped into the eternal morning."

Another paper, The Toledo Chronicle of Jan. 13, 1887, said, "MR. GRANGER was a member of the M.E. church for over forty years but had recently been connected with the Congregational. He was always an earnest Christian wherever found.---Thus another of the old landmarks has been removed, and an earnest Christian father, neighbor and friend has been taken from among us to the bourne of that land from which no traveler returns.

"George Stoakes came from school at Vinton to attend the funeral of his grandfather, MR. GRANGER."

Both of BELLE'S brothers, Theodore and George, went to school there. A pamphlet advertised it as "Tilford Collegiate Academy at Vinton, Iowa, The Cheapest and Best Patronized Academy in the West. Fine, Excellent and Thorough Courses of Study. Academic, Normal, Fine Art, Musical and Commercial. Prepares for College. Fits for Teaching and for Business."

A Tama history says, "Young people were sent to Tilford Academy, to Grinnell College, Iowa State College, Waterloo High School. But after all there was little education beyond the country school for a great majority."

However, by this time, a high school had opened in Traer and a couple of classes had already graduated.

Sometime, probably in the late eighties as deducted from all ages and dates known, WILLIAM and Thomas Pollock received the news that their mother had died in Scotland. An undated newspaper clipping pasted in the front of a small photograph album, mostly of pictures taken in Scotland, and now owned by Thomas' granddaughter, Mamie DeGroote of Humboldt, Iowa, says: "WILLIAM and Thomas Pollock have received news of their mother's recent death in Scotland. She was over eighty years of age, and their father is still living." This would have been their step mother. According to the Edinburgh registry their own mother, MARY SCOTT POLLOCK, apparently had died and their father had married Elizabeth Robertson and had more children before the boys were teen agers.

Ten years had passed since Jennie Pollock had started to teach in the country. During these years, she had bettered her qualifications by attending State Normal School at Cedar Falls. Now in 1887 she was realizing a dream come true by beginning to teach in Fort Dodge. Her first position was as a grade teacher at Lincoln school.

Lincoln school house was a stately three story brick building with a magnificent dome overhead and a large, ornate, inviting front porch on the front. When the school was built, a dozen years before Jennie came, on the site of a former school known as "the schoolhouse on the prairie," the new building had cost $45,000. The building occupied one of the highest spots in the entire area and could be seen for many miles of surrounding countryside. Parents at first were dubious about sending their children to this school "way out on the prairie" even though it was a magnificent structure. The grassy hill on which Lincoln stood was covered with violets and had long been a favorite spot for picnicking and flower gathering excursions. The plot abounded in shade trees. The school was ample size to house the entire school population of Fort Dodge, from the beginners through high school, all twelve grades-----well over 500 scholars---until the first separate high school structure was erected in 1897 and Lincoln became solely a grade school.

Jennie had been teaching a year in Fort Dodge when death messages came twice to her mother in the stone house out on the farm. Two of MARY POLLOCK'S brothers had died: Robert Beates, her oldest brother at age 65 of diabetes at their old home in Delaware county, New York, near Downsville; and Gurdon Beates (or Bates), her youngest brother at age 56, at Junction City, Kansas. These brothers were each Sunday School superintendents and each had served in a state legislature, Robert in New York and Gurdon in Kansas. GRANT, who was 24 now, one winter had visited his Uncle Gurdon in Kansas and GRANT remembered him as "a good natured man who loved to read." At that time Gurdon was working on some special bill to present to the legislature. Gurdon had a little farm and not especially well off. He had married a woman of considerable means who was quite interested in material things, while Gurdon's interest ran to the printed page and more academic interests.

Now just MARY and her one brother, James, the Methodist minister, were left. Their parents, two sisters and two brothers were dead.

Time was marching on. The last oxen was gone from Webster county. Up at Rolfe, a Presbyterian church, a frame structure, was dedicated in 1888. The first issue of the Rolfe Reveille was printed.

In Tama county, the barbecue of 1888 outclassed all other political rallies and was staged in the interest of the presidential candidate Benjamin Harrison, Republican from Ohio. Old JOHN STOAKES and his older brother William, now both deceased, had fought under this Harrison's grandfather, William Henry Harrison of Tippecanoe fame as young men from Ohio in the War of

1812. William Henry had himself become president. Now his grandson was trying for the highest office in the land, too.

The Tama history says of the barbecue, "In the morning parade, each man carried the tallest corn stalk he could find. One thousand flags were provided. A low wagon with twenty chairs, back to back, carried Tippecanoe voters (men who had voted for Harrison's grandfather.) Logs were provided to build a Tippecanoe cabin in the part. Speakers included James Wilson (A Tama county man who later was to serve 16 years as national secretary of agriculture.) An ox was roasted in a pit. The ladies served an estimated 2500 dinners – 500 at a time. Later in the afternoon, we children peeped over the edge of the pit at the bare carcass of the ox. After the torchlight procession in the evening when twenty ladies and as many men rode horseback, the eloquent Robert Cousins gave the main speech of the day. Everyone sang 'Tippecanoe and Tyler, Too.'"

Of course, Benjamin Harrison was successful in becoming president and served one term.

In 1889 WILLIAM POLLOCK added more acres to his farm, this time 76 acres at a cost of $684 from the Des Moines and Fort Dodge Railroad, according to an old warranty deed. That year Thomas Pollock's daughter Mary Jane died at age 22. She was a single girl.

The big excitement of the year, especially in northwest Iowa, was the tremendous skyrocket that went sizzling through the air with a roar across the sky above Estherville carrying in its wake a brilliant fire and a trail of smoke. It suddenly exploded with a thunderous noise scattering molten rock. It was a meteorite. The rock buried itself in the ground, the biggest hole made was 12 feet across and 15 feet deep, a cone shaped hole ploughed into the ground! Wagons and rigs, loaded with curios persons, swarmed north from town to see what had happened.

Two young men dug up the largest rock weighing 400 pounds and after displaying it in a local window for awhile and realizing the interest in it, they began traveling with it by wagon from town to town and charging to see it. Before long some other folk began realizing the value of the huge meteorite and complicated litigation for ownership started. The young men lost ownership. Eventually the meteorite was sold to the British Museum where it was divided into three parts and is now exhibited in London, Paris and Vienna. Scientists say the Estherville meteorite was the second largest ever to fall. One fell in Hungary in 1866 and weighed 547 pounds. Besides the one huge rock at Estherville, there were some small pieces. The University of Minnesota bought the second largest piece and still exhibits it at the university museum. All that is left in Iowa are small pieces picked up by curious spectators.

That was the year that Anna Jensen, a girl still in her teens, was teaching the last term of school in the old brick schoolhouse at old Rolfe. While she taught she lived in the Hait house, the first frame building in Pocahontas county. She was fond of both Mr. and Mrs. Hait who had helped found Old Rolfe and had built this fine home. On weekends Anna walked across the prairie six miles northwest to her parents' home. She says if the weather was good she often slipped off her shoes and stocking and went barefoot. Part way home she sometimes rested at a pioneer home and had tea with a girl named Laura who later became Anna's sister-in-law. (In 1963 when this chronology was being assembled, these "two girls" frequently see each other in Anna's apartment in Fort Dodge or on the old Jensen homestead where Laura still lives.)

As a young lady, Anna also taught south of the new town of Rolfe, and each day walked from her boarding house to her school. One time when Anna was attending institute in Pocahontas, she looked across a large room and saw another teacher sitting in a window. Anna thought the girl the prettiest girl she had ever seen. The pretty girl taught in the general vicinity where Anna did and drove a buggy to and from school along the same route Anna walked. The girl often stopped to give Anna a ride and they became friends. The girl was Minnie LeHane, an Irish girl, from Pocahontas.

GRANT'S oldest brother, Will, called Billy Pollock by his friends, was thirty years old and operating a grocery store in Gilmore City. That is 12 miles east of Pocahontas and 12 miles southeast of Rolfe. Billy met this pretty teacher Minnie LeHane and took her as his bride in 1890. He was the first of WILLIAM and MARY POLLOCK'S children to marry. Thus, later when Anna married another of the Pollock brothers, Jim, the two teachers became sister-in-law.

Visitors, a man and woman, came unannounced to WILLIAM and MARY POLLOCK'S home on the Lizard one day. As the story comes to us through GRANT'S telling, his father WILLIAM and some of the young members of the family met the visitors in the yard and learned who they were. Going inside, MARY at first did not recognize the visitors until the man laughed. Then she knew! It was her brother James! They had not seen each other for more than 30 years – not since she had left her girlhood home in New York state and come West. She was a young woman then and now she was 62 and he was 59. They were the only two left – their parents and two brothers and two sisters were dead.

GRANT remembered that his Uncle James, the preacher, was enthusiastic about Iowa and used glowing words to describe the beauties of the West including the prairie chickens. GRANT remembers this with pleasure. But he remembers James' wife as afraid of many things.

Emma wrote of this visit in a letter from Clare dated Nov. 30, 1890 to Bates cousins back in New York State, "Ma didn't know Uncle James when he came, not until he had been in the house some time......he commenced talking about the East. Ma looked at him and he laughed and asked if she had ever seen him before." It was a happy reunion.

Emma and Mae followed Jennie into the teacher field. Emma wrote in this same letter, "my school begins tomorrow. I am glad of it, for I am quite anxious to get back at school work again. I have almost made up my mind to go back to Cedar Falls next fall and stay until I graduate. It would take two years to do it." Jennie and Emma and Mae all attended Normal School at Cedar Falls, Anna Pollock says, and all taught. Exie, the youngest, stayed at home and kept the home for her parents.

The first brick schoolhouse was erected in the new town of Rolfe in 1890.

Three days after Christmas in 1890, U.S. army men in Dakota had arrested 250 or more Sioux Indian men, women and children, thinking some trouble was brewing among the Indians who were looking for a Messiah. The army men had the Indians in camp, surrounded with guns on them, and were searching and disarming the Indian men one by one. Some gun went off and then the army men started firing into the Indians. Twenty-nine soldiers were killed and every Indian man, woman and child was gunned down with the exception of a scant few who may have gotten away. This was the Battle of Wounded Knee in South Dakota – the last of the Indian battles.

In 1891, Jim Pollock, 25, was looking over the far West. He and his brother GRANT had been farming the home place all of their lives except for little trips here and there.

In April 1891, Emma wrote to cousins in the East, decendants of Robert Beates, "My brother Jas. Has left us for awhile; he is out in Bucoda, Wash. Now, he seems to like it real well so far. It seems to us as if he was quite aways from home, as he has never been away any length of time before. We haven't any idea how long he will stay; it will depend greatly on how he likes it there.

"GRANT is the only boy at home now; we tell him that he will be spoiled before the summer is over, there being so many girls, and only one boy at home. But he doesn't seem to think so......

"I am going to Humboldt county to teach during the summer, then I think very likely I will go to Cedar Falls to attend school for two years."

She closed with, "I have company in the other room; I can't write very well when the other young folk are talking and laughing; I will have to go and join them."

She did go to Humboldt county for she wrote again June 11, 1891, "I have been teaching in Humboldt county for seven weeks and last Monday my school was closed on account of the scarlet fever scare. Of course my time will go on just the same; won't I have a pleasant time visiting and getting paid for it?"

Jim apparently came home for Emma speaks of "the boys" in the next paragraph and Will is married and living in Gilmore City and he and Minnie had their first child, a girl, in 1891. "The boys" must mean GRANT and Jim. Emma writes, "We had quite a time fishing the other evening, the boys fixed a torch and went down to the river to fish, us girls went too, of course. Well, things went on nicely for awhile, but pretty soon we grew tired of the sport, and started for home just as a thunder storm was coming up, but it was so dark in the woods that we couldn't see anything but a slight reflection of the torch behind us. I got hit in the eye with something; one of the girls fell over a stump and hurt herself, after wandering around the brush, gooseberry bushes and the like, we found our way back to where the boys were. While waiting there one of the boys tried throwing a fish out hit a stone instead and struck my sister in the forehead; she didn't get over it for quite awhile, so then we fixed another torch and started for home, we got on a road that led us home alright. And left the boys to fish alone. After that when they wanted to go fishing, they are not bothered with us girls teasing them to let us go along too. The boys went the other evening and caught eighty fish."

Her last paragraph says, "I expect to graduate from Normal School next month; but, oh, how I hate to have my graduation exercise, to have to get up before a whole house full of smart folks and read or say a little something."

Robert Pollock, who had tried life in southern Africa and in Australia, now a man of 48 years, came with his Scotch wife Jean to America and settled in Allegheny, Penn. where he stayed for a period of years. WILLIAM and Thomas had not seen this brother since he was a lad of 8 and ran down the lane crying to go with them to America.

Anna Pollock says that WILLIAM frequently made trips around the country to far places to G.A.R. conventions to see his old war buddies. One time when he went to Cleveland, Ohio, he took Jim with him. One time WILLIAM went back to Pennsylvania. Whether that trip might have been to see Robert, no one knows.

GRANT, 29 years old, went in 1893 to Chicago to the Columbian Exposition, the 400th anniversary of Columbus' landing. The fair started a year late but made up for its year's tardiness with three wonders: 1-the electric light, powered by George Westinghouse's new generator, which flooded the Fair creating a great "White City"; 2- the present day Museum of Science and Industry; and 3- the first Ferris Wheel – Chicago's answer to the Eiffel Tower, not so tall, but more fun to go up in.

WILLAIM, 66, and MARY, 65, left the farm that year and moved into Fort Dodge. There WILLIAM built three houses on Second Avenue North. The first were two story white framehouses on the south side of the street, at least one of which MARY and he lived in for awhile. Then he built a large two story brick house across the street on the north side at 1702 and when it was completed that was their home the rest of their lives. It had a large porch on two sides and stood on a corner lot. On the back of the lot he built a small building of the same bricks for a workshop.

GRANT and Jim stayed on the farm and lived in the stone house and farmed. The sisters kept house for them. Emma filled this role more than the others. The brothers used to laughingly remember that when they'd go out to do chores in the morning, they's hardly get started in the barn before Emma would call out to them, "Breakfast is ready!"

BELLE was an eleven year old girl in Tama county then. Her oldest brother Theodore was married that year. Her Aunt Jane was widowed for the third time with the death of John Wilson. John Wilson was the father (in an earlier marriage) of Tama Jim Wilson who served for 16 years as United States Secretary of Agriculture.

And BELLE'S GRANDMOTHER GRANGER died. She had continued to make her home with her daughter Mary Wightman after GRANDFATHER GRANGER had died six years earlier. She did, however, make occasional visits to the nearby homes of her other daughters, Lizzie Kober and ELIZA STOAKES.

The Story of the Granger Family says, "In June of 1893 she went to her daughter Elizabeth Kober to visit for awhile. While there she suffered a paralytic stroke while sitting in her chair sewing. She just went to sleep and never awakened. She slept for forty-eight hours and then passed away peacefully on June 17 at the age of 84." She was laid to rest beside her husband in Buckingham.

ELIZABETH NEWMAN GRANGER had come to America from England as a bride of one year with a tiny baby in her arms. She crossed New York State with her husband and baby on the Erie Canal and then by steamboat to Ohio. They settled there and later in Illinois and then to Iowa, these moves all by covered wagon. Now death had broken this last thread to the old country. All the ancestors in BELLE'S family who had come from Europe were now dead.

BELLE had not known her paternal grandparents for they were dead before she was born. Her GRANDFATHER GRANGER had died when she was five. Now her GRANDMOTHER GRANGER was gone and BELLE was eleven.

BELLE had a carefree happy childhood. She attended rural school one mile south and one and a half miles west of her parent's country home, a school her mother had once taught, Sarah Stoakes says. BELLE did have the misfortune to fall into the lye barrel head first one time and most of her blonde hair came out but it grew back in again. A lye barrel held wood ashes and water, a pioneer method of leaching lye. Lye was needed in making homemade soap. Farm folk saved all of the grease from cooking and once a year or twice combined it with lye, cooked it, and poured it out into flat boxes to cool. This was cut in bars and made a household supply of soap for months to come.

As a young girl BELLE learned to sew and was always an expert seamstress. She learned to play the piano. She liked to help her mother peel and slice apples and string them on threads to dry after being hung up. Sometimes they were spread loose with a netting over them to dry. Dried apples, cooked in winter, made a tasty sauce.

She strung popcorn and cranberries with the other children to decorate the Christmas tree at holiday time. The ELEAZER STOAKES family and the Kobers always celebrated Christmas, New Years and GRANDMA GRANGER'S birthday together, Sarah Stoakes says. They did not get together at Thanksgiving because often the men were still picking corn. Sarah remembers one Christmas when they couldn't find the right kind of a tree for a Christmas tree. So Theodore Stoakes bore holes in a post and put boughs into these holes building a symmetric, lush tree – the loveliest one they ever had, she says.

Although life was mostly kind to BELLE in her growing up years, as an adult she used to recall the winter she had only one dress to wear to school – a plaid one. Money was scarce for the Stoakes and BELLE said it was because of a mortgage.

That likely was the great depression of 1893 when she was eleven years old. These bad times brought on the colorful presidential campaign between William J. Bryan, the silver tongued orator advocating silver 16 to 1, and William McKinley who stood for protective tariff.

GRANT, then a man of 30, later recalled these days of industrial and financial unrest by telling of Coxey's Army of unemployed men marching on Washington, D.C. A branch known as Kelley's Army crossed Iowa. Jack London, famous author, joined the army to get material for stories. The ragged men slept in barns as they crossed the state or wherever they could find shelter, and Iowans were obliged to give the hungry men food as they traveled toward the East.

Antonin Dvorak, the great composer of Humoresque, was living and writing at Spillville, Iowa. There, sitting on the slope of a hill that overlooked the beautiful valley of the Turkey River, he heard the music of nature which wove into the parts of the symphony – and forever more the sounds of the Largo movement would take Iowans "going home" to the prairies.

Billy Sunday, who became the ward of an Iowa orphanage at 12 and later a wildly cheered outfield hero and base-runner for the Chicago White Sox, "hit the sawdust trail" (his own words) in 1895 at Garner, Iowa. He was in immediate demand as an evangelist and for forty years would stump the whole country to save souls, plead for righteousness, lead lost men back to God. His enthusiasm, his force of personality, his earnestness, and his sublime confidence in the grace of God led thousands upon thousands of men and women down the sawdust trail to kneel down in front while strains of soft music swept over them. He spoke in the colorful speech of the prairie and the baseball field and was a bitter foe of liquor traffic which he promised to fight "until hell freezes over."   GRANT used to tell his children about Billy Sunday but whether GRANT had seen or heard Sunday in person we do not know – probably had.

Within a year after Mrs. GRANGER'S death, the Wightmans moved to a farm at Marion, near Cedar Rapids, and BELLE and her sister Ella were receiving letters from the Wightman twin girls Eva and Evah, in which they speak of the farm, the church activities of Pa, Ma, Lyman, Elmer and Cora. The twins were the youngest of this family of five children. The Wightmans were milking eight cows and had a new churn and were making twenty pounds of butter a week. The churn "is a barrel on rockers and it rocks back and forth." The twins each told of receiving for Christmas, "A book, a stick pin, a Christmas card, the bookmarks you girls sent us and some candy."
Eva wrote, "Our Sunday School teacher gave us the Christmas cards for learning twelve golden texts and repeating them. Mine has a horseshoe with purple, pink and red pansies, green leaves and a vine. Evah's has a fan with pink flowers and green leaves." That was Christmas 1894.

The following year BELLE started to high school in Traer. She stayed in town with her Aunt Jane, her father's thrice widowed sister, then 74 years old. BELLE loved this aunt and when BELLE was married she made trips with her little ones back to Traer to visit Aunt Jane when she was seriously ill. BELLE went to school in the red brick schoolhouse which had had two additions, one built in 1885 and the other in 1894 making the latter brand new when BELLE was a freshman. The year after BELLE graduated, this structure was replaced with a white stone and pressed brick schoolhouse with a red tile roof. It burned in 1917.

Before school started in the fall of 1897, the Wightman twins made a train trip to Traer to visit their cousins, and apparently had a good time. Returning home, they wrote back to Ella and

BELLE, "........How is your wheel getting along after so many riding it?.....We had a great time telling the boys about out visit and how the old place looked."

BELLE had a handicap with so many Stoakes around as revealed in a letter from the twins in 1898, "Well, BELLE does your mail still get mixed with your cousin Belle Stoakes yet? We still direct our envelopes to you, Ella, so that you girls will be sure to get them."

Family Lines Converge at Rolfe

In 1898 GRANT, 34, and Jim, 31, went into the grocery business for themselves at Rolfe under the firms name of "The Pollock Brothers Grocery" and with the trademark "Good Things to Eat." The brothers had apprenticed for awhile with their oldest brother Will in his store at Gilmore City before starting a store of their own. Their first store was in a frame structure on the east side of the street, about where the new bank in Rolfe stands in 1963.

Prior to this, nearly all of their lives had been spent on the family farm at Clare. When GRANT and Jim left there, the farm was rented to Mr. and Mrs. Bill Burk. Sometime after that both the stone house and the barn burned – at different times. Mrs. Burk put some grease on the stove to make doughnuts and had gone outdoors. The grease caught afire and the stone house was gutted. WILLIAM built a two story frame house up by the road. That made the seventh house he had built for himself: two log cabins, the stone house, two frame houses and a brick house in town, and now this frame house on the farm.

BELLE graduated from high school Friday evening, June 9, 1899 at the opera house in Traer. She was 17 years old. Her particular part on the program was to give a talk, presumably self composed, "Into Each Life Some Rain Must Fall." Her cousin Esther Stoakes had as her subject, "A Lie a Necessity?" This class of 17 students, the fourteenth class to graduate at Traer, had as its colors Rose and Gray, and class mascot the Four-leaf Clover. (a fifty year reunion was held in 1949 but only two members were present, one being R.P. Young who had married Esther Stoakes, and the other was Martha Fleming. Esther and BELLE were both deceased.)

The Wightman twins wrote from Marion regretting that they couldn't attend the graduation. Eva was still envious of BELLE'S wheel. "I suppose you are having oceans of rides on your wheel this summer. I want a wheel so bad I don't know what to do. If I only had a bike I believe I could be nearly happy."

The Wightmans moved in the fall of 1899 to a farm at Hart, Michigan where the twin's mother, Mary Granger Wightman lived out her years, her death coming in 1925.

BELLE'S brother George was married a month after she graduated from high school to Minnie Vogt. He built a two story frame house for his bride and himself on his parent's farm, just a ways east from their house.

Death messages seemed always coming to the WILLIAM POLLOCK home. In 1899 MARY'S only remaining brother, James the minister, died at age 68. MARY was 71 now and the last surviving one of her brothers and sisters. Jared Fuller passed away the next year leaving only his one son Eddie surviving. Markie Fuller had been killed in some war – a Mexican border skirmish or the Spanish-American war.

MARY, contrary to her own fear that she might not live to rear her own family to maturity, was always blessed, along with her husband and all seven of their children, with constant good health and longevity. MARY lived to 85 (1828-1913) and WILLIAM to the same age (1827-1912). The children all lived past sixty and GRANT the longest of all, a goal he used to chuckingly aspire to as he approached it. GRANT was 87 (1864-1951). Emma 85 (1869-1954); Jennie 80 (1861-1942); Jim 72 (1866-1939); Mae 68 (1872-1940); Exie 64 (1875-1939); Will 63 (1859-1922). GRANT used to marvel and feel especially blessed that he had lived in a large family that had not been touched by severe illness or death until old age, and he sometimes spoke of how fortunate he was with his wife and their children who seemed blessed with the same good health.

BELLE'S next oldest sister Ella was not so fortunate. She suffered from the age of 15 with arthritis.

Anna Jensen during the late nineties was clerking in the Crahen's General Store at Rolfe. The store was open from 8 a.m. to 10 p.m. each week day except Saturday when it remained open until midnight or whenever the last loafer decided to go home. She received a salary of $42.50 a month.

While working there, she took her first trip to Lake Okoboji. The man and woman in whose home she boarded, their two small sons, the lady's mother, a teen age niece, and Anna made the trip by spring wagon. They left Rolfe in the morning with a well filled provision basket. They drove "over wagon trail roads around sloughs and over knolls covered with prairie grass" and reached Ruthven that night and stayed with friends. A second day was needed to reach the lake. They stopped in Milford for kerosene to use in lamps and stoves, and for groceries.

For swimming Anna and her land lady had made their own bathing suits out of dark outing flannel – made like union suits with sailor collars trimmed with red wool braid. Short puffed sleeves and the bottoms of the below-the-knee bloomers were trimmed with the braid also. With these the women wore long black stockings and knee length skirts.

The year after GRANT and Jim went into business at Rolfe, a cyclone hit the town. GRANT, who was in the store at the time, made a hasty dash for the protection of the basement seeing the air full of flying debris as he went. The storm hit at 9:13 in the evening.

Three men were injured. Buildings were demolished in town and in the country. Two of the men were injured by flying glass: one in Hotel Tremain where timbers crashed through the window, and the other at the Challand's Restaurant when a board came through the window. The other man was in the haymow of the Pete Johnson Livery Stable when the building was hit and badly damaged. As the wind rose, Johnson had sent the man to the mow to close the doors. He carried a lighted lantern. Just seconds before the crash, the man threw the lantern through the door to the street below fearing fire. The next instant he was beneath a pile of ruins but was not badly hurt.

Many barns were demolished and others extensively damaged. A goodly number of houses lost their chimneys. Roofs were twisted and ripped up. Four or five hundred feet of board walk was torn up.

No damage was done to the Crahan Opera House, next door to the Livery Stable. Two hundred people were in the opera house at the time.

WILLAIM POLLOCK, in the leisure of his old age, enjoyed himself in his workshop back of his home. He cut flower urns, figures of animals, and of people out of stone. His daughter-in-law Anna Pollock quotes him as saying "I like to do something pleasing to the eye."

He liked especially to cut figures of lions. W.D. McEwen commissioned Pollock to cut a pair for the lawn of the McEwen mansion at Rolfe. One still stands there and hundreds of school children have sat on its back.

Another can be seen in Fort Dodge by the Driveway on the north side of Tenth Avenue just east of Twenty-Second street. One that the Fort Dodge school children fondly called "Leo the Lion" through the years and has been moved now from near the school to Olson Park is sometimes credited to WILLIAM POLLOCK. The quality of the workmanship is far inferior to the other work. GRANT says that his father, WILLIAM, was trying to teach Thomas to cut a lion and that Leo was Thomas' initial effort.

Anna Pollock thinks one of WILLIAM'S finest pieces was the bust of a neighbor girl, perfect in each detail even to each plait in her braided hair. WILLIAM admired President William McKinley and cut a statue of him. McKinley was shot in 1901.

Anna Pollock wrote, "When WILLIAM POLLOCK became and old man with long white whiskers, a slowed walk and a slightly stooped back, he sent for a large granite stone and had it put in his shop. He had his own picture taken at a local photography shop. It was a good portrait of himself sitting in a big arm chair. On his head he wore his old fur cap with a bill on the front of it. His long white whiskers covered his shirt bosom. He was wearing his work jacket. His left arm was laid on the arm of the chair, and with his right hand he held a book in his lap. His feet rested on a rectangular block of stone on which the name of "Pollock" was inscribed.

"The lifelike photograph was hung in his workshop and served as the pattern for the

statue which he carved out of brown granite. It was a life sized monument. He had it taken to Oakland Cemetery and placed on the family burial lot where it was easily seen from Highway 169. It remained there until sometime after his death and burial."

The statue was later removed and a conventional large granite stone was put in its place. What became of this statue, and the above described pieces, this writer does not know.

Best known of WILLIAM POLLOCK'S work is the Civil War Soldier in Oakland Cemetery at Fort Dodge. On the front of the monument are these words: "Erected in Memory of Unknown Soldiers of the Union Army 1861-1865 By Fort Donelson Post Number 236 Fort Dodge and Citizens of Webster County Iowa. Unveiled May 30, 1900."

In the late nineteen fifties, Ed Breen of the Fort Dodge television station compiled and telecast a program at Memorial Day time on the history of this Civil War Monument. On the program was Mrs. John W. Gustlin of 1602 Third Avenue North in Fort Dodge, who as a little neighbor girl had watched WILLIAM POLLOCK cut the statue in his workshop, and who had the privilege of unveiling the figure at the dedication. She recalled that on the day of the dedication, carriages of people from Fort Dodge and surrounding countryside had gathered for the ceremony. The dignitaries were assembled. The program was about to begin when someone missed WILLIAM POLLOCK and a carriage was immediately dispatched toward town to pick him up. The carriage met him walking toward the cemetery and hurried him there so the program could begin.

Seventeen year old BELLE STOAKES taught rural school one mile north of her parent's home the year after she graduated from high school, Sarah Stoakes said when interviewed on the subject in 1961.

Happy days for BELLE at State Normal School at Cedar Falls started in 1901. A Tama history says, "Even in the nineties, North Tama was notable for the number of students sent to college by well-to-do farmers and town parents.....A long list of young teachers went out from North Tama to other communities each fall. Few other lines of work were open to girls then."

BELLE'S cousin and high school classmate, Esther Stoakes, went with BELLE to Cedar Falls. They lived with a group of girls in Mrs. Howe's boarding house at 2104 Olive Street not far from the tree shaded campus.

From the many letters that flowed back and forth among these girls at vacation time and through the following years, many of which BELLE kept and treasured, they had a gay, fun filled time at Normal School. They were constantly delighted to meet new people. The girls wrote each other about mutual friends, about new clothes and patterns, what boys were going with which girls, and who was seen in church with whom. BELLE joined the Clio and Oria Society.

BELLE had pretty clothes for her college days. (As children we used to be privileged to dress up in these on rainy days although they were kept in good condition in a neatly packed trunk in the storeroom.) The skirts with their 22 inch waistbands and fitted hiplines swept the floor with a fullness in the back suggestive of a train. One light weight wool, a subdued lovely winter blue skirt had two shirtwaists to match. One was trimmer in fine, silk ecru lace, and the other in white pleated silk with narrow black velvet ribbons. A green and brown changeable taffeta was a rustley gown. A beige wool two piece dress with big leg-of-mutton sleeves and jet bead trim was a more practical costume. The loveliest of all was the summer dress of lemon yellow with the trim of narrow black velvet ribbon edging the two ruffles around the bottom of the skirt, the little puffs at the wrists of the sleeve, and around the ruffle that edged the white eyelet yoke. BELLE and her sister Alice had made dresses alike of this material and pattern. Alice joined BELLE at Normal School in Cedar Falls for the summer session in 1903.

BELLE liked school, and as she did when in grade and high school, she made good grades. Arithmetic, reading, grammar, music and deportment brought her highest grades, in the high nineties. Orthography didn't rank so high.

She liked to sing and one of her treasured college experiences was singing in Handel's Messiah. She took interest in the concerts given by the 20 voice Minnesingers, the college male group.

BELLE had a season ticket to the ISNS baseball games. Sports on the Cedar River was part of college life and included boating and ice skating.

In January of 1902, BELLE received word of the death of a boy, Emery Blair Roseberry, in an explosion at Arch Springs, Pa. He worked for a railroad company. Two others died in the same explosion. Apparently this was a boy she had known at Traer. She corresponded with his sister and mother in Arch Springs for a year or two afterward.

BELLE'S keepsakes included many engraved invitations to receptions, wedding, graduation exercises including an invitation to attend her cousin B. Frank Thomas' commencement at Law School in Iowa City. She received many little thank-you notes for gifts sent, including flowers. There were notes announcing picnics and telling her to come.

Anna Jensen and James Pollock were married early in the new century. Their first child was named Gurden after the Uncle Gurdon in Kansas.

In the fall of 1903, BELLE went to Rolfe to teach sixth and seventh grades and the other girls were a bit envious of her good job and told her so in letters. The schoolhouse, a three story brick structure with a steeple, had a faculty of nine teachers and the superintendent. Esther Stoakes went back to Traer to teach and subsequently married her high school sweetheart. BELLE'S special correspondent from Normal School was Clara Van Pelt whom BELLE had apparently taken home to Traer for visits. BELLE'S mother also wrote to Clara on occasion.

At Rolfe, BELLE and two other teachers rented a flat above a store in the business district and kept house. One friend wrote, "I think you must have your hands full looking after so many kids......I'll warrant you girls have a fine time keeping house. I would like to stop in sometime if I were acquainted with the other two, but I think it will pay to do it if board is high."

While BELLE taught, letters come from friends and cousins telling of weddings, marriage plans, and new boy friends. At Rolfe, like at Cedar Falls, there were invitations to parties, weddings and picnics.

Her father sent her baskets of fruit from the farm and her mother wrote her often: "Father says if he can get time to go to Traer in the next day or two he will send you a basket of peaches, so you can look for them at the express office." Another time, "We have sent your box by North Western. We thought your yellow comforter was hardly clean enough so we sent another....We send our paring knife. Alice says it is sharp enough to cut you. Hope you are well and doing well. Did you get your certificate?"

Another of her mother's letters said, "We received your very welcome letter last Friday.....Sarah was here this morning to get a basket of grapes to make jelly. They do not ripen enough to be good to eat. She said Theodore started at four o'clock this morning to help Uncle John drive his fat cattle to Traer. He ships them today, will go to Chicago with them.....George and Minnie and Fred went to Traer this morning. It is raining this morning and roads are just as muddy as rain can make them but they had to go.......Kate V. is going to have a new piano......Callie is at Uncle George's now....Wallace Gaston and family were at George's to dinner last Sabbath, they came over and visited at our house about two hours, just had a fine visit. Wish you had been here, we roamed all over the orchard and everywhere else......We are busy today making bread and plum butter......I must stop writing or I won't get any chicken and noodles, they are just going to the table so good bye write when you have time to your loving mother, Eliza A. Stoakes, Traer Sept. 15th, 1903."

A short note said, "If weather is favorable and the plums ripen I think we will send you a basket tomorrow.....am making pickles and plum jelly today will can tomatoes this afternoon. Good bye Your mother E.A. Stoakes."

Sister Alice wrote, "We took Fan and Bess (family horses) and went hazel nutting yesterday. Uncle John's boys and girls went along with us. We took our dinner and ate in the timber." The letter says that Sarah and boys, Minnie and Fred, and Ella all on the outing.

In the spring, along with other teachers, BELLE was a special guest at the graduation exercises of the Class of 1904 in the Crahan Opera House. Blanche Cuff, Mac Kent, W. Don McEwen, Frank Ritchey, Fae Squires, Gustave Everson, Mayme Crahan and T.R. Campbell were among the graduates who made speeches. A brass quartette of Messrs. Hille, Kent, Hille and Campbell played, and there was a cornet duet by the Hille brothers, Fred and Hans.

Belle spent the summer of 1904 at her parents' home. She had not been home very long when she received a letter from the grocerman at Rolfe written June 3. He said in part, "I suppose you will be very surprised to get this......I would be very pleased to hear from you......Well I must close the store and go home. Yours truly, GRANT POLLOCK." He wrote again in three weeks, June 21, pleased to have heard from her and referred to a fishing trip they had had together......"Jim was visiting in Ft. Dodge all this week......Think it is my turn to go next.....I would like to be down there and help you pick strawberries wouldn't that be fun......I would like to peep in at your cooking for five men – of yes I believe you could do it all right......Well I must ring off and go sell some prunes. Now write a nice long letter."

GRANT did take his turn at being away from the store and went on a pleasure trip to Colorado visiting, Pike's Peak, Garden of the Gods, Denver, Colorado Springs and his brother Will and family who had moved in 1902 to Monte Vista to farm and ranch. GRANT also visited James Beates in Denver – likely a cousin.

GRANT kept a little diary. Entries, in part, include:

"Saturday, July 16, 1904 – Spent the afternoon at City Park looking at the animals.

"Sun. July 17 – Forenoon in seeing Denver.....Guide said it was 65 miles to snow capped mountains that looked about two miles......

"7/8- Left Denver at 8 o'clock and got to Col. Springs at 10......Went to a ball game......5 to 4 favor of Col. Springs.

"7/19 – made a trip up the mountain on a burrow.....got up where I could see Seven Falls and H.H. grave. Took several views. Gave a big fat woman a ride on my burrow. Went to a show at night. It was good.

"7/20 Went to Manitou and climbed up the mt. and ate my little lunch and picked spruce gum. Got caught in a rain and hail storm. Had to crawl under some rocks to get out of the storm.

"7/21......Started from Manitou at 2:30 on a burro for Pike's Peak. Had a fine trip up to the camp. Everyone was keeping his eyes on the pack mule.....The supper tasted fine.

"7/22 – Started on our journey for the peak about 12:30. Had not climbed for more than an hour when I got sick....Climbed over rocks until sunrise when we got to the top. Oh my but we came near freezing. Got down to Manitou at about 2 o'clock tired and dusty. Went to see Sioux City and Colo. Springs play two games of ball in the afternoon

"7/23 – Took my Kodak to get it fixed.......In the afternoon went to the Garden of the Gods.

"7/24 – Went to the park. Paid 25 cents to get in. Saw Seven Falls and Helen Hunt's grave. Took a picture. Got caught in a rain. Got under a rock for awhile and then got in a barn. Stayed about two hours. Got back to town about starved. Eat 35 cents worth of supper and then went for the train to go to Monte Vista.

"7/25 – Slept some on the train. Woke in time to see the mountains. They were a fine sight. Climbing mountains and going through tunnels......got the train to stop at Palma. Found (Will's) folks all well. Went hunting. Did not get anything. Had a big ride after wild horses.

"7/26 –Went hunting in the evening. Did not get a shot.

"7/27 – Drove twenty miles to the hills fishing for trout.....Got a shot at a coyote coming home but did not even scare him.

"7/28 – Went fishing.....Had a run away. I climbed in over dash board and caught the lines and kid and stopped them.

"7/29 – Went hunting on a pony. Got one shot at a cottontail.

"7/30 – Went fishing in the canyon.....saw a lot of little fish. Shot five morning doves for Sunday dinner.

"8/2 – Went out to see the country. Drove between forty-five and fifty miles.

"8/3 – Played ball with the boys (Clarence 10, Raymond 7, Kevin 4. The first born, Avis, died when one year old.)

"8/4 – Will took me to Alamosa to take the train for Colo. Springs.

"8/6 – Went to Seven Falls to take several pictures......

"8/7 – Sunday. Went to Manitou. Climbed up the mt. until I got tired. Read Denver Post until I got tired of that. Went up higher and took some pictures.. Went to Presbyterian church in eve.

"8/8 – Went to bronco busting......best show yet. Band concert in evening in park.

"8/9 – Took the 9:15 train for Denver. Had a bath, hair cut and shave. Found James. Went out to Beates.

"8/10 –James and I went walking....got on train."

GRANT wrote BELLE from Monte Vista July 30, "Miss Stoakes – Dear Friend – Yours received while I was in Colorado Springs.....I have four reasons for being here. I came for a rest, sight seeing, health and to see my brother. I expect to be gone from Rolfe about a month..... This is the southern part of Colorado, the San Louis Valley. Oh my but this is wild country. I have been fishing, riding horseback and hunting until my face is so badly burned it is pealing off....I think you are foolish to work so hard. Thought you were having a vacation to rest. When the work got to crowding me I skipped out and came West....The potatoes are going to be good at Rolfe this year. I think you girls can have all you want to eat. Are you girls going to keep batch this year again?.....I would be very pleased to find a letter from you at Rolfe when I get home."

August 17, 1904 – M. BELLE STOAKES received a Pocahontas county teacher's certificate good for another twelve months. Music and arithmetic were again her high grades, 98 and 95, and orthography trailing last.

BELLE was back at her Rolfe teaching job in September but this year she was boarding rather than doing her own cooking. She roomed with Mable Rogers.

Alice wrote to BELLE from Traer Oct. 16, "Had my first experience with Barney (their horse) and an automobile. We met one but he didn't act bad." A seamstress had been helping Alice with her sewing.

Nov 7 – ELIZA wrote, "My Dear BELLE – FATHER and I are alone in the house again. Alice and Ella have just started for Cedar Falls, Pa has gone to take them to Traer. Ella is going to take treatments of Dr. Weigert (of Waterloo). She seems very much pleased to go. Alice goes to take care of her...Well, BELLE, we have concluded it is not very far from this ranch to Waterloo (25 miles): FATHER went to see the doctor who was not home; George took three horses to the horse sale, sold old Bes and little Jim brought Bob back. Drove Spot in the old buggy.......Minnie, Fred and Kate went and got new things too numerous to mention......FATHER and Alice went again and saw the doctor about treatments for Ella...... Aunt Callie is at Uncle Hugh's......George's masons have not come yet the cellar is dug and waiting.... write when you can but don't worry. It is not good for you health. As ever your loving mother ELIZA A. STOAKES."

Then she wrote to BELLE again Nov. 13, "......sorry to hear that you are getting homesick you had better give that up. We are getting along all right. You know it does not take much to keep FATHER and me going.......Theodore sold six loads of hogs......George and FATHER drove 66 head to Traer the same day..."

On Nov. 20, MOTHER wrote again to BELLE, ".....Yes, BELLE, FATHER and I are alone now will be until 28th of Nov. Then I go to Waterloo to stay with Ella and FATHER will board at George's and sleep at home. Alice and Millie will go to school as they calculated to. We do not know how long Ella will take treatments (for arthritis).......Now don't you worry but give you undivided attention to your school and make a success of it. That is where your work is for the present. I have got the work done up so I can leave things in pretty good shape for FATHER. I may not be gone very long, cannot tell.......Every your loving FATHER and MOTHER E and E A STOAKES."

Minnie wrote a week later: "........you MOTHER goes to Waterloo tomorrow to stay with Ella. Alice commences school Tuesday. The folks are going to drive across they want to get started at four in the morning if possible so your FATHER can get home before dark. Your FATHER expects to take his meals here but we can not convince him to stay all night he thinks he ought to be over there to keep fires at night. We would much rather he would come here and stay all night.....Someone just went down the road with a lantern. I guess it was Theodores. I phoned a little while ago and was telling them about the folks going away and I guess they thought they had better come down and say good bye."

Nov. 30 from Waterloo, ELIZA writes," FATHER and I came here last Monday drove up with Barney and the new buggy had it pretty well loaded." They had taken much produce for light housekeeping...."We expect to stay a month. Ella seems about the same as far as I can see......the doctor begins tomorrow to give her electric treatments in connection with the rubbing.....Fred, oh, how I miss the little fellow he used to come to see me so often when I was home alone."

Theodore was in Waterloo within a couple of weeks taking provisions from the farm. He wrote BELLE, "......I could not see that Ella had gained much......I saw FATHER this morning. He is well working away as hard as ever. I think he gets a little lonesome but he does not say much. I invited him and George and Minnie up for Christmas dinner and tree likewise you..... I will send you a Christmas present in a separate package."

From ELIZA in Waterloo Dec. 13 – "----about going home for Christmas, you must really do as you think best.......Ella and I cannot go home......Ella takes three treatments a day.......rubs her and works her joints, applies hot towels to her elbows and knees, takes sweat baths.......write when you can to you sister and MOTHER."

E. STOAKES wrote from Traer Dec. 5, 1904, "Dear DAUGHTER......You say you are always tired. I think you do too much that does not belong to you school work you will haft to do that if you hold your place in the school. But outside I would not do aney more than the other teachers do You seem to do more than your share but you ought to know best......As to coming home for the holidays, I don't think I would in fact there is no home here to come to I am here at night and sleep here but I take my meals at George's."

He wrote again Dec. 23rd "Dear DAUGHTER, I will write you a few lines to let you know we are all well. Alice is at home. She got here yesterday. We are going to have a Christmas tree at Theodore's......I thought I wod send you a Christmas present or something to buy you one. You can buy you one that will suit you better than I can. E. STOAKES."

BELLE did go home for Christmas and there a few days after the holiday she received a letter from Rolfe written on Pollock Bros. letterhead and with a salutation, "My Dear Little Girl......I received your first letter yesterday morning. Jim happened to know that I got a letter yesterday morning and when he went to the PO this morning and got another he did not say a word but put on a very knowing smile. Was glad to hear you are better and are having a good time.... Things were very quiet Christmas. Had turkey......and went to the Presbyterian church at night. I got a Bible for a Christmas present through the mail. There was someone in when I got it so it was only a short time until everyone knew what I got for Christmas.....Oh my but this is a wild night......Trains all late......I have not called 162 all week. I will tell you the rest Sunday. GRANT."

A storm prevented BELLE from getting to Waterloo to see her mother and sister at holiday time. Their stay in Waterloo stretched on and on, rather than a month, they were there three months.

In February, Minnie wrote, "Well, BELLE, your FATHER was telling me that your MOTHER would be home the 14th of this month again. It surely has been a long lonesome time for her and I know your FATHER will be glad for he can't help but be lonesome for he always goes home right after supper and has to spend the evenings alone......she will be more than tickled to get home again. I guess it will be Happy, Happy for both of them. Only hope Ella will be contented and improved. I know there is no use to think she will be well for that is impossible." She was an invalid with arthritis the rest of her life.

Mother and daughter did go home Feb. 16 by train although they were detained a day because the railroad was blocked with snow.

March 12, Theodore wrote, "The folks down home are all well. George and FATHER are to ship their fat cattle tomorrow. Geo. is going with them. I shipped mine the last of January."

A few days later "FATHER had a growth cut out of his face," Alice wrote Mar. 17, "The bunch was a little larger than a hazel nut. FATHER is well and his face is healing nicely.....I cannot see that Ella has improved one bit this winter. Mother rubs her in the morning and we put hot clothes on her knees toward night."

George and Minnie had a baby girl in March and named her Florence.

ELEAZER tried something new for him. He tapped the maple trees in the front yard and made syrup. He did his spring butchering. ELIZA was busy with the first settings of baby chicks and expecting more.

On April 6, 1905, ELEAZER and ELIZA received a letter that their daughter BELLE was thinking of being married. ELIZA sat right down and replied, "MY Dear BELLE, We received your letter today between one and two o'clock. I read it to FATHER. We concluded as we do not know MR. POLLOCK we really can not advise you what to do, so will leave it to yourself as you think best. Remember it is for life. Be sure, consider it well and be <u>sure</u> that he is the one man in all the world you want. If you truly love him (for marriage without love would be a dreary life) and he is an honorable man one that you feel you can love and cherish while life lasts. We will be willing and may God bless and keep you both to be a blessing to each other."

Almost immediately the spring housecleaning started in the Stoakes home although the weather was still cold. ELIZA had the sitting room, both stairways, the kitchen, BELLE'S and Alice's room, and Aunt Callie's room papered. ELIZA wrote, "The sitting room will be green with a green and white border and ceiling and white picture molding."

BELLE wanted her mother to come to Rolfe to visit but received this reply, "I would like to come to see you BELLE but I do not know how I can this spring and it will not be very long until you are home. You know I was away so long last winter they do not think they can let me go."

Belle Stoakes   Grant Pollock

When BELLE'S school was out, GRANT accompanied her home on the train to meet her family. They had not announced their plans but they were riced as they got on the train.

BELLE'S roommate Mabel Rogers writes about it, "......Well, I should say that I had a serious time answering questions and trying not to tell any black ones just a few white ones. After the train pulled out that evening the crowd that did the 'riceing act' looked for me to pump all they could but I was no where to be seen, had slipped back into the depot......The next day it was reported all over town that you were married and nearly everyone I met would yell out 'Is Miss STOAKES married?' I would say no. They would say they did not know whether to belive me or not......Nearly everyone seems to know that you will be back again soon, for soon after GRANT came home the report came to me from several different ones that GRANT had bought the store and the house and that you were to be married within a few weeks......I suppose you know they are cleaning and getting the house all ready. I have been thinking that I would begin to pack up our stuff tomorrow night. I am going to stay with Nell."

GRANT did buy Jim's interest in the store and Jim's and Anna's house. They moved into a rental place for a short time. They had a year old son Howard. Their first born Gerden died. Soon Jim and his family headed West so he could investigate copper mines and possible locations in Colorado, Idaho and California.

GRANT came home from Traer by train via Iowa Falls and Fort Dodge, according to a letter he wrote back to BELLE. He wrote from Fort Dodge, "I believe we decided you were to buy the dishes in Traer. You could do that the first time you get any time and have him pack them and bill them to Pollock Bros. and send the bill to us. You spoke of lamps and such things too........Do you suppose they will meet me with pocketsfull of rice? How did Spot feel after her hard drive?......."

He wrote again when he was back in Rolfe, "......Oh mister but they did jump on me when I came. They had it all over town that we were married. (H.D. and Nellie) Brinkman came home on the same train. There was about a hundred down there with rice for them. I was looking for them so I got out of the front end of the smoker and was half way up town before the crowd got out of the car......Will Shirk got our wallpaper and will be ready to put it on next week.....Mr. Cassidy (the school superintendent) was in asking Jim if there was any truth in the report about us. Do you want me to tell him?"

BELLE was busy at home at Traer   "........Yesterday I was in town half of the day waiting on dress makers. Brought one home with me. She's at it this morning hard, but I can only have her today. Then Theodore's wife is coming down. I want everything finished by Saturday evening if possible......GRANT, are you coming Saturday evening so as to be here Sunday.....I'll meet you. If you come on that 3:55 train so much the better. No one will be up to sell gawk seed. Then you can rest as long as you like out here. You might as well come Saturday evening as Monday. Remember we are early birds. Six in the morning is the hour. I expect the cards today.   As to that list of names, I want a list of the ones you want to receive announcements......Don't you wish it were today? BELLE."

BELLE had gone to the James Black Dry Goods Company in Waterloo and bought sheeting, tablecloths, D. Napkins, towels, yards of silkoline and French lawn all for $29.65.

At the W.P. McIntire store at Rolfe, they purchased such things as two rockers, a couch, rugs, carpets sideboard, pair of pictures, center table and many other things for a total of $225.70.

Theodore's wife Sarah recalls that while she was sewing, BELLE went outdoors where her FATHER was cutting wood and told him she'd like to have Aunt Lizzie's and Uncle John's family come for the wedding. Her FATHER said, "Not unless you can invite 'Uncle' Matt and all the rest of the uncles and aunts and cousins." That she could not do because they were too numerous, so just the immediate members of her family were present for the wedding. Sarah says that she picked June peas from the garden for the breakfast which was served after the ceremony. Minnie Stoakes' sister served the breakfast.

Petite, blonde, blue eyed BELLE wore a white silkoline gown fashioned with an embroidered net yoke outlined with a wide ruffle of silkoline edged with rooshing and pleated silk ribbon. The full upper sleeves tapered into fitted sleeves below the elbow and the lower sleeve was of embroidered net. The skirt with its 21 inch waist was shirred and fitted at the top and fell into a full skirt with a pleated ruffle at the bottom.

After the ceremony at 6 a.m., June 21, 1905, the breakfast, the newlyweds took the Rock Island train from the depot on the east edge of Traer, and went to Clear Lake for their honeymoon. They were delighted and pleased that cousins and friends had gathered at the wrong depot to give them a send-off and missed them entirely.

The wedding announcements said "at home after July twelfth at Rolfe, Iowa." Once more they gave their friends the slip and were in the dark, one story, gingerbread trimmed house when well wishers, headed by a neighbor-to-be, Fred Hille, came and busied themselves outdoors decorating the exterior of the house. A board with old shoes tied to it stuck out of the chimney and a baby buggy was put on the front porch. GRANT and BELLE sat on an unrolled rug and watched the activity through the dark windows.

A new home was starting here at 902 Elm Street. Sailing ships, steamships and stage coaches were a thing of the past. The iron horse had created this new little town of Rolfe just 22 years ago. One automobile had come to Rolfe. A few months before the wedding, the first automobile trip across the United States, New York to San Francisco, had been made in ten weeks. Orville and Wilbur Wright had taken their first successful flight in a heavier-than-air mechanically propelled airplane at Kitty Hawk, N.C. the previous December.

Five children, Cora Belle, Robert, Margaret, Mary and Jean, would come to bless this home. The house itself would be enlarged to more than twice its size. A half century later, when the children were departed to lives of their own and BELLE and GRANT had lived out their allotted years, a friend would pause in front of the old house and sum up the years. "There was much good living in that old house."

902 Elm Street, Rolfe, Iowa, 1905